THE PICKERING MASTERS

THE COMPLETE SHORTER POETRY OF GEORGE ELIOT

Volume 1

To Graham Handley, who urged me to start work on this edition and remained on hand with valuable support and advice.

THE COMPLETE SHORTER POETRY OF GEORGE ELIOT

Edited by
Antonie Gerard van den Broek

Consulting Editor
William Baker

Volume 1

Routledge
Taylor & Francis Group
LONDON AND NEW YORK

First published 2005 by Pickering & Chatto (Publishers) Limited

Published 2016 by Routledge
2 Park Square, Milton Park, Abingdon, Oxon OX14 4RN
711 Third Avenue, New York, NY 10017, USA

Routledge is an imprint of the Taylor & Francis Group, an informa business

BRITISH LIBRARY CATALOGUING IN PUBLICATION DATA
Eliot, George, 1819–1880
The complete shorter poetry of George Eliot.
(The Pickering masters)
1. Eliot, George, 1819–1880 – Criticism and interpretation
I. Title II. Van den Broek, A. G. III. Baker, William, 1944–
823.8

LIBRARY OF CONGRESS CATALOGUING-IN-PUBLICATION DATA
Eliot, George, 1819–1880.
[Poems. Selections]
The complete shorter poetry of George Eliot / edited by Antonie Gerard van den Broek ; consulting editor, William Baker.
p. cm. – (Pickering masters)
Includes bibliographical references (p.) and index.
ISBN 1–85196–796–6 (acid-free paper)
I. Van den Broek, A. G. II. Baker, William, 1944– III. Title. IV. Series.
PR4666.A1 2005
821'.8–dc22 2004028463

ISBN-13: 978-1-85196-796-4 (set)

New material typeset by P&C

CONTENTS

ACKNOWLEDGEMENTS

A project like this is always a collaborative effort since it is difficult for the lone editor to keep up with George Eliot's extraordinary range of interests. I have been fortunate to lean on the scholarship of Gordon S. Haight, John Clark Pratt, Victor A. Neufeldt, Joseph Wiesenfarth, William Baker, John C. Ross, Thomas Pinney, Jane Irwin, Margaret Harris and Judith Johnston, and others whom I have acknowledged in notes – but none more than Cynthia Ann Secor. My copy of her unpublished dissertation, 'The Poems of George Eliot' (1967), has been a constant companion, and I am deeply indebted to her pioneering work.

I would also like to thank the following libraries for their efficient and courteous responses to my many requests for assistance and material: the British Library; Dr Williams's Library, London; the Dreadnought Library, Greenwich University; and the Beinecke Rare Book and Manuscript Library, Yale University.

I am grateful to Jonathan G. Ouvry, the great-great-grandson of George Henry Lewes, for giving me permission to quote from copyright material.

I want to thank family, friends and colleagues who have helped me at various stages by generously offering assistance, advice, translations and/or proof-reading services: my mother Kathleen van den Broek, my aunt Patricia Piperno, Sr Bridgid, Tiree Macgregor, Marcus

Pethers, Francisco Montero, Adrienne Gould, Mary McKenzie, Ruth Davis, Beryl Gray, William Baker and my editor Julie Wilson at Pickering & Chatto.

I also owe a debt of gratitude to my wife, Judy, and daughter, Stacy, who have remained wonderfully cheerful and supportive throughout.

Finally, I want to acknowledge Graham Handley for his generosity, friendship, encouragement and help over the years. In partial repayment I dedicate this edition to him.

All facsimile pages are reproduced by permission of the British Library, with the exception of the *Jubal* 1878 title pages and the extract from Rose Cleveland, *George Eliot's Poetry and Other Studies* (1885), both of which are reproduced from Antonie van den Broek's personal collection.

PREFACE

Antonie Gerard van den Broek's edition of *The Complete Shorter Poetry of George Eliot* makes available a fascinating and important genre by one of Victorian Britain's greatest writers. George Eliot's poetry has been neglected. Part of this neglect is due to the lack of access; so few of her poems are available in recent selections from her writings. For instance, A. S. Byatt and Nicholas Warren's *George Eliot: Selected Essays, Poems and Other Writings* (1990) publishes three poetic extracts. The first is the second scene from 'Armgart' (1870), a dramatic poem focusing upon a woman who turns down marriage to concentrate on her singing career and subsequently loses her voice. The second consists of a selection from the first and third books of the lengthy dramatic poem set in Spain just before the 1492 expulsion of its Jewish population. Byatt and Warren choose the opening of *The Spanish Gypsy* (written in 1867, published in 1868) and the passage where Fedalma, the Gypsy princess, accepts the renunciation of her love for a Spanish Duke, Silva. They also print, in their entirety, the eleven poems constituting Eliot's Shakespearean sonnet sequence 'Brother and Sister'. First published in *Jubal and Other Poems* in 1874, these sonnets are intensely autobiographical, having as their foundation Eliot's complex relationship with her estranged brother Isaac. Written in 1869, Eliot draws upon the same relationship as she did for the central plot of *The Mill on the Floss*, published in 1860.

The eleven 'Brother and Sister' sonnets are included in Daniel Karlin's *The Penguin Book of Victorian Verse* (1998), and in Thomas J. Collins and Vivienne J. Rundle's *The Broadview Anthology of Victorian Poetry and Poetic Theory* (1999), which also includes, with very sparse introduction and notation, 'O May I Join the Choir Invisible', extracts from the first and third books of *The Spanish Gypsy* and 'Armgart'. Byatt and Warren provide brief overall introductions to their selections, no more than a page each in length. Their annotations are limited to six explications of lines from *The Spanish Gypsy.* This is at least more detailed than the annotation provided in Lucien Jenkins's *George Eliot Collected Poems*, published in 1989. With the exception of four notes by Eliot on *The Spanish Gypsy* no annotation is provided, only a short 'Note on the Text' and an 'Introduction'. Before van den Broek's present edition the most authoritative edition of Eliot's poetry was Cynthia Ann Secor's unpublished Ph.D. thesis. Her 'The Poems of George Eliot: A Critical Edition with Introduction and Notes' is a Cornell dissertation presented in September 1969. An eight-page 'Preface to the Text' is followed by an 'Introductory Essay' of just under one hundred pages. Each poem is prefaced by the instance of its first publication and texts collated. Textual variations follow at the foot of the page and there is an extensive commentary on the poem. This encompasses date of composition, its biographical context and other points of interest. The first poem in Secor's work is 'Knowing that shortly I must put off this tabernacle'. First published in the *Christian Observer* in January 1840, Eliot sent her teacher and friend, the Evangelical Maria Lewis, a copy in a letter she wrote to her dated 17 July 1839. This poem is in fact the second in the present edition; the first being 'On Being Called a Saint', omitted from Secor and first published in Gordon S. Haight's definitive *George Eliot: A Biography* (1968). Found in Eliot's notebook kept during her school days, it was 'probably written by Mary Anne herself' and dates, from the paper evidence provided by the notebook, to the early 1830s.[1] Secor's unpublished edition is unavailable and, in view of the quality of primary Eliot documentation which has been published since its appearance, especially in the area of her notebooks, rather dated. It remained, until the publication of van den Broek's edition, to which he has provided an introduction both scholarly and critical, the most extensive, detailed and authoritative edition of Eliot's poetry.

Placing Eliot's poetic output in a wider context, she wrote poems, non-fiction prose (letters, reviews and review essays, articles for Victorian periodicals) and, of course, fiction. Her notebooks are a mixture of prose notation from various eclectic sources in diverse languages and extracts from poems also from different languages in addition to English. Unlike her contemporaries Charles Dickens, Wilkie Collins, Charles Reade and the slightly later Henry James, Eliot did not write for the theatre. She writes in her poetry and fiction about actors, actresses and opera singers, but refrained from theatrical ventures, unlike her partner George Henry Lewes, whose theatrical experiments ceased with their union. Lewes wrote singly or collaborated in at least ten plays belonging to the period of the 1840s or

1. Gordon S. Haight, *George Eliot: A Biography* (Oxford and New York, Oxford University Press, 1968), p. 20; see also this volume, p. 4

the early 1850s, but apparently not to the period past 1854 when he and Marian Evans left London for Weimer, where he prepared his definitive biography of Goethe, published in 1855. Lewes wrote in many genres, unlike his contemporary Matthew Arnold, whose output is confined to non-fictional prose and poetry, although the latter ceases to be a major preoccupation later on in Arnold's life. Amongst other contemporaries of Lewes and Eliot, Thomas Carlyle primarily wrote non-fiction prose and, of course, the fictional extravagant exuberant *Sartor Resartus* ('The Tailor Retailored'), first published in 1833 and 1834. He also produced around forty poems which, with his translations, have been forgotten. Carlyle seems to have had an antipathy to the form, remarking in a letter 'It is one of my constant regrets, in this generation that men to whom the gods have given a genius … will insist, in such an earnest time as ours has grown, in bringing out their divine gift in the shape of verse, which now no man reads entirely in earnest'.[2] Of Eliot's other contemporaries, Robert Browning is remembered for his verse, including dramatic monologues and lengthy poems, and he also produced closet dramas. Of the Brontë sisters, all three wrote poetry in addition to creating a most complex fictional world. Thomas Hardy, who lived on until the end of the second decade of the twentieth century, and who primarily wished to be a poet, devoted many years to his lengthy historically-based poetic drama *The Dynasts*, set at the time of the Napoleonic Wars. George Eliot wrote poetry throughout her life, took her poetry seriously, and allowed some of it to be published.

2. *The Collected Letters of Thomas and Jane Welsh Carlyle*, eds Charles Richard Sanders, Kenneth J. Fielding, et. al., 30 vols (Durham, NC, Duke University Press, 1970–2003), Vol. 22, p. 16.

The motivation to write for the theatre was mixed. In the instances of Wilkie Collins, Charles Reade or Henry James, to cite but three, they may well have wished to make a lot of money (certainly Collins did) with a smash hit, gain recognition, or seek direct audience response (as in the case of Henry James). Poetry, on the other hand, usually implies slower recognition and no direct audience response. Response primarily coming in the form of letters, of course, took time. Tennyson is an obvious case of a Victorian who made a good deal of money from poetry and gained enormous celebrity status, but he is an exception rather than the rule. Eliot naturally favoured poetry from her youth, and she also wrote poetry for money. For instance, she received the relatively large sum of £250 from *Macmillan's Magazine* in 1878 for the 838-line 'A College Breakfast-Party', based on her May 1873 visit to Cambridge.

Eliot and Lewes, after their union, were regular theatre-goers, not to music halls, comedy or farce, but to Shakespeare, serious drama and, of course, the opera. Lewes protected her from the 'aves vehement'; the applause of the vulgar crowd, the London theatrical mob and newspaper and journal criticism of her fiction. Growing up in the East Midlands, removed from any major city, there were few opportunities in her youth for theatrical experience, but many for private meditation, reflection and verse. Inspiration came from the great poetry of the Bible and the mellifluous cadencies of its translations. For instance, 'Knowing that shortly I must put off this tabernacle' is a forty-line poetic meditation in ten stanzas of four lines each. Each quatrain concludes with the single line 'Farewell!'. This meditation, based on the biblical line from '2 Pet. 1.16', was not republished in Eliot's lifetime. As van den Broek indicates in his headnote commentary on the poem, sentiments in the verses echo biographical problems its author experienced with her father. The poet, the 'I' of the poem, expresses the 'somewhat unorthodox wish to take the Bible with her to heaven' (this volume, p. 8). This parallels comments she makes in letters to her teacher and friend Maria Lewis, dated 17 July 1839 and slightly earlier, on 20 May 1839, when she alludes to problems associated with church attendance.

Eliot's poetry dating from the late 1830s and early 1840s, the period when she was in her late teens and early twenties, provides insight into her state of mind, personal preoccupations and dilemmas. Some of the poems are found in letters written to Maria Lewis and did not resurface until the publication, in 1954, of the first volume of George Eliot's letters in the monumental edition edited by Gordon S. Haight. She uses the traditional form, the sonnet, in a poem sent in the text of a letter to Maria Lewis on 4 September 1839. In her letter Eliot speaks of leading 'so unsettled a life and [having] been so desultory in my employments'. She also revealingly observes that 'her mind presents just such an assemblage of disjointed specimens of history, ancient and modern, scraps of poetry picked up from Shakespeare, Cooper, Wordsworth, and Milton'. Other sources include 'newspaper topics, morsels of Addison and Bacon, Latin verbs', and so on 'all arrested and petrified and smothered by the fast thickening every day accessions of actual events, relative anxieties, and household cares and vexations'.[3] In the 'Sonnet' there is no attempt at a persona: 'my' is used in the second and thir-

3. *The George Eliot Letters*, ed. Gordon S. Haight, 9 vols (New Haven, Yale University Press; London, Oxford University Press, 1954–78), Vol. 1, p. 29.

teenth line; 'me' in the sixth line. The first person 'I've' occurs twice – in the sixth and eleventh line. 'I' has a single occurrence – in line nine. Rarely, if ever, in her later poetry does she use such personal forms or subject matter. Her themes are childhood, loneliness, reflection, dreams and the pilgrimage of life; all also themes of her fiction. She prefaces the poem in a self-deprecatory tone, writing to Maria Lewis, 'To prevent myself from saying anything still more discreditable to my head and heart I will send you a something between poetry and prose expressive of an idea that has often been before my child's eye. For want of an humbler title I will call it a Sonnet', and the poem follows.[4] This lack of self-confidence rarely left Eliot. She had to be protected by Lewes from hostile reviews and needed continuing encouragement. Interestingly the manuscript of *Daniel Deronda*, her last completed novel, now in the British Library, contains lines from Shakespeare's Sonnet 29. This is a sonnet full of self-doubt written by an isolated person in need of reassurance. Her mature poetry is not, on the whole, short and is not personal but focused on historical, musical or other subjects. She used recognized conventional forms and diction often based on classical or other poetic models.

Translation from others, from other literature and tradition provided comfort and models to follow. An early example is found in 'Question and Answer', a twelve-line poetic translation from an unidentified German poetic source. Using couplets and three quatrains she 'put the idea ... into English doggrel which', Eliot writes to Maria Lewis in a letter dated 10 October 1840, 'quite fails to represent the beautiful simplicity

4. Ibid., Vol. 1, p. 30; see also this volume, p. 13.

and nature of the original'.[5] Following the translation Eliot reflects upon lines in the thirty-first chapter of Isaiah. Many instances of translations and variations upon translations are found throughout her poetic output, published and unpublished and in her notebooks. The original, sometimes with a translation, at times recurs in her fiction. For instance, the epigraph for chapter fifty-five of *Daniel Deronda*, the chapter in which Grandcourt drowns, is three lines from Dante, cited twice by Eliot in her notebooks.[6] Imagery in the translations, of entwined fingers, of the relationship between a child and father, of appearances and deception, of individuality and social pressures, prefigure again the novels. Many of Eliot's finest poems are based upon translations. For instance, 'How Lisa Loved the King' was first published in *Blackwood's Edinburgh Magazine* in May 1869 and separately published in book form by Ticknor and Fields in Boston.[7] The poem, in 646 lines, is, as van den Broek explains in his informative headnote, 'a more or less faithful rendering of Boccaccio's *Decameron* X.7' (this volume, p. 137). The verse form reveals indebtedness to Chaucerian metrical format and to the dexterous use of alexandrines, bringing the verse paragraphs to a graceful conclusion.

Turning away from translations and moving to another period of George Eliot's life and productivity, 'In a London Drawing Room' is indicative of mood,

5. *Letters*, Vol. 1, p. 69; see also this volume, p. 17.

6. See *George Eliot, A Writer's Notebook, 1854–1879, and Uncollected Writings*, ed. Joseph Wiesenfarth (Charlottesville, University Press of Virginia, 1981), p. xxxviii.

7. See William Baker and John C. Ross, *George Eliot: A Bibliographical History* (New Castle, DE, Oak Knoll Press; London, British Library, 2002), pp. 387–9.

attitude and poetic productivity. As van den Broek indicates in his headnote, the dating of these nineteen lines is uncertain. It remained unpublished until Bernard J. Paris included it in his 'George Eliot's Unpublished Poetry'.[8] The poem's theme, 'the indifference of the human world', clearly echoes elements in her letters and fiction. In his insightful commentary on the poem in *Experiments in Life: George Eliot's Quest for Value* (1965), Paris draws intertextual parallels with sentiments expressed by George Eliot in a 4 June 1848 letter she wrote to her friend Sara Sophia Hennell. In her letter Eliot writes: 'Alas for the fate of poor mortals which condemns them to wake up some fine morning and find all the poetry in which their world was bathed only the evening before utterly gone'. Instead they confront 'the hard angular world of chairs and tables and looking-glasses staring at them in all its naked prose'.[9]

> The world of the poem is urban, commercial London. Its motifs are sameness and hurry. Its dwellings are not human, individual; instead of providing interest, room for speculation, allowing the consciousness to expand and take hold of something outside itself, they will it in. There is no variety of color, light and shade, for the factory smoke has obscured the sun.

Paris adds 'Each human being is alone, self-enclosed, hurrying on, unconscious of the things and people around him, preoccupied with his own private business

8. Bernard J. Paris, 'George Eliot's Unpublished Poetry', *Studies in Philology*, LVI (July 1959), pp. 539–58.

9. *Letters*, Vol. I, p. 138; cf. Bernard J. Paris, *Experiments in Life: George Eliot's Quest for Value* (Detroit, MI, Wayne State University Press, 1965), p. 138.

or mission'.[10] Parallels may be made with character situations in the fabric of George Eliot's fiction. In the opening chapter of *Silas Marner* the weaver 'has everything that makes his life human and meaningful stripped away from him'. The novel depicts his 'despair and alienation from the human world; it is the story also of his slow rehabilitation and integration into the life of Ravelve'.[11] Experience of despair, of social and moral isolation, frequently a product of the lack or disappearance of communal associations, is also seen in *Adam Bede*, *The Spanish Gypsy*, *Romola* and *Daniel Deronda*, to cite but four examples from many in Eliot's output. Hetty's pregnancy forces her to depart from Hayslope. Don Silva, a Spanish military commander in *The Spanish Gypsy*, is placed in an impossible position, forcing him to leave his community and to kill the father of his beloved. Romola's realization that Savonarola is not what he appears to be necessitates her leaving Florence. Gwendolen Harleth, in despair following the drowning of Grandcourt, her husband, reveals to Daniel Deronda that her life is one of personal entrapment. Deronda gives her a dose of reality when he tells her 'some real knowledge would give you an interest in the world beyond the small drama of personal desires'.[12]

Van den Broek's edition includes George Eliot's epigraphs to her last three completed novels, *Felix Holt, the Radical* (1866), *Middlemarch* (1871–2) and *Daniel Deronda* (1876). Poetic fragments written by her are found scattered throughout her notebooks. Her fiction also draws upon other writers. For instance, the epi-

10. Ibid., p. 137.
11. Ibid., pp. 138, 140.
12. *Daniel Deronda*, ed. Graham Handley, Oxford World's Classics (Oxford, Oxford University Press, 1988), p. 387.

graph to *Adam Bede* (1859) is taken from the sixth book of William Wordsworth's *The Excursion*, the section 'Churchyard among the Mountains'. The lines pinpoint powerful motifs such as remoteness, trials and suffering, present in both the novel and the poem. The lines drawn from Wordsworth's 'Michael', with which Eliot prefaces *Silas Marner* (1861), draw attention to, amongst other elements, the themes of rejuvenation in both Wordsworth's poem and her novel. As George Eliot's art matured she increasingly drew upon her own poetry. In addition, there are many poetic lines in her poetry which she did not use in her fiction. For instance, unused epigraphs, or as she prefers to call them 'mottoes', for *Romola* (1863) are available as 'Appendix B' in Andrew Sanders's edition.[13] David L. Higdon's 'George Eliot and the Art of the Epigraph',[14] summarized by van den Broek, 'argues that Eliot primarily used' her own epigraphs, and those she took from others, 'to create structural allusions, abstractions, ironic refractions, and metaphoric evaluations'. Van den Broek observes that Eliot uses epigraphs to 'describe characters indicating their unconscious thoughts and arguing for realistic presentation'.[15] George Eliot's own mottoes are stylistically highly varied. In *Daniel Deronda*, for instance, they extend from seven lines of blank verse, akin to lines from a Robert Browning poetic dramatic monologue, prefacing each of the four separate volumes of the work, to

13. George Eliot, *Romola*, ed. Andrew Sanders (Harmondsworth, Penguin, 1980).

14. David L. Higdon, 'George Eliot and the Art of the Epigraph', *Nineteenth Century Fiction*, 25 (1970), pp. 127–51.

15. Antonie van den Broek, 'Epigraphs' in John Rignall (ed.), *Oxford Reader's Companion to George Eliot* (Oxford, Oxford University Press, 2000), p. 100.

five lines of narrative verse introducing chapter nine. Sixteen lines of verse dialogue between two 'gentlemen' head the tenth chapter and, to take one other example, two cryptic poetic lines, seemingly advocating altruism, preface chapter sixty-seven: 'The godhead in us wrings our nobler deeds / From our reluctant selves' (see Vol. 2, p. 161). The inclusion in *The Complete Shorter Poetry of George Eliot* of such epigraphs creates the opportunity to explore a most neglected terrain of their creator's complex eclectic art.

In common with many of her other poems, a composition such as 'In a London Drawing Room' illuminates the themes, preoccupations, images and situations in Eliot's other writing. Recent authoritative studies of Victorian poetry unfortunately have given George Eliot's poetry short shrift, although she herself makes interesting observations on 'Versification', revealing her own concerns and those, too, of her contemporaries. There are two essays on the subject of 'verse', both of which are included in the present volumes. One, 'Notes on Form in Art' belongs to the period of *The Spanish Gypsy*, 1868. The other, 'Versification', to the following year. Both exhibit her thoughts on form and verse. In the first she clarifies what poetry means to her: '*Poetry* begins when passion weds thought by finding expression in an image; but *poetic form* begins with a choice of elements, however meagre, as the accordant expression of emotional states' (Vol. 2, p. 182). The form of poetry develops as 'the beautiful expanding curves of a bivalve shell' (Vol. 2, p. 183). Her language is pervaded with the scientific, psychological language and imagery found, for instance, in George Henry Lewes's *Seaside Studies* (1858). A. S. Byatt perceptively indicates in her introduction to *George Eliot: Selected Essays, Poems and*

Other Writings, that for George Eliot 'Poetry combines the particular with the ideal, the "true and universal" in its rhythms, its images, its sequences. Poetry, she says has been defined to mean fiction, but fiction itself is only the expression of *predominant* feeling in "an arrangement of events in feigned correspondences"'.[16]

'Versification' expands upon such ideas. It is a reaction, as van den Broek indicates in his headnote, to, amongst other writings on verse forms, her friend James J. Sylvester's *The Laws of Verse: or, Principles of Versification*, published in 1870, which she had an advance copy of, and used when working on *Middlemarch*.[17] Sylvester's edited volume contains attempts to formulize, almost mathematically, varieties of verse. For instance, in her notebooks for *Middlemarch*, George Eliot copies almost verbatim from Sylvester: 'I am satisfied that ... Edgar Poe is perfectly right in his "Rationale of Versification", that the substitution of measure is time; that an accented syllable is a long syllable, and that an unaccented syllable is a short one of varying degrees of duration, & that feet in modern metre are of equal length'.[18] 'Versification' reacts to contemporary poetic theoretical formulations and specifically focuses upon what constitutes 'English blank verse'. It is replete with examples drawn from such poets as technically and historically diverse as Byron, Shakespeare and Milton.

16. *George Eliot: Selected Essays, Poems and Other Writings*, eds A. S. Byatt and Nicholas Warren, intro. A. S. Byatt (London, Penguin Books, 1990), p. xxxi.

17. See Baker and Ross, *Bibliographical History*, p. 459.

18. Cited in George Eliot's *'Middlemarch' Notebooks: A Transcription*, eds John Clark Pratt and Victor A. Neufeldt (Berkeley, University of California Press, 1979), pp. 87, 164. Eliot is reacting to Sylvester's *Laws of Verse*, pp. 64–8.

The reprinting in the present volumes of 'Versification' is an interesting addition to George Eliot's poetic reflections and deliberations. It also provides access to a by no means insignificant nineteenth-century primary document. 'Versification' and George Eliot herself are largely ignored in two recent influential studies of Victorian poetry. Isobel Armstrong, in *Victorian Poetry, Poetics and Politics* (1993), affords Eliot only a passing reference. The lengthiest discussion in a work devoted to the exploration of neglected Victorian poetry concerns explication of *The Spanish Gypsy.* The choice of this work illustrates why Armstrong may well neglect Eliot's poetic output. Armstrong is concerned with female poets and their importance. She does note that 'questions of the status of women's experience … dominate George Eliot's poetry, perhaps more than they figure in her prose'. The poem 'is an attempt to see how the feminine principle might be the source of a new humanist myth'. For Armstrong, Eliot 'seems to have used poetry both to consider consolations which were simpler than those of her novels and to explore a devastating scepticism which was often harsher than her novels intimate'. Eliot, however, for Armstrong, is ambivalent towards 'the "feminine tradition"'.[19]

There is a single passing reference to George Eliot in the thirteen essays found in Joseph Bristow's *The Cambridge Companion to Victorian Poetry* (2000), and this reference is not to Eliot's poetic output but to her translations of Friedrich Strauss's *Life of Jesus*.[20] Even in the

19. Isobel Armstrong, *Victorian Poetry: Poetry, Poetics and Politics* (London and New York, Routledge, 1993), pp. 370, 372, 371, 370.

20. Daniel Brown, 'Victorian Poetry and Science' in Joseph Bristow (ed.), *The Cambridge Companion to Victorian Poetry* (Cambridge, Cambridge University Press, 2000), pp. 137–58; p. 150.

context of the exploration of Eliot's writing, there is still neglect of her poetry. This is exemplified, for instance, in George Levine's *The Cambridge Companion to George Eliot* (2001), which does not devote an essay to her poetry. Poems, such as *The Spanish Gypsy*, are only mentioned in passing reference. Signs that the critical current is shifting, and the importance of George Eliot's poetic output to Victorian poetry, and to an understanding of her own writing, is being recognized, are evinced in the present edition and in other recent studies. Louise Hudd's 'The Politics of Feminist Poetics: "Armgart" and George Eliot's Critical Response to Aurora Leigh' reveals how important Eliot's verse drama, with its tale of the opera singer who loses her voice, has become for feminist criticism.[21] Charles La Porte's 'George Eliot, the Poetics as Prophet' draws from poems in the 1874 and 1878 *Jubal* editions in order to demonstrate why Isobel Armstrong was so reluctant to afford Eliot's poetry much attention. George Eliot's 'well-known ambivalence toward "feminine" writing is amply documented'. For La Porte, 'Eliot's ambivalence conceals what became a complex position on the feminine in art'. The explication of ambiguities in 'O May I Join the Choir Invisible', 'The Legend of Jubal' and the much neglected 'The Death of Moses', form part of an extensive illumination of 'the prophetic element of Eliot's poetry'.[22]

21. Louise Hudd, 'The Politics of a Feminist Poetics: "Armgart" and George Eliot's Critical Response to *Aurora Leigh*' in Kate Flint (ed.), *Poetry and Politics* (Cambridge, D. S. Brewer, 1996), pp. 62–83.

22. Charles La Porte, 'George Eliot, the Poetics as Prophet', *Victorian Literature and Culture* (2003), pp. 159–79; pp. 159, 174.

A judicious overall assessment of Eliot's poetry and its relation to her fiction is found in Margaret Reynolds's entry on the 'Poetry of George Eliot' in John Rignall's *Oxford Reader's Companion to George Eliot*. Reynolds writes that 'George Eliot's poetry functions as a parallel text to the novels; many of the same concerns and themes are taken up there, and quite often a poetic text, composed at about the same time as a novel, will reflect and enlarge upon the prose'. The obvious well-cited instance of this is 'Armgart', written whilst she was at work on *Middlemarch*. Reynolds observes that 'the connected web of images in "O, May I Join the Choir Invisible"' relating to 'poetry, music, singing, breath, and self-expressiveness' constitute 'a recurring theme which is particularly notable in George Eliot's poetry', as it is in her fiction. The sonnet sequence 'Brother and Sister' is preoccupied with 'questions to do with the constrictions of gender and the conventions of contemporary sexual difference [which] dominate in the poetry to be closely followed with related questions of race and identity'. *The Spanish Gypsy* and other poems explore the themes of 'social conditioning and cultural expectations' prevalent in the novels.[23]

George Eliot is not buried amongst the great poets and other national worthies in Westminster Abbey. She lies alongside philosophers such as Herbert Spencer and George Henry Lewes and poets such as James Thomson, buried in Highgate Cemetery in 1882, and Christina Rossetti in 1894, amongst others representative of 'the middle – and upper middle-class respectable

23. Margaret Reynolds, 'Poetry of George Eliot' in Rignall (ed.), *Oxford Reader's Companion to George Eliot*, pp. 304–8; pp. 304, 305, 306.

market' for burial.[24] Van den Broek's edition of *The Complete Shorter Poetry of George Eliot* provides an invaluable service. His scrupulous and thorough editing of her otherwise inaccessible poems presents the evidence for the continuing revaluation of George Eliot's *oeuvre*. An important addition to Victorian scholarship in general, it presents the documentation for an assessment of the importance of poetry to her own work, and to a revaluation of its place in Victorian poetry as a whole. Above all, van den Broek's edition ensures that Eliot's poetry is not destined to 'rest in unvisited tombs'.[25]

Dr William Baker
Presidential Research Professor
Department of English/University Libraries
Northern Illinois University

24. Samantha Matthews, *Poetical Remains: Poets' Graves, Bodies, and Books in the Nineteenth Century* (Oxford, Oxford University Press, 2004), p. 190.
25. *Middlemarch*, eds Margaret Harris and Judith Johnston, Everyman Series (London, Dent, 1997), p. 747.

GENERAL INTRODUCTION

These two volumes bring together all of George Eliot's shorter poetry, including unascribed novel and chapter epigraphs, with a complete set of textual variants and editorial notes. Also included are Eliot's essays, 'Notes on Form in Art' (1868), 'Versification' (1869) and 'Leaves from a Note-Book' (no date), because they shed interesting light on her views regarding poetry. Such an edition has not been produced since Cynthia Ann Secor wrote her unpublished doctoral dissertation for Cornell University in 1969. The only other authoritative editions of some of Eliot's poetry are the two that Eliot oversaw in 1874 and 1878. It is, therefore, high time that a comprehensive, readily accessible edition is made available. Eliot was very keen to see her mature poems of the 1860s and 1870s in print, and these extensive products of a major nineteenth-century writer deserve to be brought to the attention of twenty-first-century readers – together with the necessary apparatus to help them better appreciate the poems' artistic and intellectual merits.

Some readers may still question why I have bothered. Eliot's poems have been largely neglected because they are seen as inferior verse, certainly not in the same artistic category as her novels. Like many others, I have wondered why she published her poetry. It is one thing to write verse for private consumption; another for the public. And yet, if the quality and interest of the poems are so uneven or indifferent, is it possible that the woman who wrote the sometimes scathing article 'Silly Novels by Silly Women Novelists' (October 1856) could have been so blind about her own poetic abilities? Did she write poetry for money, knowing that her reputation as a novelist would ensure publication? They certainly made money (see below and the headnotes to 'Agatha', 'How Lisa Loved the King', 'Jubal', 'A College Breakfast-Party' and 'Armgart'). However, that intent seems unlikely, given the reverence with which she approached all art. Besides, she wrote poetry most of her life and did not try to publish everything. And as she told Cara Bray, in a letter dated 7 May 1868, in which she expressed her gratitude that George Henry Lewes always encouraged her literary interests, regardless of financial gain, she could earn hundreds of pounds for her poems but thousands for her novels.[1] Other possible reasons, put forward but dismissed by an early commentator, George W. Creel, are Lewes urging her on, her wish to emulate writers like Fielding and Scott, who also turned their hands to verse, and because she enjoyed the role of poet.[2] From Eliot's 'How I Came to Write Fiction' we know that Lewes was there from the very beginning of her novelistic career,[3] and he remained on hand to support her in all her endeavours. If Eliot partly

1. *Letters*, Vol. IV, p. 438. Cf. also her observation, dated July 1868, about the promising sales of *The Spanish Gypsy*: 'I care for the sales, not in a monetary light (for one does not write poems as the most marketable commodity) [but] because sale means large distribution'. She went on to say that she and Lewes were financially secure enough to pursue non-lucrative interests (*Letters*, Vol. IV, p. 466).

2. Creel, pp. 18–19.

3. Cf. *Letters*, Vol. II, pp. 406–10, where the essay is reprinted.

turned to poetry for publication because she believed it her artistic right to be as versatile as other literary figures, that conviction did not impress her contemporary critic, W. Fraser Rae:

> Great writers are exposed to a double temptation (1) they are tempted to try whether they can succeed in a new field as well as they have done in that wherein their laurels were won; and (2) they are tempted to believe that their friends are not deceived in pronouncing the new effort a splendid triumph.

Citing the plays of Scott and Tennyson as cases in point, he asked, 'who reads these plays now? How many readers can honestly admire them, or refrain from wishing that they had never been written?'[4] Secor has some very plausible things to say about Eliot's motive in writing verse: that she was seeking a prophetic voice, wanting 'to achieve poetic stature of the kind described in Shelley's *A Defence of Poetry*'.[5] What is certain is that she valued her poetry. In a letter to her friend François D'Albert-Durade, written in July 1868, she said about it, 'I seem to have gained a new organ, a new medium that my nature had languished for',[6] and the textual variants alone indicate how much time and effort she spent practising and honing her new organ/medium, sometimes returning to revise aspects years later. I address the question of poetry's importance to Eliot in the headnote to Appendix C in Vol. 2, but here I want to outline the history of how some of the poems came into print, how

4. W. Fraser Rae, 'George Eliot's Life and Writings', *International Review*, 10 (1881), pp. 447–58, 497–509; pp. 499–500.
5. Secor, p. 21.
6. *Letters*, Vol. IV, p. 465.

critics received them, and to suggest that all the poems have intrinsic interest when seen as integral to our understanding of George Eliot the artist.

Early Verse

These poems are mainly of interest because they predate 'George Eliot' and reflect some of Mary Anne Evans's thoughts and feelings during the 1830s and 1840s. Her early poem 'Question and Answer' is a translation from German, 'As tu vu la lune se lever' an attempt at French verse, while the rest are 'largely derivative in sentiment and style', as Margaret Reynolds has said. Like many other young women of her time, Mary Anne learned certain 'formulas and themes' from the 'many annuals and album books designed for female readership'.[7] Her School Notebook furnishes plenty of copied-out examples: 'The Forsaken', 'He whispered praises in my ear / Oh! I remember well', 'The Unwilling Bride', 'Forget Thee?', 'My Father's at the Helm', 'Death hath been there since last we met', 'If sometimes in the haunts of men / Thine image from my breast may fade' – and so on.[8] The speaker in 'Sonnet' sounds a lit-

7. Margaret Reynolds, 'Poetry of George Eliot' in John Rignall (ed.), *Oxford Reader's Companion to George Eliot* (Oxford, Oxford University Press, 2000), pp. 304–8; p. 305. Reynolds points out that *The Keepsake* for 1832 is discussed in chapter 27 of *Middlemarch*, and that 'the effeminate feebleness of the "Keepsake" style' is mentioned in 'The Natural History of German Life' (1856).

8. Cf. School Notebook [1833?–1835?], Yale IV, 13, ff. 1–30. The handwritten introductory page, by a member of staff at the Beinecke Rare Book and Manuscript Library, reads, in part, 'Verses by Alaric A. Watts, N. T. H. Bayly, Thomas Dale and others, mostly extracted from annuals and magazines'. See also the headnote to 'On Being Called a Saint'.

tle like another adolescent, in the 'The Indian Girl's Song', who pines for home, despite being 'in a lovely clime / Of bright and glowing flowers', presumably England: 'This bright clime throws no spell o'er me / Oh! none like my native land!' (ll. 1–2, 15–16).[9] Of particular interest, however, are 'On Being Called a Saint', because it may well be one of Eliot's first poems; 'Knowing that shortly I must put off this tabernacle', her first published work; and 'Mid the rich store of nature's gifts to man', written at the time when she had turned her back on Christianity. Given the pressure brought to bear on her by family and friends to change her mind about not attending church, it is little wonder that she urged 'sympathy', the 'best image' of the 'Great Spirit [bidding] creation teem / With conscious being and intelligence' ('Mid the rich store', ll. 10, 4–5). Generally, however, it is the later poems of the 1860s and beyond that merit closer study.

The 1874 and 1878 editions of *Jubal*

On 6 March 1874 George Eliot sent her publisher, John Blackwood, a small collection of poems, including 'Agatha' (1869), 'How Lisa Loved the King' (1869), 'The Legend of Jubal' (1870) and 'Armgart' (1871), which had 'already been printed in fugitive form'.[10] She

9. School Notebook [1833?–1835?], Yale IV, 13, f. 11. The author of 'The Indian Girl's Song' is not identified.

10. The order of the 1874 *Jubal* is: 'The Legend of Jubal', 'Agatha', 'Armgart', 'How Lisa Loved the King', 'A Minor Prophet', 'Brother and Sister', 'Stradivarius', 'Two Lovers', 'Arion' and 'O May I Join the Choir Invisible'. For full publication details, see the respective headnotes. See also the 'Facsimile Title Pages', Appendix D in Vol. 2, pp. 211–19.

told Blackwood, 'Mr. Lewes wishes me to get [them] published in May ... and every one of those I now send you represents an idea which I care for strongly and wish to propagate as far as I can. Else I should forbid myself from adding to the mountainous heap of poetical collections.'[11] When he and Eliot were compiling the Cabinet Edition of her collected works (1878–80), four more poems were added to *Jubal*, this time for more pragmatic reasons. John Blackwood's nephew, William, who had begun to take over the publishing business from his ailing uncle, wrote to her on 7 August 1878, 'The other Volume [of shorter poems] will take some planning and scheming to swell it out to the required length unless you have any other poems you wish to insert in it. Will you kindly let me know as to this at your early convenience?' Two days later, she wrote back, 'As to the "Jubal" volume, there will, I hope be added enough to save you from difficulty as to the size'. Her reply indicates she had already completed or, perhaps, was still composing, one or two of the additional poems. She wrote again to William Blackwood on 15 August, 'For the volume of miscellaneous poems, there will be (retaining the present page of 20 lines) enough additional material to make the volume about 300

11. *Letters*, Vol. VI, pp. 25–6. Blackwood received them with customary diplomacy and expedient encouragement:

> I have had a copy of the proofs lying in my dressing room and have been reading and rereading the Poems at night. They are very beautiful. There is a solemn cadence and power, almost a warning voice about them all, which becomes very impressive when thought over. You must have been thinking if not writing Poetry all your life, and if you have any lighter pieces written before the sense of what a great author should do for mankind came so strongly upon you, I should like very much to look at them. (*Letters*, Vol. VI, p. 37)

pages, which I see from the volumes of "Scenes of Clerical Life" will be a suitable size to run with the other works'. John Blackwood advised her on 29 September, 'Willie tells me they are ready in the printing office for the additional matter you propose for the second volume of poetry so will you send it to Edinburgh'; and she wrote to William Blackwood once more on 3 October, 'I send by today's post the additional matter for the reprint of "Jubal" etc.'[12] The additional poems were 'A College Breakfast-Party',[13] 'Self and Life', 'Sweet Evenings Come and Go, Love' and 'The Death of Moses'. Unfortunately, Eliot's diary for 1878 has disappeared,[14] making it impossible to verify if any of the additional poems were written that year.[15]

The sales of *Jubal* started off well. In early May 1874, Blackwood had 1,609 copies of the first edition on sale for six shillings each.[16] (A second printing of 1,313 copies of the first edition, with minor corrections, followed in July 1874.)[17] Later in May, John Blackwood reported they had already sold 800 copies; by August 1874, 1,609 copies; and on 16 September 1874, William Blackwood told Eliot that *Jubal* was still selling well.[18]

12. *Letters*, Vol. VII, pp. 51, 55, 58, 69, 70.

13. 'A College Breakfast-Party' was first published in *Macmillan's Magazine* in July 1878.

14. Cited in *Journals*, p. 149.

15. I have followed what is presumably Eliot's ordering of the 1878 *Jubal* poems under the heading '*The Legend of Jubal* (1878) Poems'. There is no correspondence confirming she determined the order, but it is unlikely that she left it to her publishers, given her habitual interest in all other details (thickness and tint of paper, colours of book covers, type and size of fonts, size of margins and so on).

16. *BH*, p. 509.

17. *Letters*, Vol. VI, p. 57.

18. *Letters*, Vol. VI, pp. 50 n. 73, 80.

In 1875, Blackwood's ledger charges recorded 742 copies still 'boarding', but a further 257 copies were sold in 1875 and the rest by 1880.[19] American, German and Canadian editions of *Jubal* also appeared in 1874.[20] The 1878 *Jubal* was priced five shillings, and a total of 3,414 copies were printed for the nineteen- and then twenty-volume Cabinet Editions published between December 1878 and May 1881.[21] Blackwood sent Eliot a bank order for £777.12.6 on 27 January 1879, of which £212.11.4 was for the Cabinet Edition of her collected works, which, he said, had been selling extremely well.[22] However, on 13 February 1880, William Blackwood's statement of sales to Eliot recorded only four copies of the 1878 *Jubal* sold, compared with thousands of copies of her novels, the declining sales mirroring *Jubal*'s critical reception.[23]

Early Criticism

During her lifetime, what Eliot was keen to propagate in poetry received polite reviews; immediately after her death, it tended to be dismissed altogether. A brief anonymous notice in the *Westminster and Foreign Quarterly Review* announced that the 1874 *Jubal* will 'assuredly take a foremost place in the literature, not only of our day, but of the world'. Noting that the poetry is concerned with the doctrine of self-sacrifice, a common theme in Eliot's novels, the reviewer said *Jubal*

19. *BH*, p. 513.
20. Cf. *BH*, pp. 515–22; *Letters*, Vol. VII, p. 364.
21. 788 copies were printed in December 1878, June 1879 and January 1881, and 1,050 copies in May 1881 (*BH*, pp. 595–6).
22. *Letters*, Vol. VII, pp. 97–8.
23. Cf. *Letters*, Vol. VII, pp. 251–2.

treats it with 'greater power and deeper insight'. He added, 'The whole teaching of the "Legend of Jubal" … is summed up in lines which certainly are unequalled in modern literature for power, depth of thought, and beauty of language'. Other poets simply do not measure up. 'Will any one of the writers of the thin little octavos before us read George Eliot's "Brother and Sister," and then their own compositions? If this experiment does not convince them that they have not the "faculty divine" no words of ours can.'[24] However, even before this glowing endorsement by someone apparently unwilling to criticize Britain's greatest living novelist, the tone had been set for the sort of criticism that has predominated ever since. H. Buxton Forman, better known today as Thomas J. Wise's partner in 'forgery' than as an astute literary critic,[25] wrote an article in *Tinsley's Magazine* in December 1868, in which he considered Eliot's unascribed epigraphs in *Felix Holt*. He predicted that it was unlikely she would 'surpass, or even equal, her prose achievements by anything produced in verse … and that opinion has been recently confirmed by the publication of *The Spanish Gypsy*' (June 1868). The epigraphs, he said, are 'charming' instances of high prose reared up into verse 'for the sake of a holiday, and no more'. Some are 'forcible' and 'admirable in thought and applicability to the respective chapters', but they lack all 'traces of that clearly-defined individuality of

24. Anonymous, 'Belles Lettres', *The Westminster and Foreign Quarterly Review*, XLV (1874), pp. 574–90; p. 582. See 'Contemporary Reviews', Appendix F in Vol. 2, pp. 229–67; p. 244. For a similar, albeit more qualified assessment, see the headnote to 'Will Ladislaw's Song'.

25. For more on Wise and Forman's forgeries, see the headnote to 'Agatha' and *BH*, pp. 391, 393–9.

style which all great serious, and accomplished practitioners of verse betray in even so small a compass as these headings'. Some of the epigraphs, he went on, are marked by 'condensation', but even here they are imitative of Shakespeare, Samuel Butler, Wordsworth and Elizabeth Barrett Browning: 'it is hardly necessary to enforce here that the power of assimilation, or reproduction, however large, is far from an infallible index of self-existent poetic faculty'.[26] Edward Dowden, Professor of English at Trinity College, Dublin, considered the 'fugitive' poems in an article for the *Contemporary Review* (1872) and judged them 'honest failures':

> The poems are conspicuously inferior to the novels, and a striking indication that poetry is not George Eliot's element as artist is this, that in her poems the idea and the matter do not really interpenetrate; the idea stands above the matter as a master above a slave, and subdues the matter to its will … A large rhythm sustains the verse, similar to the movement of a calmly musical period of prose; but at best the music of the lines is a measurable music; under the verse there lies no living heart of music, with curious pulsation, and rhythm, which is a miracle of the blood … The author was acquainted with the precise position of the vocal organs in singing; the pity is she could not sing.[27]

The novelist and critic Henry James followed Dowden's lead, highlighting the problem of form and spontaneity

26. H. Buxton Forman, 'George Eliot', *Tinsley's Magazine*, 3 (December 1868) pp. 565–78; pp. 568–9, 577.

27. Edward Dowden, 'George Eliot', *The Contemporary Review*, reproduced in *Littell's Living Age*, 115 (October–December 1872),

in the poems. He called them 'interesting failures': 'Our author's verse is a mixture of spontaneity of thought and excessive reflectiveness of expression, and its value is generally more in the idea than in the form ... you get the substance of her thought in the short poems, without the somewhat rigid envelope of her poetic diction' that you get in, say, 'Armgart', which, although 'the best thing', would have been even better had it been written in prose.[28]

For James, and some others mentioned below, it was not just the absence of music in the verse but also Eliot's agnosticism that undermined her poetry. Armgart shares the 'almost gratuitously sad' fate of Eliot's other heroines, James said, because even though Eliot has 'an ardent desire and faculty for positive, active, constructive belief of the old-fashioned kind ... she has fallen upon a critical age and felt its contagion and dominion'. Had she been blessed with 'passionate faith', she 'would have achieved something incalculably great'.[29] In an obituary, the writer in the *London Quarterly Review* focused on the lines 'The faith that life on earth ... / Throbbing responsive to the far-off orbs' ('A Minor

---

pp. 100–10; pp. 100–1 (see Vol. 2, pp. 231–42). For similar comments, see 'George Eliot', *London Quarterly Review*, LVII (October 1881 and January 1882), pp. 154–760; p. 173; W. Fraser Rae, 'George Eliot's Life and Writings', *International Review*, 10 (1881), pp. 447–58, 497–509; Margaret Lonsdale, *George Eliot: Thoughts Upon Her Life, Her Books, and Herself* (London, Kegan Paul, Trench & Co., 1886), pp. 1–52; p. 31; Joseph Jacobs, *George Eliot, Matthew Arnold, Browning, Newman: Essays and Reviews from the 'Athenæm'* (London, David Nutt, 1891), pp. 3–73; pp. 14–15; Frederick Harrison, 'George Eliot's Place in Literature', *The Forum*, XX (September 1895–February 1896), pp. 65–78; pp. 74–6.

28. Henry James, 'George Eliot's Legend of Jubal', *The North American Review*, CXIX (1874), pp. 484–9; pp. 485, 488–9 (see Vol. 2, pp. 245–51).

29. James, 'George Eliot's Legend of Jubal', p. 489.

Prophet', ll. 286–325), citing them as evidence of Eliot's 'instinctive belief in development of good, as of other things, which seems to have been especially bestowed on the nineteenth century to comfort it in its many sorrows'. But this, he went on to say, is a poor substitute for a belief in Christ. Even the promise of immortality through 'joining that choir invisible' is not enough, since it is accessible 'only if genius of intellect or character has been vouchsafed to him'.[30] Rose Elizabeth Cleveland, in *George Eliot's Poetry and Other Studies*, found the verse

> a labyrinth of wonder and beauty; crowded with ethics lofty and pure as Plato's; with human natures fine and fresh as Shakespeare's; but a labyrinth in which you lose the guiding cord! With the attitude and utterance of her spirit confronting me, I cannot allow her verse to be poetry. She is the *raconteur*, not the *vates*; the scientist, not the seer.

This is partly, according to Cleveland, because poetry and agnosticism are incompatible. Real poetry always offers at the very least some glimpse of immortality, which agnosticism denies.[31] In the *Spectator*'s obituary, the writer also felt Eliot's poetry lacking in 'inspiration' and full of the 'speculative melancholy' found in the novels, except that in the verse it 'predominates fatally'. 'Throughout her poems she is always plumbing the deep waters for an anchorage, and reporting "no sound-

30. Anonymous, 'George Eliot', *London Quarterly Review*, LVII (October 1881 and January 1882), pp. 154–76; pp. 164–5.

31. Rose Elizabeth Cleveland, *George Eliot's Poetry and Other Studies* (New York and London, Funk & Wagnalls, 1885), pp. 9–23; p. 23 (see Vol. 2, pp. 252–67).

ings"'. 'Jubal' is a case in point, he said. It tries to teach us that our moral standing is improved in death, 'as though the loss of self were the loss of selfishness, which it not only is not, but never could be, since selfishness can only be morally extinguished in a living self'. Eliot's teaching, he added, amounts to 'a moral gloss put on the face of a bad business'.[32]

Social Evolution and Immortality

However, at least two of Eliot's best critics saw that her verse returns again and again to ideas of social evolution and the consolation of immortality. Concentrating on the 'tragic aspect of life' in the poems, Dowden, despite his lament about the singer, valued Eliot's song. In his review he talks about the self-renunciation that heroines in Eliot's novels and poetry variously experience. Maggie, Romola, Fedalma and Armgart, he said, are alike insofar as they are suddenly, or after long ordeals, forced to renounce the talents, passions and joys which help to distinguish them. Why? Because, Eliot teaches us, there is no individual life after death, although the larger life in which we all participate goes on. Individual life is short, filled with joy and suffering, and the only immortality on offer is through binding ourselves to the 'higher rule' of this world. By contributing to the needs of others, instead of themselves, Eliot's heroines go on to enrich their larger worlds. Their personal hopes and aspirations are crushed and this is painfully sad, but then 'The world is sad ... and being sad, the world needs sympathy more than it needs joy – joy which in its

32. Anonymous, 'George Eliot', *The Spectator*, reproduced in *Littell's Living Age*, 148 (January–March, 1881), pp. 318–20; p. 320.

blindness is cruel'. Jubal's joy is cruel, too, returning home only to be beaten and rejected by the people singing his praises. 'This is tragic', Dowden says, 'His apotheosis and martyrdom were one'; his consolation, however, is being 'incorporate' in

> A strong persistent life
> Panting through generations as one breath,
> And filling with its soul the blank of death. (ll. 245–7)[33]

The critic Charles Gardner, writing in the early years of the twentieth century, when Eliot's entire critical reputation was in steep decline, also saw that her poetry deals with immortality above all else. As he put it, for Eliot, 'Man's immortality is in his after effects'. We see this in the stories of Jubal and Moses: one lived on in 'the larger life of Music', the other 'as Law', and the idea of living on is summed up and given concise expression in 'O May I Join the Choir Invisible'.[34] 'Self and Life' similarly articulates in abstract terms the philosophy of living on through love. Self demands that 'Changeful' Life 'Justify thyself to me' (ll. 1, 6), since age has mainly brought 'Fear' and 'loathing' for 'the law' (ll. 19, 57, 60) before which Self has been made to bow down. Life's answer is, 'I brought a love' that 'Filled, o'erflowed [thee] with tenderness' (ll. 61, 69), which assuages Self to accept that 'Life is justified by love' (l. 78).

33. Dowden, 'George Eliot', p. 110.

34. Charles Gardner, *The Inner Life of George Eliot* (London, Sir Isaac Pitman & Sons, Ltd., 1912), pp. 198, 199–200. Summing up Eliot's poetic achievement, Gardner says, 'We claim no high place for George Eliot's poetry – it was not her proper medium. But to a student of her inner life it is valuable, as she expressed herself in it very directly' (pp. 213–14).

In the words of 'Ex Oriente Lux', since the early days of our planet, life has evolved towards 'sublimer union': 'While yet the western half was cold and sad', 'Asia was the earliest home of light' (ll. 20, 7, 9). In time, Earth's young race 'Clove sense & image subtilly in twain, / Then wedded them, till heavenly Thought was born' (ll. 21–2). That same belief in social evolution lies behind the assertion in 'A Minor Prophet' that things are 'being shaped / To glorious ends':

> that great faith
> Is but the rushing and expanding stream
> Of thought, of feeling, fed by all the past.
> Our finest hope is finest memory (ll. 286–92)[35]

And 'finest memory' is best achieved through the legacy of love, as the sonnet sequence 'Brother and Sister' illustrates. Recalling the many times brother and sister went rambling through the countryside, the sister-narrator says

> Those hours were seed to all my after good;
> My infant gladness, through eye, ear, and touch,
> Took easily as warmth a various food
> To nourish the sweet skill of loving much. (Sonnet V, ll. 5–8)

All the sights, sounds and textures of those early days 'are part of me, / My present Past, my root of piety'

35. For a discussion of Eliot's views on social evolution, see K. K. Collins, 'Questions of Method: Some Unpublished Late Essays', *Nineteenth-Century Fiction*, 35:3 (December 1980), pp. 385–405. In an untitled, late essay, in which she responded to aspects of theories of social evolution, Eliot wrote, 'The mere fact that mankind has a conception of what is pure & lovely, might be fairly taken as a ground of faith in the human nature out of which the conception was born, & the proper attitude of faith is bravery'. The essay was first published as part of Collins's article.

(Sonnet VI, ll. 13–14), even now after the 'dire years whose awful name is Change / Had grasped our souls still yearning in divorce' (Sonnet XI, ll. 9–10). Nevertheless, in the words of 'Self and Life', 'Half man's truth must hidden lie / If unlit by Sorrow's eye', and Sorrow teaches 'Willing pain of ministry' (ll. 51–2, 54), or love in the widest sense of that word. Having learned from pain to love, and having seen the connection with memory, the sister finishes the sonnets with 'But were another childhood-world my share, / I would be born a little sister there' (Sonnet XI, ll. 13–14).

'Agatha', 'How Lisa Loved the King' and 'Stradivarius' offer more proof of the legacy of love. Agatha's saint-like goodness is celebrated in the song sung at feasts and weddings, which includes the verse full of 'gentle jesting with the three old maids' (l. 311):

> Here the three old maidens dwell,
> Agatha and Kate and Nell;
> See, the moon shines on the thatch,
> We will go and shake the latch.
>   Heart of Mary, cup of joy,
>   *Give us mirth without alloy!* (ll. 342–7)

The nobility, purity and unselfishness of Lisa's love, expressed in the music and words of Minuccio and Mico, move King Pedro to take notice of a lowly maid, thereby ensuring that she will be remembered. For his part, Stradivarius's unwavering devotion to his craft guarantees that he is remembered long after his death. Thus, not only Bach and Joachim

> made our joy to-day:
> Another soul was living in the air
> And swayed it to true deliverance
> Of high invention and responsive skill (ll. 16–19)

Hearing with Eyes

Music is a predominant theme in the poems, closely linked to the idea of immortality. 'It is noteworthy, by the way', Henry James wrote, 'that three of these poems [in the 1874 *Jubal*] are on themes connected with music, and yet we remember no representation of a musician among the multitudinous figures which people the author's novels'.[36] In the novels before 1874 there are no musicians resembling Armgart, Arion, Jubal, Klesmer, Mirah and the Princess Leonora Halm-Eberstein, but, as Beryl Gray rightly says, commenting on an extract from Eliot's Journal, 14 April 1858,

> 'music that stirs all one's devout emotions blends everything into harmony, – makes one feel part of one whole, which one loves all alike, losing the sense of a separate self'. This sense of music-engendering unity is conveyed to the novels (and poems) as an organising principle.[37]

That stirring of 'devout emotions' is achieved through 'hearing with eyes', which Jubal illustrates.

In a section on music in one of George Eliot's Pforzheimer notebooks, comprising extracts and paraphrases from John Pike Hullah's *The History of Modern Music, A Course of Lectures Delivered at the Royal Institute of Great Britain* (1862), Eliot indicates what she means by 'hearing with eyes'. Specifically, the notebook includes a comment on Guido Aretino's emphasis on '*hearing with the eye*', resulting in an 'absolutely timeless' music, a 'plain-song', '[extolling] a kind of respect'

36. James, 'George Eliot's Legend of Jubal', pp. 487–8.

37. Beryl Gray, *George Eliot and Music* (Houndmills and London, Macmillan, 1989), p. x. See also Delia da Sousa Correa, *George Eliot, Music and Victorian Culture* (Basingstoke, Hampshire, Palgrave, 2003), pp. 1–10.

whenever it is heard.[38] 'Hearing with eyes' is based on the last line of Shakespeare's Sonnet 23, 'To hear with eyes belongs to love's fine wit'. In *Felix Holt*, Eliot misquotes Shakespeare's line in one of the double epigraphs to chapter XXVII: 'To hear with eyes is part of love's rare wit'. Nevertheless, the epigraph is apt since Felix, in the language of the sonnet, is like the frightened 'unperfect actor' or some 'fierce thing replete with too much rage' who 'decays' in his 'own love's strength'; and Esther, ennobled by his often severe, moral example and the story of Rufus Lyon and Annette, eloquently pleads for love's 'dumb presages' – first in the courtroom scene when she speaks on Felix's behalf and later when she comforts the ruined Transomes and brings mother and son together. In *Middlemarch* the line is misquoted again, this time to describe Mrs Vincy's feelings towards the ailing Fred: '"to hear with eyes belongs to love's rare wit", and the mother in the fullness of her heart not only divined Fred's longing, but she felt ready for any sacrifice in order to satisfy him'.[39] The variations on Shakespeare's line in *Felix Holt* and *Middlemarch* indicate that Eliot quoted it from memory – which, in turn, points to the power of its abiding influence on her.

Eliot's interest in hearing with eyes points to her moral vision. Aretino and Shakespeare gave her a metaphor for the human experience of very real and direct feelings of

38. Eliot's entry reads, in part, 'Of Guido Aretino we hear first early in the Eleventh Century as resident in the Benedictine monastery of Pomposa between Ferrara & Ravenna' (cf. *Pforzheimer*, Vol. 1, pp. 145–8).

39. Cabinet Edition, Vol. 1, p. 406. The line from Sonnet 23 also appears in the Berg notebook under *Shakespeare's Sonnets* (cf. Pratt and Neufeldt, pp. 209–13, 265–6); in 'A Writer's Notebook, 1854–1879' (cf. Wiesenfarth, pp. 49, 177); and in the 'Quarry for *Romola* and *The Spanish Gypsy*' (Bodleian Ms. Don. G. 8, f. 20).

love, respect, sympathy, understanding, tolerance, reverence. Why such feelings occur remains a mystery, but that they occur is undeniable, since music and poetry often bring them about. For Eliot, I suspect, the same feelings could be prompted by any revelatory experience making intelligible life's mysterious workings. Most of Eliot's characters are 'unperfect actors on the stage[s]' of her novels and poetry, experiencing some sort of 'despair' as they reflect on their lives with a 'widening retrospect' (cf. 'O May I Join the Choir Invisible', l. 15). Often they inflict pain and suffering on themselves and others, because they do not hear with eyes, yet they are redeemed or at least consoled after learning to use this extraordinary, verifiable faculty. Throughout her fiction Eliot emphasized the difficulties involved in the struggle towards right moral conduct, but, insofar as she believed in its attainability, she remained optimistic about the future.[40]

That philosophy of life is clearly articulated in 'The Legend of Jubal', tracing the origin of music and its redemptive power. Jubal quite literally hears with eyes while observing Tubalcain hammering away at his forge:

> Jubal, too, watched the hammer, till his eyes,
> No longer following its fall or rise,

40. I am grateful to William Baker for giving me permission to reprint parts of my brief article in *The George Eliot George Henry Lewes Newsletter*, 12–13 (September 1988), pp. 6–11. Delia da Sousa Correa also draws attention to the 'hearing with eyes' lines in 'The Legend of Jubal', arguing

> Aside from the specific figurative overlaps of hammering and speech, Eliot is also explicitly describing the forging of a particular kind of language. Her employment of musical figures in 'Jubal' and elsewhere revivifies the clichéd alliance of music and poetry as 'sister' arts to address questions about the formation of literary language. (*George Eliot, Music and Victorian Culture*, p. 194)

Seemed glad with something that they could not see,
But only listened to – some melody,
Wherein dumb longings inward speech had found,
Won from the common store of struggling sound. (ll. 248–53)

Hearing with eyes results in him grasping

That love, hope, rage, and all experience,
Were fused in vaster being, fetching thence
Concords and discords, cadences and cries
That seemed from some world-shrouded soul to rise
Some rapture more intense, some mightier rage,
Some living sea that burst the bounds of man's brief age.
(ll. 262–7)

In other words, he intuits a 'higher rule', to which everyone is necessarily subject, but which simultaneously offers individuals escape from the 'unnamed discontent' of the sort that continues to gnaw away at Cain and his people in their land of plenty (cf. ll. 404–9). Once Jubal's music is heard, the younger generation 'Thrilled towards the future' (l. 433), while Cain 'who had lived through twice three centuries',

Dreamed himself dimly through the travelled days
Till in clear light he paused, and felt the sun
That warmed him when he was a little one;
Felt that true heaven, the recovered past,
The dear small Known amid the Unknown vast,
And in that heaven wept. (ll. 424–32)

Thus, Jubal's music is a trigger, a means to an end: it reveals to his people a form of immortality, 'their larger soul' (l. 469), offering hope to some and consolation to others. The mistake Jubal makes is thinking that his discovery somehow exempts him from obedience to that 'higher rule'. In *As You Like It*, one of Eliot's most frequently quoted Shakespearean plays, Duke Senior 'Finds tongues in trees, books in the running brooks, / Sermons in stones, and good in everything' (II.i.16–17) precisely because he has humbled himself before nature. Jubal sets off on a similar quest of learning, but he is mistakenly intent on appropriating nature for selfish ends, so that 'My life shall grow like trees both tall and fair' (l. 487). Predictably, he fails and returns home a bruised soul, doubly so when his unwitting votaries reject him. For their part, they have made the mistake Ludwig Feuerbach talks of in *The Essence of Christianity*, turning Jubal into a god and hence rejecting him when he appears in the flesh.[41] It is left to the Voice of his Past to console him: he will die, but, thanks to his gift of music, he will achieve immortality by living on in the memory of future generations (ll. 778–9).

Significantly, the stories of Jubal and Moses resemble each other: Jubal lies 'tombless on this sod' ('Jubal', l. 776); Moses 'has no tomb' ('The Death of Moses', l. 121); angels lift Moses to heaven (cf. 'Moses', ll. 109–14); and the deliberately ambiguous last nine lines of 'Jubal' just about avoid saying that he is similarly rewarded. The parallels are surely deliberate. For Eliot, Jubal is as important as Moses because he unlocked a timeless, universal language, which can move people to see that there is goodness beyond frequently unhappy lives. In that sense, the myth of Jubal, which originated with Eliot, is like the story of Moses, since it also looks forward to the promise of a better future and freedom

41. Discussing how it is that the idea of God is turned into an objective 'reality', Feuerbach says, 'in conceiving God, man first conceives reason as it truly is, though by means of the imagination he conceives this divine nature as distinct from reason, because as a being affected by external things he is accustomed always to distinguish the object from the conception of it' (Ludwig Feuerbach, *The Essence of Christianity*, trans. George Eliot (1854; New York, Hagerstown, San Francisco and London, Harper Torchbooks, 1957), p. 37).

from human bondage, despite moments of bitter personal disappointment.[42]

It is against this understanding of immortality that 'Arion' should be read. The song the titular hero sings moments before his death is a sort of secular prayer to the 'All-creating Presence', which Jubal is dimly aware of as he '[quits] mortality' ('Jubal', ll. 790–1). Fortified with 'inward fire' (l. 42), Arion sang, 'Fearless of death or other wrong' (l. 50), and majestically 'leaped on high' (l. 61), sure of his sublimation. This is also the consolation Walpurga and Leo impress on Armgart. Like Jubal, she is initially wrong to think her extraordinary gift of music gives her dispensation from the 'higher rule'. The extra 'trill' in her magnificent performance of Gluck's *Orfeo ed Euridice*, which exercises Leo and is laughingly dismissed by her (cf. ll. 72–97), hints at her Jubal-like arrogance. Similarly, there is a touch of vanity in the scene where she turns down the Graf's proposal of marriage, telling him 'I sing for love of song and that renown / Which is the spreading act, the world-wide share, / Of good that I was born with' (ll. 276–8). Loving song is commendable; loving renown, though understandable, is not.[43] All this is not to dismiss the genuine conflict of interests Armgart experiences, and to which I refer in my headnote to the poem, but to dwell too much on Armgart's sorrow is to ignore her consolation.

42. Lewes told Alexander Main in a letter dated 21 October 1871, 'It is pure myth – and a myth of her own creation too, which few readers suspect. The fact is, it reads so like an old Saga that no suspicion arises as to its origin' (*Letters*, Vol. V, p. 205).

43. Creel draws attention to Minuccio's description in 'How Lisa Loved the King', 'He was a singer of most gentle fame – / A noble, kindly spirit, not elate / That he was famous, but that song was great' (ll. 250–2), and comments, 'Armgart when she is famous, *is* elated, and not simply glad that song is great' (Creel, p. 129 n.). In 'The

Recent Criticism and Conclusion

In the past twenty-five years or so, and mainly among feminist critics, 'Armgart' has been Eliot's most frequently considered poem, the rest mostly neglected.[44] This is because, together with *Daniel Deronda*'s Princess Leonora Halm-Eberstein, Armgart bitterly comments on '"The Woman's Lot: a Tale of Everyday"' ('Armgart', l. 689), suggesting that there may be more than ameliorative teaching in Eliot's attitude to gender. Sandra M. Gilbert and Susan Gubar briefly look at 'Jubal' and 'Self and Life' before turning to the heroine they call Eliot's 'Satanic Eve'.[45] Like some other Eliot heroes and

---

Politics of a Feminist Poetics: "Armgart" and George Eliot's Critical Response to *Aurora Leigh*' in Kate Flint (ed.), *Poetry and Politics* (Cambridge, D. S. Brewer, 1996), pp. 62–83, Louise Hudd argues that Armgart's 'egoism has serious political, not just moral, consequences' insofar as it not only betrays an elitist attitude towards ordinary women but marginalizes them. For a discussion likening Armgart to a monster, see Britta Zangen, 'That Monsterous Self: Armgart and the Alcharisi', *George Eliot – George Henry Lewes Studies*, 46–7 (September 2004), pp. 79–87.

44. But see Bonnie J. Lisle, 'Art and Egoism in George Eliot's Poetry', *Victorian Poetry*, 22:3 (Autumn 1984), pp. 263–78; Gillian Beer, 'Voice and Vengeance: The Poems and *Daniel Deronda*' in *George Eliot* (Brighton, The Harvester Press, 1986), chapter 7; Kristin Brady, *George Eliot* (Houndmills and London, Macmillan, 1992), pp. 152–8; Isobel Armstrong, '"A Music of Thine Own": Women's poetry – an expressive tradition?' in *Victorian Poetry: Poetry, Poetics and Politics* (London and New York, Routledge, 1993), chapter 12.

45. Sandra M. Gilbert and Susan Gubar, *The Madwoman in the Attic: The Woman Writer and the Nineteenth-Century Literary Imagination* (New Haven and London, Yale University Press, 1979), pp. 451–2. They see 'Jubal' and 'Self and Life' as reflecting Eliot's own anxieties about authorship. Jubal belongs to a group of characters resembling their author, all suffering from 'passivity, illness, and impotence … directly related to their visionary insight'. For more discussions that consider some of the poems, including 'Armgart', in

heroines, Armgart's 'divine powers', they say, are 'never fully achieved'; she is 'cursed' for being far from 'paternal grace', she has 'demonic energy' and she ends up in a 'secondary position'.[46] For Kathleen Blake, 'Armgart' offers 'a double critique of the conflict of love and art for a woman': on the one hand, love and art are reconciled when Armgart determines to teach music in the Freiburg where Walpurga was born; on the other hand, love and art remain divided insofar as Armgart remains contemptuous of the common lot of women that she has necessarily had to reconcile herself to, following the loss of her voice.[47] Louise Hudd develops a point raised by Kathleen Blake: seeing 'Armgart' as part of Eliot's extensive response to Elizabeth Barrett Browning's *Aurora Leigh* (1857), which began with 'Mr. Gilfil's Love-Story' (1857) and ended with *Daniel Deronda* (1876). Specifically, Hudd says, 'Armgart' questions Barrett Browning's 'problematic depiction of class politics and social reform'. By insisting that Romney's blinding 'had to be', by encouraging fellow poets to focus on their artistic vision and nothing else, and by having Marian reject Romney's offer of marriage, Barrett Browning propounded a theory of art and politics

---

the light of authorial anxiety or self-division, see Lisle, 'Art and Egoism in George Eliot's Poetry'; Rosemarie Bodenheimer, 'Ambition and its Audiences: George Eliot's Performing Figures', *Victorian Studies*, 34:1 (Autumn 1990), pp. 7–33; Pauline Nestor, *George Eliot* (Basingstoke, Palgrave, 2002), pp. 22–3, 125–7; Delia da Sousa Correa, *George Eliot, Music and Victorian Culture*, pp. 91, 153–67; and my headnote to 'Jubal'.

46. *The Madwoman in the Attic*, pp. 452–3.

47. Kathleen Blake, '*Armgart* – George Eliot on the Woman Artist' in Angela Leighton (ed.), *Victorian Women Poets: A Critical Reader* (Oxford and Cambridge, MA, Blackwell Publishers Ltd., 1996), pp. 82–7.

both unrealistic and elitist. In contrast, 'Armgart' explores the 'obligations of the exceptional woman to her society and to other women, raising the issue of what it means to be marginalized in the interest of a political action which might liberate only the exceptional few rather than the many'. Most of the criticism on 'Armgart' has drawn attention to the 'egoism of artistic ambition' that Eliot is often seen to have experienced herself, Hudd goes on to argue; however, 'Armgart' is more than 'just a psychodrama; its discourse of revolution reveals that egoism has serious political, not just moral, consequences'. Armgart's egoism is not only associated with Graf Dornberg but also Walpurga and, in letting Walpurga criticize Armgart's egoism, the poem attacks the attitude that accepts that ordinary women like Walpurga are in some way inferior or subservient to the gifted, artistic woman. In so doing, Eliot champions the ordinary woman and 'broadens the base of Barrett Browning's feminist aims'.[48]

Thus, a few of the ideas that Eliot cared for strongly and wished to propagate still continue to spawn limited debate, while the poetry as a whole continues to be dismissed.[49] That is surely a pity, because, as the writer of her obituary in *Blackwood's Magazine* put it:

> If George Eliot fell short of being a poet, it was not for want of many of the higher qualities of the poetic faculty. Apart, however, from their

48. Hudd, 'The Politics of a Feminist Poetics'. See also Jennifer Uglow, *George Eliot* (London, Virago Press, 1987), p. 198; Brady, *George Eliot*, pp. 156–8; and Renata Kobetts Miller, 'The Exceptional Woman and her Audience: *Armgart*, Performance and Authorship', *The George Eliot Review*, 35 (2004), pp. 38–45.

49. Cf. Lisle, 'George Eliot remains at best a second-rate poet. That the poems are so pedestrian, in fact, may tempt us to overlook

intrinsic merits, her poems derive an interest from her prose works, and will continue to be read by all who desire to fathom the fullness of her genius, and to comprehend the true character of the power which she was able to put forth in her prose writings.[50]

their real importance ... Whatever their dubious merits as verse, the poems embody "ideas" that afford us insight into the writer and her fiction' ('Art and Egoism in George Eliot's Poetry', p. 263). Cf. also Kerry McSweeney, *George Eliot (Marian Evans) A Literary Life* (Houndmills and London, Macmillan, 1991), p. 112; and Nestor, *George Eliot*, p. 125.

50. Anonymous, 'George Eliot', *Blackwood's Magazine*, reproduced in *Littell's Living Age*, 148 (January–March, 1881), pp. 664–74; p. 672.

ABBREVIATIONS

AM	*Atlantic Monthly Magazine*
Beichner	Paul E. Beichner, 'The Medieval Representation of Music, Jubal or Tubalcain?' in A. L. Gafriel and J. N. Garvin (eds), *Texts and Studies in the History of Mediaeval Education*, No. II (Notre Dame, The Mediaeval Institute, University of Notre Dame, 1954), pp. 5–27
BEM	*Blackwood's Edinburgh Magazine*
BH	William Baker and John C. Ross, *George Eliot: A Bibliographical History* (New Castle, DE, Oak Knoll Press; London, British Library, 2002)
Biography	Gordon S. Haight, *George Eliot: A Biography* (Oxford and New York, Oxford University Press, 1968)
Cabinet Edition	George Eliot, *The Works of George Eliot*, Cabinet Edition, 20 vols (Edinburgh and London, William Blackwood & Sons, 1878–80)
CO	*Christian Observer*

Creel	George W. Creel, 'The Poetry of George Eliot' (Ph.D. dissertation, University of California, 1948)
Cross	*George Eliot's Life as Related in her Letters and Journals*, ed. J. W. Cross, new edn (Edinburgh and London, William Blackwood and Sons, n.d.)
Folger Notebook	'Miscellaneous quotations', Notebook MS M.a.13, The Folger Shakespeare Library, Washington
IELM	*Index to English Library Manuscripts, Part IV, 1800–1900*, eds Barbara Rosenbaum and Pamela White (London and New York, Maunsell, 1982), Vol. 1
Irwin	*George Eliot's Daniel Deronda Notebooks*, ed. Jane Irwin (Cambridge, Cambridge University Press, 1996)
Journals	*The Journals of George Eliot*, eds Margaret Harris and Judith Johnston (Cambridge, Cambridge University Press, 1998)
1874 *Jubal*	*The Legend of Jubal and Other Poems* (Edinburgh and London, William Blackwood & Sons, 1874)
1878 *Jubal*	*The Legend of Jubal and Other Poems, Old and New* (Edinburgh and London, William Blackwood & Sons, 1878), Cabinet Edition, Vol. 10
Letters	*The George Eliot Letters*, ed. Gordon S. Haight, 9 vols (New Haven, Yale

	University Press; London, Oxford University Press, 1954–78)
MM	*Macmillan's Magazine*
M.S. Add. 34,038	'Jubal M.S.', British Library Add. 34,038. Collection of poems, bound with George Eliot's inscription to George Henry Lewes
Paris	Bernard J. Paris, 'George Eliot's Unpublished Poetry', *Studies in Philology*, LVI (July 1959), pp. 539–58.
Pforzheimer	*Some George Eliot Notebooks: An Edition of the Carl H. Pforzheimer Library's George Eliot Holograph Notebooks, MSS 707, 708, 709, 710, 711*, ed. William Baker, 4 vols (Institut für Anglistik und Amerikanistik Universität Salzburg, A–5020 Salzburg, Austria, 1976–85)
Pinney	*The Essays of George Eliot*, ed. Thomas Pinney (London, Routledge and Kegan Paul, 1963)
Pratt and Neufeldt	*George Eliot's Middlemarch Notebooks A Transcription*, eds John Clark Pratt and Victor A. Neufeldt (Berkeley, Los Angeles and London, University of California Press, 1979)
Secor	Cynthia Ann Secor, 'The Poems of George Eliot: A Critical Edition with Introduction and Notes' (Ph.D. dissertation, Cornell University, Ithaca, NY, 1969)

Wiesenfarth	*George Eliot, A Writer's Notebook, 1854–1879, and Uncollected Writings*, ed. Joseph Wiesenfarth (Charlottesville, University Press of Virginia, 1981)
Yale Poetry Notebook	George Eliot. Holograph MS notebook, The Beinecke Rare Book and Manuscript Library, Yale Univerisity, MS Vault Eliot, Section IV. George Eliot. Writings. Box Folder 21. 7. Notebook, copied about 1873–6

USE OF SYMBOLS IN TEXTUAL VARIANTS

All variants in the MSS and printed versions of the poems have been included. Eliot's original spelling and punctuation have been retained, even where non-standard. On rare occasions where missing punctuation could cause confusion, small amendments have been made; these are listed in the variants. Wherever possible, I have tried to demonstrate rather than describe textual variants. So, for example, if a MS has a double underlining beneath a letter, because Eliot wanted the printer to render the word with a capital letter, I show what she wrote: 'change' or 'death'. Line breaks are shown with a spaced forward slash (/). Where I cannot usefully show what a variant looks like, I describe it. Such editorial insertions are included within square brackets.

Symbols used throughout:

- Superscript, lower case letters identify individual variants, starting with 'a' on each new page.
- In the 'Textual Variants' section, the copy-text word(s), phrase(s) or line(s), listed by page number and letter, is followed by a square bracket

followed by the variant in the MS and/or the printed version. Thus,

b hollow:] hollow; *MS*

indicates that variant 'b' records a change in punctuation: Eliot wrote a semi-colon in the MS but this was changed (in the proofs by Eliot or by her publisher? –it is very rarely clear who made the change and/or when) to a colon. Again,

l her] her, *1869*, *Atlantic Monthly*

means that variant 'l' records that the 1869 edition of the poem and the printed version in the *Atlantic Monthly* include a comma which is omitted in the copy-text.

- Eliot's insertions are recorded with curly brackets and arrows indicating whether the changes appear above or below the original entries. For example,

f France by the Rhine,] The Rhine-edged France {France by the Rhine↑}*MS*

indicates that the copy-text phrase, 'France by the Rhine', was arrived at after Eliot first wrote 'The Rhine-edged France' in her MS and then wrote above that 'France by the Rhine' (in this case, without the comma after 'Rhine'). Here, she did not cancel her original entry.

- Changes involving cancelled but still readable words are shown this way:

g monks] monks {~~Benedictines~~↑} *MS*

In this case, Eliot wrote 'monks' in her MS and then 'Benedictines' above it, before changing her mind.

- Eliot frequently crossed out words so heavily and thoroughly that they are unreadable. In instances where a single word is cancelled, the variant appears like this:

c the garden] ~~& the little~~ {~~xxxxx~~ the garden↑} *MS*

The copy text phrase 'the garden' originally began as '& the little' in the MS; this was crossed out and a heavily scored, now unreadable word, indicated as '~~xxxxx~~', was then written above the original entry, followed by 'the garden'. Whether the first word was crossed out after the three words were written or before (because Eliot made an obvious error?) is not known. The entry simply shows what appears in the MS.

- In cases where two or more words have been cancelled and made unreadable, the symbol '~~xxxxx xxxxx~~' is used. Thus,

  a as mothers] ~~xxxxx xxxxx~~ {as mothers↑} *MS*

  shows the original MS entry consisting of two or more words now totally unreadable with 'as mothers' written above.
- In cases where a line has gone through several stages of change, each change is indicated. Thus,

  h And ever … ears.] ~~But xxxxx oft again xxxxx he xxxxx till the heights~~. / ~~Had shown him ocean with its liquid light~~. / ~~And till he heard its multitudenous roar~~ / ~~Its plunge and hiss upon the pebbled shore~~ {And ever […] ears. [left margin]} *MS*

  Here, the copy-text lines 'And ever … ears.' was arrived at after Eliot wrote four lines, which she then crossed out, making some words unreadable.

She then added the copy-text line in the left margin of the MS. Again, in the example below,

j Yet … blent,] ~~But with the feast some hunger still was blent~~ {Yet […] blent.↑}; {~~Yet with joy's nectar some strange~~ ~~thirst was blent~~ [left margin]} *MS*

the copy-text line, 'Yet … blent,' was settled on after (or at some stage during the writing of?) two discarded lines, one of which appears in the left margin.

EARLY EXPERIMENT IN VERSE

ON BEING CALLED A SAINT

This poem was first published in Haight's *Biography* (p. 20), with some of the stanzas omitted. The copy-text is found in Eliot's 'School Notebook', Yale IV, 13, ff. 26–7, described by the Beinecke Rare Book and Manuscript Library as:

> the earliest known Eliot manuscript, contain[ing] poems copied from various sources, rules and illustrative problems in arithmetic, an essay on 'Affectation and Conceit,' and a story, 'Edward Neville.' 66 leaves. Purchased from J. H. P. Pafford with the Library Associates Fund. (*Yale University Beinecke Rare Book and Manuscript Library General Collection of Rare Books and Manuscripts, George Eliot and George Henry Lewes Collection, Ms Vault Eliot* by Gordon S. Haight and Marjorie G. Wynne (1999; New Haven, Connecticut, 1975))

The introductory page of the notebook notes that 'Marianne Evans / March 16th 1834' is written on a pasted-down flyleaf.

The MS dates from her time at the Miss Franklins' School in Coventry, which Eliot began attending when she was thirteen and left in late 1836. The paper of the notebook is watermarked 1830 (cf. Yale note on introductory page to MS and *Biography*, p. 552) and contains

'On Being called a Saint', which Haight suggests was 'probably written by Mary Anne herself' (*Biography*, p. 20). Haight's hesitation to ascribe the poem unconditionally is justified: the handwriting in the notebook differs in places, allowing for the possibility that the poem, which appears to be a fair copy, was written by one of Eliot's school friends.

The version below includes the verses omitted by Haight.

On Being Called a Saint

A Saint! O would that I could claim
The privileg'd, the honour'd name
And confidently take my stand
Though lowest in the saintly band!

Would though it were in scorn applied
That term the test of truth could bide
The kingly salutations given
In mockery to the King of Heaven.

A saint and what imports the name
Thus lauded in decision's game?
"Holy and separate from sin
If good, nay even to God akin"

Is such the meaning of the name
From which a Christian shrinks with shame
Far dazzled by the glorious light
He owns his crown is all too bright

And ill might sons of Adam dare
Alone such honoured might to bear
That fearlessly he takes the load
United to the son of God

Saint! Oh! saviour give some sign
Some seal to prove the little kind
And [unreadable word] thanks thou shalt command
Thou bringing kingdoms in thy hand

Oh for an interest in that name
When hell shall ope its jaws of flame
And sinners to their doom be hurl'd
While scorned saints 'shall judge this world.'

How shall the name of Saint be prized
Tho' now neglected and despised
When truth

KNOWING THAT SHORTLY I MUST PUT OFF THIS TABERNACLE

The poem was first published in the *Christian Observer* (January 1840). Eliot sent Maria Lewis a copy of it on 17 July 1839, commenting:

> I thank you very heartily for your kind note, and I send you in return some doggrel lines, the crude fruit of a lonely walk last evening, when the words of one of our martyrs occurred to me. You must be acquainted with the idiosyncrasy of my authorship, which is that my effusions, once committed to paper, are like the laws of the Medes and Persians that alter not [cf. Daniel 6:8]. My attempt at poetry will serve to amuse you, if no more, and you love a laugh so well that it would be ungenerous to withhold the occasion of one. (*Letters*, Vol. I, pp. 27–8)

When reproducing the letter and poem in his *Life*, Cross said 'there is the first allusion to authorship, but, from the wording of the sentence, the poem referred to has evidently not been a first attempt'. In his transcription of the poem, Cross omitted stanzas 6 and 9. He then recollected Eliot having told him the poem had been published somewhere, and added, 'After a long search, I found it in the "Christian Observer" for

January 1840. That version is complete and is signed "M. A. E."' Cross also emended the biblical reference to 2 Peter 1:14 ('Knowing that shortly I must put off *this* my tabernacle, even as our Lord Jesus Christ hath shewed me'), and included a note from the editor of the *Christian Observer*:

> We do not often add a note to a poem: but if St. John found no temple in the New Jerusalem, neither will there be any need of a Bible; for we shall not then see through a glass darkly, – through the veil of Sacraments or the written word – but face to face. The Bible is God's gift, but not for heaven's use. Still, on the very verge of heaven we may cling to it, after we have bid farewell to everything [ea]rthly; and this perhaps is what M. A. E. means. (*The Christian Observer* (London, J. Hatchard and Son, Piccadilly, 1840), p. 38; and *Life*, pp. 28–9)

With respect to Eliot's somewhat unorthodox wish to take the Bible with her to heaven, Secor draws attention to Eliot's letter of 20 May 1839 to Maria Lewis, where she mentions her 'oscillating judgments':

> On no subject do I veer to all points of the compass more frequently than on the nature of the *visible* church. I am powerfully attracted in a certain direction but when I am about to settle there, counter assertions shake me from my position. I cannot enter into details but when we are together I will tell you all my difficulties. (Secor, pp. 98–9)

These 'difficulties' worsened and, on Sunday, 2 January 1842, she broke with orthodox religion altogether, refusing to attend church. That threatened the relationship between father and daughter, the two only reaching a compromise towards the middle of May 1842, when she 'agreed to attend church with him as usual, and he tacitly conceded her the right to think what she liked during service' (*Biography*, p. 44).

The copy-text is Eliot's letter to Maria Lewis, and I have followed Secor's lead in not naming the poem 'Farewell', as Haight did (cf. *Biography*, p. 585). She rightly points out that both versions sent to the *Christian Observer* and Maria Lewis bear the biblical title (Secor, p. 98).

Knowing that shortly I must put off this tabernacle

– 2 Pet. 1. 16.[a]

As o'er the fields by evening's light I stray,
I hear a still, small whisper – "Come away!
Thou must to this bright, lovely world soon say
Farewell!"[b]

The mandate I'd[c] obey, my lamp prepare,
Gird up my garments, give my soul to pray'r,
And say to earth and all that breathe earth's air
Farewell![d]

Thou sun, to whose parental beam I owe
All that has gladden'd me while here below, –[e]
Moon, stars, and covenant confirming bow,[f]
Farewell![g]

Ye verdant meads, fair blossoms,[h] stately trees,
Sweet song of birds, and soothing hum of bees,
Refreshing odours, wafted on the breeze,[i]
Farewell![j]

Ye patient servants of creation's[k] lord[l]
Whose mighty strength is govern'd by his word,
Who raiment, food[m] and help in toil afford,[n]
Farewell![o]

Ye feebler, freer tribes, that people air,
Fairy like[a] insects, making buds your lair,
Ye that in water shine, and frolic there,[b]
Farewell![c]

Books[d] that have been to me as chests of gold,
Which, miser like, I secretly have told,
And for them[e] love, health, friendship, peace have sold,[f]
Farewell![g]

Blest volume! whose clear truth-writ page,[h] once known,
Fades not before heaven's sunshine or hell's moan,
To thee I say not, of earth's gifts alone,[i]
Farewell![j]

Dear kindred, whom the lord to me has given,[k]
Must the dear tie that binds us,[l] now be riven?
No! say I *only* till we meet in heaven,[m]
Farewell![n]

There[o] shall my newborn senses find new joy,
New sounds, new sights[p] my eyes and ears employ,
Nor fear that word that here brings sad alloy,
Farewell![q]

SONNET

The sonnet is found in Eliot's letter to Maria Lewis, dated 4 September 1839 (*Letters*, Vol. I, p. 30). It was probably written immediately before it was sent, since it reflects, as Haight suggests, Eliot's state of mind at that time, as she pondered on the vanity of human wishes (*Biography*, p. 26). In her letter, she talks about having 'lately led so unsettled a life and [having] been so desultory in my employments':

> How deplorably and unaccountably evanescent are our frames of mind, as various as the forms and hues of the summer clouds. A single word is sometimes enough to give an entirely new mould to our thoughts; at least I find myself so constituted, and therefore to me it is pre-eminently important to be anchored within the veil, so that outward things may only act as winds to agitating sails, and be unable to send me adrift.
>
> … To prevent myself from saying anything still more discreditable to my head and heart I will send you a something between poetry and prose expressive of the idea that has often been before my mind's eye. For want of an humbler title I will call it a
>
> Sonnet [the lines then follow].

The above letter serves as the copy-text.

Sonnet

Oft, when a child, while wand'ring far alone,
That none might rouse me from my waking dream,
And visions with which fancy still would teem
Scare by a disenchanting earthy tone;
If, haply, conscious of the present scene,
I've marked before me some untraversed spot
The setting sunbeams had forsaken not,
Whose turf appeared more velvet-like and green
Than that I walked and fitter for repose:
But ever, at the wished-for place arrived,
I've found it of those seeming charms deprived
Which from the mellowing power of distance rose:
To my poor thought, an apt though simple trope
Of life's dull path and earth's deceitful hope.

QUESTION AND ANSWER

The copy-text for 'Question and Answer' is found in a letter from Eliot to Maria Lewis, dated 1 October 1840 (*Letters,* Vol. I, p. 69). It was first published in Cross's *Life*, although not altogether accurately (see Textual Variants, below, pp. 190–1).

The poem is a translation. In her letter to Maria Lewis, she said,

> I have made an alteration in my plans with Mr. Brezzi [her Coventry language teacher], and shall henceforward take Italian and German alternatively so that I shall not be liable to the consciousness of having imperative employment for every interstice of time. There seems a greater affinity between German and my mind than Italian, though less new to me, possesses. I am reading Schiller's Maria Stuart and Tasso. I was pleased with a little poem I learnt a week or two ago in German, and as I want you to like it I have just put the idea it contains into English doggrel which quite fails to represent the beautiful simplicity and nature of the original, but yet I hope will give you sufficiently its sense to screen the odiousness of the translation. Eccola:
>
> [the poem then follows]

> I was this morning deeply struck by a figure in I think the 31 chapter of Isaiah [31:4] where a picture is given of a young lion tearing the flock and fearlessly continuing his work of destruction though a multitude of shepherds be assembled against him – this to shadow forth the works that God doeth, the desolations He maketh in the earth, unobstructed by all the mustered array of human power and skill.

The original German poem remains unidentified.

Question and Answer

"Where[a] blooms, O my Father, a thornless rose?"[b]
"That[c] can I not tell thee, my child;
Not one on the bosom of earth e'er grows,
But wounds whom its charms have beguiled."[d]

"Would[e] I'd a rose on my bosom lie![f]
But I shrink from the piercing thorn;[g]
I long, but I dare not its point defy,[h]
I long, and I gaze forlorn."[i]

"Not[j] so, O my child,[k] round the stem again
Thy resolute fingers entwine –[l]
Forego not the joy for its sister pain,[m]
Let the rose, the sweet rose, be thine!"[n]

MID THE RICH STORE OF NATURE'S GIFTS TO MAN

The poem is part of a letter from Eliot to Maria Lewis, dated 18 February 1842 (*Letters,* Vol. I, p. 127): it was first published in Cross's *Life*, pp. 66–7, although not altogether accurately. He altered the punctuation (see Textual Variants, below, p. 191) and also omitted parts of the letter to Maria Lewis. Haight restored both in *Letters*.

The date of composition is difficult to determine. 'Mid the rich store' was sent after Eliot's refusal to attend church. On 2 January 1842, Robert Evans wrote in his journal, 'Went to Trinity Church in the forenoon. Miss Lewis went with me. Mary Ann did not go. I stopd the sacrement and Miss Lewis stopd also' (*Letters*, Vol. I, p. 124). It was not until May 1842 that Eliot agreed to resume her church going, thereby putting an end to the 'Holy War' at home (*Letters*, Vol. I, p. 133). Given that the poem is part of an outlining of Eliot's changed religious convictions, it may well have been composed earlier than February 1842, even though other poems sent to Maria Lewis were written or translated immediately before they were sent.

Maria Lewis had joined Eliot's family in unsuccessfully urging her to reconsider her new philosophy, and Eliot's resultant stress during this period is reflected in the letter to her former teacher, which accompanied the poem:

> How go you for society, for communion of spirit, the drop of nectar in the cup of mortals? But why do I say the drop? The mind that feels its value will get large draughts from some source if denied it in the most commonly chosen way.
>
> [the poem then follows]
>
> Beautiful ego-ism! to quote one's own. But where is not this same ego? The martyr at the stake seeks its gratification as much as the court sycophant, the difference lying in the comparative dignity and beauty of the two egos. People absurdly talk of self-denial – why there is none in Virtue to a being of moral excellence – the greatest torture to such a soul would be to run counter to the dictates of conscience, to wallow in the slough of meanness, deception, revenge or sensuality. This was Paul's idea in the 1st chapter of 2d Ep[istle] to Timothy [2 Timothy 2:5–12] (I think that is the passage).
>
> ... I have had a weary week and you have the fag end. At the beginning more than the usual amount of *cooled* glances, and exhortations to the suppression of self-conceit. The former are so many hailstones that make me wrap more closely around me the mantle of determinate purpose – the latter are needful and have a tendency to exercise forbearance that well repays the temporary smart. The heart knoweth its own whether bitterness or joy [Proverbs 14:10] – let us, dearest beware how we *even with good intentions* press a finger's weight on the already bruised. The char-

ity that thinketh no evil is loudly professed – but where is it in persons who to nurse their reliance on their own sentiments positively as I have heard a lady do today attribute perseverance in lovely conduct to a proud determination to disappoint the expectations or fall? O this masquerade of a world! But I shall weary you. May you be happy and healthy and continue to love.

Eliot's steadfastness in her convictions, despite the pressures at home, is seen in a letter to Charles Bray's sister, Mrs Abijah Hill Pears, of 28 January 1842:

Never again imagine that you need ask forgiveness for speaking or writing to me on subjects to me more interesting than aught else, – on the contrary believe that I really enjoy conversation of this nature; blank silence and cold reserve are the only bitters I care for in my intercourse with you. I can rejoice in all the joys of humanity; in all that serves to elevate and purify feeling and action; nor will I quarrel with the million who, I am persuaded, are with me in intention though our dialect differ. Of course I must desire the ultimate downfall of error: for no error is innocuous, but this assuredly will occur without my proselyting aid, and the best proof of a real love of the truth, – that freshest stamp of divinity, – is a calm confidence in its intrinsic power to secure its own high destiny, – that of universal empire. Do not fear that I will become a stagnant pool by a self-sufficient determination only to listen to my own echo; to read the yea, yea, on my own side, and be most comfortably deaf to the nay, nay. Would that all rejected *practically* this maxim! To *fear* the examination of any proposition appears to me an intellectual and a moral palsy that will ever hinder the firm grasping of any substance whatever. For my part, I wish to be among the ranks of that glorious crusade that is seeking to set Truth's Holy Sepulchre free from a usurped domination. We shall then see her resurrection! Meanwhile, although I cannot rank among my principles of action a fear of vengeance eternal, gratitude for predestined salvation, or a revelation of future glories as a reward, I fully participate in the belief that the only heaven here or hereafter is to be found in conformity with the will of the Supreme; a continual aiming at the attainment of that perfect ideal, the true Logos that dwells in the bosom of the One Father. I hardly know whether I am ranting after the fashion of one of the Primitive Methodist prophetesses, with a cart for her rostrum, I am writing so fast. (*Letters*, Vol. I, pp. 125–6)

Mid the rich store of nature's gifts to man

"Mid the rich store of nature's gifts to man
Each has his loves, close wedded to his soul
By fine associations' golden links.
As the Great Spirit bids creation teem
With conscious being and intelligence,
So man[a] His miniature resemblance[b] gives
To matter's every form a speaking soul,
An emanation from his spirit's fount,
The impress true of its peculiar seal.
Here finds he thy best image, sympathy!"

AS TU VU LA LUNE SE LEVER

The copy-text for 'As tu vu la lune se lever' is the holograph letter to Mr and Mrs Charles and Cara Bray and Sara Sophia Hennell, dated 20 August 1849. It was first published in Haight, *Letters*, Vol. I, p. 299. Cross cited the letter in *Life* (1885), but he omitted the section containing the poem, presumably because he considered it, as did Haight (cf. *Biography*, p. 72), to demonstrate bad French verse.

It was written for an album that the Marquise de St Germain was compiling while Eliot was staying in a pension in Geneva, Switzerland, following her father's death in May 1849. Addressing Sara Hennell in August of that year, Eliot writes:

> I have been invoking the French muse for the Marquise's album – since she would fain have something and it must not be in English which she cannot understand. It will make you smile – so I write it.
>
> [the poem follows]
>
> I thought it would have done admirably to put in Molière's Misanthrope or Precieuses ridicules. But the thought, dear soul, is a very true one, above all when I apply it to you. Receive it as just

what I am feeling and thinking about you. Love me ever in spite of everything, dear friends. (Haight, *Letters*, Vol. I, pp. 298–9)

As tu vu la lune se lever

As tu vu la lune se lever
Dans un ciel d'azur sans voile?
Mille gouttes de rosée réflechissent
Sa lumière, comme autant d'étoiles.

Un violet du printemps cueilles
Et le caches bien dans ton sein,
De la delicieuse odeur
Tu et res vêtements seront pleins.

Ainsi lorsqu'une belle âme se montre
Elle revêtit tant de ses charmes: –
Ainsi son souvenir gardons
Quoique, hélas! il tire nos larmes.[1]

THE LEGEND OF JUBAL (1878)
POEMS

THE LEGEND OF JUBAL

Plans for the 'The Legend of Jubal' are found in Eliot's Notebook for 1868–*c*. 70 (Folger M.a.13): '(Tubalcain) Vision of Jubal' appears under 'Themes for Poems'. In the same list Eliot also quoted from the Bible:

> (* Land of Nod in the East of Eden: 'And Lamech took unto him two wives: the name of the one was Adah, & the name of the other was Zillah, And Adah bare Jubal [*sic*; Jabal]: he was the father of all such as dwell in tents & as such as have cattle. And his brother's name was Jubal: he was the father of all such as have the harp & organ. And Zillah, she also bare Tubalcain, an instructor of every artifice in brass & iron: & the sister of Tubalcain was Naamah. Gen. IV. 19–22) (cf. Pratt and Neufeldt, pp. 72, 154–5)

Eleven notebook pages after the 'Themes for Poems', she made the following entry, clarifying for herself Jubal's genealogy (cf. Pratt and Neufeldt, pp. 78–9, 160):

City of Enoch

Cain	Female Names
|	Milcah
Enoch	Iccah
|	Hagar
Irad	Ashta
|	Loe
Mehujael	
|	
Methusaleh or Methusael	
|	
Lamech – Adah	Lamech – Zillah
|	|
Jabel	Tubalcain
Jubal	Naamah

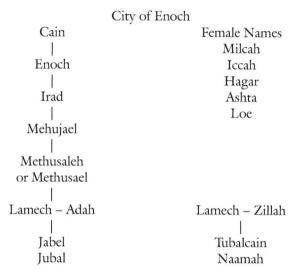

The entry '(Tubalcain) Vision of Jubal' suggests that Eliot worked from ancient sources – or at least from scholars who knew them. In medieval times, the name 'Jubal' was sometimes mistakenly copied as 'Tubal', and

> thereafter it became possible for the *Tubal* born of poor orthography to be mistaken for a shortened form of *Tubalcain*. As a result of this error, Tubalcain, the Biblical blacksmith, was sometimes credited with the musical abilities which Genesis had bestowed upon his brother Jubal. (Beichner, p. 7)

However, medieval writers 'consistently make Jubal (often spelled *Tubal*) the discoverer of music because of the reference in the Bible and not his brother Tubalcain' (Beichner, p. 27):

> Jubal's contribution to the world, and a separate debate over whether or not Pythagoras discovered music by listening to the sound of hammers, eventually led to a conflation of the two stories.

> Peter Comestor's *Historia scholastica* (1190s) records that Jubal 'discovered the art after hearing his brother Tubalcain pounding upon metals. The Greek tradition, spoken of by St. Isodore, crediting the discovery of music to Pythagoras with his hammers is thus transferred and grafted to the Biblical. (Beichner, p. 10)

This is the version Eliot follows in her poem (cf. ll. 248–67).

Further evidence of research, this time into the origins of organs, is seen in other Eliot notebook entries. Extracts from F. J. Fétis's 'Résume philosophique de l'histoire de la musique', *Bibliographie universelle des musicians et biographie générale de la musique* (Meline, Brussels, Cans et Cie, 1837), Vol. I, are found in the notebook for 1854–79 (cf. Wiesenfarth, pp. 101–3, 202–3), including the following:

> I do not wish to raise a doubt about the existence of a wind organ in the 4th century because a passage of commentary by St. Augustine on the 56th psalm leaves no doubt about the organ being known that early: 'All musical instruments are called organs, not only the ones with the specific name 'organ,' which is large and has inflatable bellows, but whatever instrument is of a certain size and is used in song is also called an organ'. (cliii–clvii *passim*)

> Without doubt the first wind organs were simply small portable boxes like those seen in some old paintings and in manuscripts dating from the twelfth and thirteenth centuries. (clvii)

> As to small portable organs which musicians carry attached to their bodies by straps and play with one hand while pumping air with the other, the size of their keyboard is very small indeed, with the hand able only to extend the space of a fifth. Such an instrument is called a *nimfali*. (Wiesenfarth's translations, p. 202)

Rosemary Ashton suggests that 'The Legend of Jubal' 'seems to be a displaced expression of her [Eliot's] anxiety about her writing past, present, and future' (*George Eliot. A Life* (London, Penguin, 1997), pp. 301–2), insofar as she, like Jubal, frequently doubted her own powers as a writer. But, given Eliot's careful research and the poem itself, another way of seeing it is as a sort of *Midrash*, a commentary on a life immortalized through music – using Scripture as a starting point. Jubal's vision has secular religious significance, because if he can replicate the melodies of the natural world in

> human voices with such passion fed
> As does but glimmer in our common speech,
> But might flame out in tones whose changing reach,
> Surpassing meagre need, informs the sense
> With fuller union, finer difference (ll. 314–18)

then he will, in the words of 'O May I Join the Choir Invisible', 'make undying music in the world' (l. 10). And creating the 'Choir Invisible', as it were, turns out to be his great achievement, as the angelic Voice reassures him towards the end of the poem:

> It is the glory of the heritage
> Thy life has left, that makes thy outcast age:
> Thy limbs shall lie dark, tombless on this sod,

Because thou shinest in man's soul, a god,
Who found and gave new passion and new joy
That nought but Earth's destruction can destroy.
(ll. 774–9)

Eliot began 'The Legend of Jubal' on 5 October 1869, writing in her Journal, '*I have begun a long-meditated poem: "The Legend of Jubal"*, but have not written more than 20 or 30 verses'. At this time Lewes's son, Thornie, had returned to them from South Africa and was dying of paraplegia (*Journals*, pp. 137, 139). On 13 October 1869, Eliot wrote in her Diary: 'My head has been sadly feeble and my whole body ailing of late. I have written about 100 verses of my poem. *Poor Thornie seems to us in a state of growing weakness*' (*Journals*, pp. 138–9). He died six days later.

In her Diary 1861–77, 'The Legend of Jubal' appears under 'Order of Writings' with the date 'January 13, 1870' (*Journals*, p. 96), corroborated by her Diary entry for 20 May 1870:

> The day after Thornie's death, the chief epochs have been our stay at Limpsfield, in Surrey, till near the beginning of December (I think we returned on the 21st November); my writing of Jubal, which I finished on the 13th January; the publication of the poem in Macmillan's Magazine (May No.); and our journey to Berlin and Vienna. (*Journals*, p. 139)

She explained her decision to sell the poem to *Macmillan's Magazine* in a letter dated 7 March 1870:

> A rather long poem which I finished about Christmas I have been induced to accept an offer for from Mr. Macmillan, who has behaved very handsomely to me. I did not mention it (the

poem) to you because I know that you do not care to have exceptional contributions to Maga [*Blackwood's Magazine*]. And the English worship of Quantity does not allow the separate publication of 800 lines, after the fashion of America (for example, Lowell's 'Cathedral'). My poem is not to be published until May, the announcement for April being a mistake. (*Letters*, Vol. V, p. 81)

Macmillan's paid £200 for 'The Legend of Jubal' and the American *Atlantic Monthly* £50 (*Biography*, p. 422). It was then revised before being included in the 1874 edition of *Jubal* and revised again for the 1878 edition. The Jubal M.S. is dated '*5 October 1869 – December 1869/January 1870*' and differs from the printed versions (see Textual Variants, below, pp. 191–203). The copy-text is the version in the 1878 *Jubal*.

Notes to the Jubal M.S. (Add. 34,038)

- MS page numbering starts on first page; later, dedication page (f. 1) and title (f. 2) were added: page numbering then altered, because of extra pages
- Eliot counted lines from the beginning, adding numbers at the bottom of pages; numbers are missing on some pages, probably because the MS was cropped when bound
- f. 2ff onwards, text on the right halves of pages, left halves for corrections and instructions to printers
- MS written in black ink; f. 1 unlined paper, no watermark; ff. 2–35 lined paper, no watermarks
- MS signed 'George Eliot', dated 'December 1865'

f. 1: [Inscription]:

To my beloved Husband, George Henry Lewes,
whose cherishing tenderness for twenty years
has alone made my work possible to me.

"And the last parting now began to send
Diffusive dread through love & wedded bliss,
Thrilling them into finer tenderness."
May, 1874 ['Jubal', ll. 99–101]

f. 2: [Title page:] 'The Legend of Jubal' [MS page has 'MS with proof to Author.' top left corner]

The Legend of Jubal

When Cain was driven from Jehovah's land
He wandered eastward, seeking some far strand[1]
Ruled by kind gods who asked no offerings[a]
Save pure field-fruits,[b] as aromatic things,[c]
To feed the subtler sense of frames divine
That lived on fragrance for their food and wine:
Wild joyous gods, who winked at faults and folly,
And could be pitiful and melancholy.
He never had a doubt that such gods were;
He looked within,[d] and saw them mirrored there.
Some think he came at last to Tartary,
And some to Ind;[2e] but, howsoe'er it be,
His staff he planted where sweet waters ran,[f]
And in that home of Cain the Arts[g] began.

Man's life was spacious in the early world:[h]
It paused, like some slow ship with sail unfurled
Waiting in seas by scarce a wavelet curled;
Beheld the slow star-paces[i] of the skies,
And grew[j] from strength to strength through centuries;
Saw infant trees fill out their giant limbs,
And heard a thousand times the sweet birds' marriage hymns.

In Cain's young city[3] none had heard of Death[k]
Save him, the founder; and it was his faith
That here, away from harsh Jehovah's law,[l]

Man was immortal, since no halt or flaw
In Cain's own frame betrayed six hundred years,
But dark as pines that autumn never sears
His locks thronged backward as he ran, his frame
Rose like the orbèd sun each morn the same,
Lake-mirrored to his gaze; and that red brand,
The scorching impress of Jehovah's hand,[4]
Was still clear-edged to his unwearied eye,
Its secret firm in time-fraught[a] memory.
He said, "My happy offspring shall not know
That the red life from out a man may flow
When smitten by his brother." True, his race
Bore each one stamped upon his new-born face
A copy of the brand no whit less clear;
But every mother held that little copy dear.

Thus generations in glad idlesse throve,
Nor hunted prey, nor with each other strove;
For clearest springs were plenteous in the land,
And gourds for cups; the ripe fruits sought the hand,
Bending the laden boughs with fragrant gold;[b]
And for their roofs and garments wealth untold
Lay everywhere in grasses and broad leaves:
They laboured gently,[c] as a maid who weaves
Her hair in mimic mats, and pauses oft
And strokes across her palm[d] the tresses soft,
Then[e] peeps to watch the poisèd butterfly,
Or little burthened ants that homeward hie.
Time was but leisure to their lingering thought,
There was no need for haste to finish aught;
But sweet beginnings were repeated still
Like infant babblings that no task fulfil;
For love, that loved not change, constrained the simple will.

Till, hurling stones in mere athletic joy,[a]
Strong Lamech struck and killed his fairest boy,[5]
And tried to wake him with the tenderest cries,
And fetched and held before the glazèd eyes
The things they best had loved to look upon;
But never glance or smile[b] or sigh he won.
The generations stood around those twain
Helplessly gazing, till their father Cain
Parted the press,[c] and said, "He will not wake;
This is the endless sleep, and we must make
A bed deep down for him beneath the sod;
For know, my sons, there is a mighty God
Angry with all man's race, but most with me.
I fled from out His land in vain! – 'tis[d] He
Who came and slew the lad, for He[e] has found
This home of ours, and we shall all be bound
By the harsh bands of His most cruel will,
Which any moment may some dear one kill.
Nay, though we live for countless moons, at last
We and all ours shall die like summers past.
This is Jehovah's will, and He[f] is strong;
I thought the way I travelled was too long
For Him[g] to follow me: my thought was vain!
He walks unseen, but leaves a track of pain,
Pale Death His footprint is, and He will come again!"[h]

And a new spirit from that hour came o'er
The race of Cain: soft idlesse was no more,
But even the sunshine had a heart of care,[i]
Smiling with hidden dread – a mother fair
Who folding to her breast a dying child
Beams with feigned joy that but makes sadness mild.
Death was now lord of Life,[j] and at his word
Time, vague as air before, new terrors stirred,

With measured wing now audibly arose
Throbbing through all things to some unknown close.[a]
Now glad Content by clutching Haste[b] was torn,
And Work grew eager, and Device[c] was born.
It seemed the light was never loved before,[d]
Now each man said, "'Twill[e] go and come no more."
No budding branch, no pebble from the brook,
No form, no shadow, but new dearness took
From the[f] one thought that life must have an end;
And the last parting now began to send
Diffusive dread through love and wedded bliss,
Thrilling them into finer tenderness.[6]
Then Memory disclosed her face divine,
That like the calm nocturnal lights doth shine
Within the soul, and shows the sacred graves,
And shows the presence that no sunlight craves,
No space, no warmth, but moves among them all;
Gone and yet here, and coming at each call,
With ready voice, and eyes that understand,[g]
And lips that ask a kiss,[h] and dear responsive hand.

Thus to Cain's race death was tear-watered seed[i]
Of various life and action-shaping need.[j]
But chief the sons of Lamech felt the stings
Of new ambition,[k] and the force that springs
In[l] passion beating on the shores of fate.
They said,[m] "There comes a night when all too late
The mind shall long to prompt the achieving hand,
The eager thought behind closed[n] portals stand,
And the last wishes to the mute lips press
Buried ere death in silent helplessness.
Then while the soul its way with sound can cleave,
And while the arm is strong to strike and heave,
Let soul and arm give shape that will abide

And rule above our graves,[a] and power divide
With that great god of day, whose rays must bend
As we shall make the moving shadows tend.
Come, let us fashion acts that are to be,[b]
When we shall lie in darkness silently,
As our young brother doth, whom yet we see
Fallen and slain, but reigning in our will
By that one image of him pale and still."[c]

For Lamech's sons were heroes of their race:
Jabal, the eldest, bore upon his face
The look of that calm river-god, the Nile,
Mildly secure in power that needs not guile.
But Tubal-Cain[7][d] was restless as the fire
That glows and spreads and leaps from high to higher
Where'er is aught to seize or to subdue;
Strong as a storm he lifted or o'erthrew,[e]
His urgent limbs like rounded granite grew,[f]
Such granite as the plunging torrent wears[g]
And roaring rolls around through countless years.[h]
But strength that still on movement must be fed,
Inspiring thought of change, devices bred,
And urged his mind through earth and air to rove
For force that he could conquer if he strove,
For lurking forms that might new tasks fulfil
And yield unwilling to his stronger will.
Such Tubal-Cain.[i] But Jubal[8] had a frame
Fashioned to finer senses,[j] which became
A yearning for some hidden soul of things,
Some outward touch complete on inner springs
That vaguely moving bred a lonely pain,
A want that did but stronger grow with gain
Of all good else, as spirits might be sad
For lack of speech to tell us they are glad.

Now Jabal learned to tame the lowing kine,
And from their udders drew the snow-white wine
That stirs the innocent joy, and makes the stream
Of elemental life with fulness teem;
The star-browed calves he nursed with feeding
hand,
And sheltered them, till all the little band
Stood mustered gazing at the sunset way
Whence he would come with store at close of day.
He soothed the silly sheep with friendly tone
And reared their staggering lambs that, older
grown,
Followed his steps with sense-taught memory;
Till he, their shepherd, could their leader be
And guide them through the pastures as he would,[a]
With sway that grew from ministry of good.
He spread his tents upon the grassy plain
Which, eastward[b] widening like the open main,
Showed the first whiteness 'neath the morning star;
Near him his sister,[9] deft, as women are,[c]
Plied her quick[d] skill in sequence to his thought
Till the hid treasures of the milk she caught
Revealed like pollen 'mid the petals white,
The golden pollen, virgin to the light.
Even the she-wolf with young, on rapine bent,[e]
He caught and tethered in his mat-walled tent,
And cherished all her little sharp-nosed young[f]
Till the small race with hope and terror clung
About his footsteps, till each new-reared brood,
Remoter from the memories of the wood,
More glad discerned their common home with man.
This was the work of Jabal: he began
The pastoral life, and, sire of joys to be,[g]
Spread the sweet ties that bind the family

O'er dear dumb souls that thrilled at man's caress,
And shared his pains with patient helpfulness.[a]

But Tubal-Cain[b] had caught and yoked the fire,
Yoked it with stones that bent the flaming spire
And made it roar in prisoned servitude
Within the furnace, till with force subdued
It changed all forms he willed to work upon,
Till hard from soft, and soft from hard,[c] he won.
The pliant clay he moulded as he would,[d]
And laughed with joy when 'mid the heat it stood
Shaped as his hand had chosen, while the mass
That from his hold, dark, obstinate,[e] would pass,
He drew all glowing from the busy heat,
All breathing as with life that he could beat
With thundering hammer, making it obey
His will creative, like the pale soft clay.
Each day he wrought and better than he planned,
Shape breeding shape beneath his restless hand.
(The soul without still helps the soul within,[f]
And its deft magic ends what we begin.)
Nay, in his dreams his hammer he would wield
And seem to see a myriad types revealed,[g]
Then spring[h] with wondering triumphant cry,[i]
And, lest the inspiring vision should go by,
Would rush to labour[j] with that plastic zeal
Which all the passion of our life can[k] steal
For force to work with. Each day saw the birth
Of various forms which, flung upon the earth,[l]
Seemed harmless toys to cheat the exacting hour.
But were as seeds instinct with hidden power.
The axe, the club, the spikèd wheel, the chain,
Held silently the shrieks and moans of pain;[m]
And near them latent lay in share and spade,[n]

In the strong bar, the saw, and deep-curved[a] blade,
Glad voices of the hearth and harvest-home,
The social good, and all earth's joy to come.
Thus to mixed ends wrought Tubal; and they say,
Some things he made have lasted to this day;
As,[b] thirty silver pieces that were found
By Noah's children buried in the ground.
He made them from mere hunger of device,
Those small white discs;[c] but they became the price
The traitor Judas sold his Master for;
And men still handling them in peace and war
Catch foul disease, that comes as appetite,[d]
And lurks and clings as withering,[e] damning blight.
But Tubal-Cain[f] wot not of treachery,
Nor greedy lust, nor[g] any ill to be,
Save the one ill of sinking into nought,[h]
Banished from action and act-shaping thought.
He was the sire of swift-transforming skill,
Which arms for conquest man's ambitious will;
And round him gladly, as his hammer rung,
Gathered the elders and the growing young:[i]
These handled vaguely and those plied the tools,[j]
Till, happy chance begetting conscious rules,[k]
The home of Cain with industry was rife,
And glimpses of a strong persistent life,
Panting through generations as one breath,[l]
And filling with its soul the blank of death.

Jubal, too, watched the hammer, till his eyes,[m]
No longer following its fall or rise,[n]
Seemed glad with something that they could not
    see,[o]
But only listened to[10] – some melody,[p]
Wherein dumb longings inward speech had found,[q]

Won from the common store of struggling sound.
Then, as the metal shapes more various grew,[a]
And, hurled upon each other, resonance drew,
Each gave new tones, the revelations dim
Of some external soul that spoke for him:
The hollow vessel's clang, the clash, the boom,
Like light that makes wide spiritual room
And skyey[b] spaces in the spaceless thought,
To Jubal such enlargèd[c] passion brought
That love, hope, rage, and all experience,
Were fused in vaster being,[d] fetching thence
Concords and discords, cadences and cries
That seemed from some world-shrouded soul to rise,[e]
Some rapture more intense, some mightier rage,
Some living sea that burst the bounds of man's brief age.

Then with such blissful trouble and glad care
For growth within unborn[f] as mothers bear,
To the far woods he wandered, listening,[g]
And heard the birds their little stories sing
In notes whose rise and fall seemed[h] melted speech –
Melted with tears, smiles,[i] glances – that can reach
More quickly through our frame's deep-winding night,[j]
And without thought raise thought's best fruit, delight.
Pondering,[k] he sought his home again and heard
The fluctuant changes of the spoken word:[l]
The deep remonstrance and the argued want,
Insistent first in close monotonous chant,
Next leaping upward to defiant stand
Or downward beating like the resolute hand;
The mother's call, the children's answering cry,
The laugh's light cataract tumbling[m] from on high;

The suasive repetitions Jabal taught,
That timid browsing cattle homeward brought;
The clear-winged fugue of echoes vanishing;
And through them all the hammer's rhythmic ring.[a]
Jubal sat lonely, all around was dim,
Yet his face glowed with light revealed to him:[b]
For as the delicate stream of odour[c] wakes
The thought-wed sentience and some image makes
From out the mingled fragments of the past,
Finely compact in wholeness that will last,
So streamed as from the body of each sound
Subtler pulsations, swift as warmth, which found[d]
All prisoned germs and all their powers unbound,
Till thought self-luminous flamed from memory,[e]
And in creative vision wandered free.
Then Jubal, standing, rapturous arms upraised,[f]
And on the dark with eager eyes he gazed,
As had some manifested god been there.[g]
It was his thought he saw:[h] the presence fair
Of unachieved achievement, the high task,
The struggling[i] unborn spirit that doth ask
With irresistible cry for blood and breath,
Till feeding its great life we sink in death.

He said, "Were[j] now those mighty tones and cries
That from the giant soul of earth arise,
Those groans of some great travail heard from far,
Some power at wrestle[k] with the things that are,
Those sounds which vary with the varying form
Of clay and metal, and in sightless swarm
Fill the wide space with tremors: were these wed
To human voices with such passion fed[l]
As does but glimmer in our common speech,
But might flame out in tones whose changing reach,

Surpassing meagre need, informs the sense
With fuller union, finer difference –[a]
Were this great vision,[b] now obscurely bright
As morning hills that melt in new-poured light,
Wrought into solid form and living sound,
Moving with ordered throb and sure rebound,
Then – Nay,[c] I Jubal will that work begin!
The generations of our race shall win
New life, that grows from out the heart of this,
As spring from winter, or as lovers'[d] bliss
From out the dull unknown of unwaked energies."[11e]

Thus he resolved, and in the soul-fed[f] light
Of coming ages waited through[g] the night,
Watching for that near dawn whose chiller ray
Showed but the unchanged world of yesterday;[h]
Where all the order of his dream divine
Lay like Olympian forms within the mine;[i]
Where fervour[j] that could fill the earthly round
With througèd[k] joys of form-begotten sound
Must shrink intense within the patient power
That lonely labours[l] through the niggard hour.
Such patience have the heroes who begin,
Sailing the first to[m] lands which others win.[n]
Jubal must dare as great beginners dare,
Strike form's first way in matter rude and bare,
And, yearning vaguely toward the plenteous[o] quire
Of the world's harvest, make one poor small lyre.[p]
He made it, and from out its measured frame
Drew the harmonic soul, whose answers came
With guidance sweet and lessons of delight
Teaching to ear and hand the blissful Right,
Where strictest law is gladness to the sense
And all desire bends toward obedience.[q]

Then Jubal poured his triumph in a song –[a]
The rapturous word that rapturous notes prolong
As radiance streams from smallest things that burn,
Or[b] thought of loving into love doth turn.
And still his lyre gave companionship
In sense-taught concert as of lip with lip.
Alone amid the hills at first he tried
His wingèd song; then with adoring pride
And bridegroom's joy at leading forth his bride,
He said, "This[c] wonder which my soul hath found,
This heart of music in the might of sound,
Shall forthwith be the share of all our race
And like the morning gladden common space:
The song shall spread and swell as rivers do,
And I will teach our youth with skill to woo
This living lyre, to know its secret will,
Its fine division of the good and ill.
So shall men call me sire of harmony,
And where great Song is, there my life shall be."[d]

Thus glorying as a god beneficent,
Forth from his solitary joy he went
To bless mankind. It was at evening,
When shadows lengthen from each westward thing,
When imminence of change makes sense more fine
And light seems holier in its grand decline.
The fruit-trees wore their studded coronal,
Earth and her children were at festival,
Glowing as with one heart and one consent –[e]
Thought, love, trees, rocks, in sweet warm radiance blent.[f]

The tribe of Cain was resting on the ground,
The various ages wreathed in one broad round.
Here lay, while children peeped o'er his huge thighs,

The sinewy man embrowned by centuries;
Here the broad-bosomed mother of the strong
Looked, like Demeter, placid o'er the throng
Of young lithe forms whose rest was movement
too –[a]
Tricks, prattle, nods, and laughs that lightly flew,
And swayings as of flower-beds where Love blew.
For all had feasted well upon the flesh
Of juicy fruits, on nuts, and honey fresh,
And now their wine was health-bred merriment,[b]
Which through the generations circling went,[c]
Leaving none sad, for even father Cain
Smiled as a Titan might, despising pain.
Jabal sat climbed on by[d] a playful ring
Of children, lambs and whelps, whose gambolling,
With tiny hoofs, paws, hands, and dimpled feet,
Made barks, bleats, laughs, in pretty hubbub meet.
But Tubal's hammer rang from far away,
Tubal alone would keep no holiday,
His furnace must not slack for any feast,
For of all hardship work he counted least;
He scorned all rest but sleep, where every dream
Made his repose more potent action seem.

Yet with health's nectar some strange thirst was blent,[e]
The fateful growth, the unnamed discontent,
The inward shaping toward[f] some unborn power,
Some deeper-breathing act, the being's flower.
After all gestures, words, and speech of eyes,
The soul had more to tell, and broke in sighs.
Then from the east, with glory on his head
Such as low-slanting beams on corn-waves spread,
Came Jubal with his lyre: there 'mid the throng,[g]
Where the blank space was, poured a solemn song,[h]

Touching his lyre to full[a] harmonic throb
And measured pulse, with cadences that sob,[b]
Exult and cry, and search the inmost deep
Where the dark sources of new[c] passion sleep.
Joy took the air,[d] and took each breathing soul,
Embracing them in one entrancèd[e] whole,
Yet thrilled each varying frame to various ends,[f]
As Spring new-waking through the creature[g] sends
Or rage or tenderness; more[h] plenteous life
Here breeding dread, and there a fiercer strife.
He who had lived through twice three centuries,
Whose months monotonous, like trees on trees
In hoary forests, stretched a backward maze,
Dreamed himself dimly through the travelled days
Till in clear light he paused,[i] and felt the sun
That warmed him when he was a little one;
Felt[j] that true heaven, the recovered past,
The dear small Known amid the Unknown[k] vast,
And in that heaven wept. But younger limbs
Thrilled toward the future, that bright land which swims
In western glory, isles and streams and bays,
Where hidden pleasures float in golden haze.
And in all these the rhythmic influence,[l]
Sweetly o'ercharging the delighted sense,[m]
Flowed out in movements, little waves that spread
Enlarging, till in tidal union led[n]
The youths and maidens both alike long-tressed,
By grace-inspiring melody possessed,[o]
Rose in slow dance, with beauteous floating swerve[p]
Of limbs and hair, and many a melting curve
Of ringèd feet swayed by each close-linked palm:
Then Jubal poured more rapture in his psalm,
The dance fired music, music fired the dance,

The glow diffusive lit each countenance,[a]
Till all the gazing elders rose[b] and stood
With glad yet awful shock of that mysterious good.[12]

Even Tubal caught the sound, and wondering came,
Urging his sooty bulk like smoke-wrapt flame
Till he could see his brother with the lyre,
The work for which he lent[c] his furnace-fire
And diligent hammer, witting nought of this –[d]
This power in metal shape which made strange bliss,[e]
Entering within him like a dream full-fraught
With new creations finished in a thought.

The sun had sunk, but music still was there,[f]
And when this ceased, still triumph filled the air:[g]
It seemed the stars were shining with delight[h]
And that no night was ever like this night.
All clung with praise to Jubal: some besought
That he would teach them his new skill; some caught,
Swiftly as smiles are caught in looks that meet,
The tone's melodic change and rhythmic beat:
'Twas easy following where invention trod –[i]
All eyes can see when light flows out from God.[j]

And thus did Jubal to his race reveal
Music their larger soul, where woe and weal
Filling the resonant chords, the song, the dance,
Moved with a wider-wingèd[k] utterance.[13]
Now[l] many a lyre was fashioned, many a song
Raised[m] echoes new, old echoes to prolong,
Till things of Jubal's making were so rife,
"Hearing myself," he said, "hems[n] in my life,
And I will get me to some far-off land,
Where higher mountains under heaven stand[o]

And touch the blue at rising of the stars,
Whose song they hear where no rough mingling mars
The great clear voices. Such lands there must be,
Where varying forms make varying symphony –[a]
Where other thunders roll amid the hills,
Some mightier wind a mightier forest fills
With other strains through other-shapen boughs;
Where bees and birds[b] and beasts that hunt or
browse
Will teach me songs I know not. Listening there,[c]
My life shall grow like trees both[d] tall and fair
That rise and spread and bloom toward fuller fruit each
year."[e]

He took a raft,[f] and travelled with the stream
Southward for many a league, till he might deem
He saw at last the pillars of the sky,
Beholding mountains whose white majesty
Rushed through him as new awe,[g] and made new song
That swept with fuller wave the chords along,[h]
Weighting his voice with deep religious chime,
The iteration of slow chant sublime.[i]
It was the region long inhabited
By all the race of Seth;[14j] and Jubal said:
"Here[k] have I found my thirsty soul's desire,
Eastward the hills touch heaven, and evening's fire
Flames through deep waters; I will take my rest,[l]
And feed anew from my great mother's breast,
The sky-clasped Earth, whose voices nurture me
As the flowers' sweetness doth the honey-bee."[m]
He lingered wandering for many an age,[n]
And, sowing music,[o] made high heritage
For generations far beyond the Flood –[p]
For the poor late-begotten human brood

Born to life's weary brevity and perilous good.[a]

And ever as he travelled he would climb
The farthest mountain, yet the heavenly chime,
The mighty tolling of the far-off spheres
Beating their pathway,[15] never touched his ears.[b]
But wheresoe'er he rose the heavens rose,
And the far-gazing mountain[c] could disclose
Nought but a wider earth;[d] until one height
Showed him the ocean stretched in liquid light,
And he could hear its multitudinous roar,[e]
Its plunge and hiss upon the pebbled shore:
Then Jubal silent sat, and touched his lyre no more.

He thought, "The world is great, but I am weak,[f]
And where the sky bends is no solid peak
To give me footing, but instead, this main –
Myriads of maddened horses thundering o'er the plain.[g]

"New[h] voices come to me where'er I roam,
My heart too widens with its widening home:[i]
But song grows weaker,[j] and the heart must break
For lack of voice, or fingers that can wake
The lyre's full answer; nay, its chords were all[k]
Too few to meet the growing spirit's call.[l]
The former songs seem little, yet no more
Can soul, hand, voice, with interchanging lore[m]
Tell what the earth is saying unto me:[n]
The secret is too great, I hear confusedly.

"No[o] farther will I travel: once again
My brethren I will see,[p] and that fair plain
Where I and Song were born. There fresh-voiced youth[q]
Will pour my strains with all the early truth

Which now abides not in my voice and hands,
But only in the soul, the will that stands
Helpless to move. My tribe remembering
Will cry "'Tis he !' and run to greet me, welcoming."[a]

The way was weary. Many a date-palm grew,[b]
And shook out clustered gold against the blue,[c]
While Jubal, guided by the steadfast spheres,[16d]
Sought the dear home of those first eager years,[e]
When, with fresh vision fed, the fuller will
Took living outward shape in pliant skill;
For still he hoped to find the former things,
And the warm gladness recognition brings.
His footsteps erred among the mazy woods
And long illusive sameness of the floods,[f]
Winding and wandering. Through far[g] regions, strange
With Gentile homes and faces, did he range,[h]
And left his music in their memory,
And left at last, when nought besides would free
His homeward steps from clinging hands and cries,
The ancient[i] lyre. And now in ignorant eyes
No sign remained of Jubal, Lamech's son,
That mortal frame wherein was first begun
The immortal life of song. His withered brow
Pressed over eyes that held no lightning[j] now,[k]
His locks streamed whiteness on the hurrying air,
The unresting soul had worn itself quite bare
Of beauteous token, as the outworn might
Of oaks slow dying, gaunt in summer's light.
His full deep voice toward thinnest treble ran:
He was the rune-writ story of a man.[17]

And so at last he neared the well-known land,
Could see the hills in ancient order stand
With friendly faces whose familiar gaze

Looked through the sunshine of his childish days;[a]
Knew the deep-shadowed folds of hanging woods,
And seemed to see the self-same insect broods
Whirling and quivering o'er the flowers –[b] to hear
The self-same cuckoo making distance near.
Yea, the dear Earth, with mother's constancy,
Met and embraced him, and said, "Thou art he![c]
This was thy cradle, here my breast was thine,[d]
Where feeding,[e] thou didst all thy life entwine
With my sky-wedded life in heritage divine."[f]

But wending ever through the watered plain,[g]
Firm not to rest save in the home of Cain,[h]
He saw dread Change,[i] with dubious face and cold
That never kept a welcome for the old,[j]
Like some strange heir upon the hearth, arise[k]
Saying "This home is mine."[l] He thought his eyes
Mocked all deep memories, as things new made,[m]
Usurping sense, make old things shrink and fade
And seem ashamed to meet the staring day.
His memory saw a small foot-trodden way,
His eyes a broad far-stretching paven road
Bordered with many a tomb and fair abode;
The little city that once nestled low[n]
As buzzing groups about some central glow,
Spread like a murmuring crowd o'er plain and steep,
Or monster huge in heavy-breathing sleep.[o]
His heart grew faint, and tremblingly he sank
Close by the wayside on[p] a weed-grown bank,
Not far from where a new-raised[q] temple stood,
Sky-roofed, and fragrant with wrought cedar wood.[r]
The morning sun was high; his rays fell hot
On this hap-chosen, dusty, common spot,
On the dry-withered[s] grass and withered man:

That[a] wondrous frame where melody began
Lay as a tomb defaced that no eye cared to scan.

But while he sank far music reached his ear.
He listened until wonder silenced fear
And gladness wonder; for the broadening stream[b]
Of sound advancing was his early dream,[c]
Brought like fulfilment of forgotten prayer;
As if his soul, breathed out upon the air,[d]
Had held the invisible seeds of harmony
Quick with the various strains of life[e] to be.
He listened:[f] the sweet mingled difference
With charm alternate took the meeting sense;
Then bursting like some shield-broad lily red,[g]
Sudden and near the trumpet's notes out-spread,
And soon his eyes could see the metal flower,[h]
Shining upturned, out on the morning pour
Its incense audible;[i] could see a train
From out the street slow-winding on the plain
With lyres and cymbals, flutes and psalteries,[18]
While men, youths, maids,[j] in concert sang to these
With various throat, or in succession poured,
Or in full volume mingled. But one word
Ruled each recurrent rise and answering fall,
As when the multitudes adoring call
On some great name divine, their common soul,
The common need, love, joy,[k] that knits them in one
  whole

The word was "Jubal!" ... "Jubal"[l] filled the air
And seemed to ride aloft, a spirit there,
Creator of the quire, the full-fraught strain
That grateful rolled itself to him again.[m]
The aged man adust upon the bank –
Whom no eye saw – at first with rapture drank

The bliss of music, then, with swelling heart,
Felt, this was his own being's greater part,
The universal joy once born in him.
But when the train, with living face and limb
And vocal breath, came nearer and more near,[a]
The longing grew that they should hold him dear;[b]
Him, Lamech's son, whom all their fathers knew,
The breathing Jubal – him, to whom their love was due.[c]
All was forgotten but the burning need
To claim his fuller self, to claim the deed
That lived away from him, and grew apart,[d]
While he as from a tomb, with lonely heart,
Warmed by no meeting glance, no hand that pressed,
Lay chill amid the life his life had blessed.
What though his song should spread from man's small race
Out through the myriad worlds that people space,[e]
And make the heavens one joy-diffusing quire? –[f]
Still 'mid that vast would throb the keen desire
Of this poor aged flesh,[19] this eventide,
This twilight soon in darkness to subside,
This little pulse of self that, having glowed
Through thrice three centuries,[g] and divinely strowed[h]
The light of music through the vague of sound,
Ached with its smallness[i] still in good that had no bound.

For no eye saw him,[j] while with loving pride
Each voice with each in praise of Jubal vied.
Must he in conscious trance, dumb, helpless lie
While all that ardent kindred passed him by?
His flesh cried out to live with living men
And join that soul which to the inward ken

Of all the hymning train was present there.
Strong passion's daring sees not aught to dare:
The frost-locked starkness of his frame low-bent,
His voice's penury of tones long spent,
He felt not; all his being leaped in flame
To meet his kindred as they onward came
Slackening and wheeling toward the temple's face:
He rushed before them to the glittering space,
And, with a strength that was but strong desire,[a]
Cried, "I am Jubal, I! . . .[b] I made the lyre!"

The tones amid a lake of silence fell
Broken and strained, as if a feeble bell
Had tuneless pealed the triumph of a land
To listening crowds in expectation spanned.
Sudden came showers of laughter on that lake;[c]
They spread along the train from front to wake
In one great storm of merriment, while he[d]
Shrank doubting whether he could Jubal be,
And not a dream of Jubal, whose rich vein
Of passionate music came with that dream-pain
Wherein the[e] sense slips off from each loved thing
And[f] all appearance is mere vanishing.
But ere the laughter died from out the rear,
Anger in front saw profanation near;
Jubal was but a[g] name in each man's faith
For glorious power untouched by that slow death
Which creeps with creeping time; this too, the spot,[h]
And this the day, it must be crime to blot,[i]
Even with scoffing at a madman's lie:
Jubal was not a name to wed with mockery.

Two rushed upon him: two,[j] the most devout
In honour[k] of great Jubal, thrust him out,[l]
And beat him with their flutes. 'Twas little need;[m]

He strove not, cried not, but with tottering speed,[a]
As if the scorn and howls were driving wind
That[b] urged his body, serving so the mind
Which[c] could but shrink and yearn, he sought the screen
Of thorny[d] thickets, and there fell unseen.[e]
The immortal name of Jubal filled the sky,
While Jubal lonely laid him down to die.[f]
He said within his soul, "This[g] is the end:
O'er all the earth to where the heavens bend
And hem men's travel, I have breathed my soul:
I lie here now the remnant of that whole,
The embers of a life, a lonely pain;[h]
As far-off rivers to my thirst were vain,
So of my mighty years nought comes to me again.[i]

"Is[j] the day sinking? Softest coolness springs
From something round me: dewy shadowy wings
Enclose me[k] all around – no, not above –
Is moonlight there? I see a face of love,[l]
Fair as sweet music when my heart was strong:
Yea – art thou come again to me, great Song?"[m]

The face bent over him like silver night
In long-remembered summers; that calm light
Of days which shine in firmaments of thought,
That past unchangeable, from change still wrought.
And gentlest tones were with the vision blent:[n]
He knew not if that gaze the music sent,
Or music that calm[o] gaze: to hear, to see,
Was but one undivided ecstasy:[20]
The raptured senses melted into one,[p]
And parting life a moment's freedom won
From in and outer, as a little child
Sits on a bank and sees blue heavens mild

Down in the water, and forgets its limbs,[a]
And knoweth nought save the blue heaven that swims.

"Jubal," the face said, "I am thy loved Past,[b]
The soul that makes thee one from first to last.[21]
I am the angel of thy life and death,
Thy outbreathed being drawing its last breath.
Am I not thine alone, a dear dead bride
Who blest thy lot above all men's beside?[c]
Thy bride whom thou wouldst never change, nor
    take
Any bride living, for that dead one's sake?
Was I not all thy yearning and delight,
Thy chosen search, thy senses' beauteous Right,
Which still had been the hunger of thy frame
In central heaven, hadst thou been still the same?
Wouldst thou have asked aught else from any god –[d]
Whether with gleaming feet on earth he trod
Or thundered through the skies –[e] aught else for[f] share
Of mortal good, than in thy soul to bear
The growth of song, and feel the sweet unrest
Of the world's spring-tide in thy conscious breast?
No, thou hadst grasped thy lot with all its pain,
Nor loosed it any painless lot to gain
Where music's voice was silent; for thy fate
Was human music's self incorporate:
Thy senses' keenness and thy passionate strife
Were flesh of *her*[g] flesh and her womb of life.
And greatly hast thou lived, for not alone
With hidden raptures were her secrets shown,
Buried within[h] thee, as the purple light
Of gems may sleep[i] in solitary night;
But thy expanding joy was still to give,[j]
And with the generous air in song to live,

Feeding the wave of ever-widening bliss
Where fellowship means[a] equal perfectness.
And on the mountains in thy wandering
Thy feet were beautiful as blossomed spring,
That turns the leafless wood to love's glad home,
For with thy coming Melody[b] was come.
This was thy lot, to feel, create, bestow,
And that immeasurable life to know
From which the fleshly self falls shrivelled, dead,
A seed primeval that has forests bred.
It is the glory of the heritage
Thy life has left, that makes thy outcast age:
Thy limbs shall lie dark, tombless on this sod,
Because thou shinest in man's soul,[c] a god,
Who found and gave new passion and new joy
That nought but Earth's destruction can destroy.
Thy gifts to give was thine of men alone:
'Twas but in giving that thou couldst atone
For too much wealth amid their poverty." –[d]

The words seemed melting into symphony,
The wings upbore him, and the gazing song
Was floating him the heavenly space along,
Where mighty harmonies all gently fell
Through veiling vastness, like the far-off bell,
Till, ever onward through the choral blue,
He heard more faintly and more faintly knew,
Quitting mortality, a quenched sun-wave,
The All-creating Presence for his grave.[e]

AGATHA

Eliot told Alexander Main that 'Agatha was written after a visit to that St. Märgen described at the beginning of the poem. There was really an aged woman among those green hills who suggested the picture of Agatha' (*Letters*, Vol. VI, p. 49). The Leweses took that trip to Germany from 26 May to 23 July 1868, after Eliot had finished *The Spanish Gypsy*, visiting Bonn, Baden, Petersthal and Freiberg. It was during their time in Freiberg that they made a side trip to St Märgen, from where Eliot wrote to Blackwood on 7 July 1868:

> We got your letter yesterday here among the peaceful mountain tops. After ascending gradually (in a carriage) for nearly four hours, we found ourselves in a region of grass, corn, and pine-woods, so beautifully varied that we seem to be walking in a great park laid out for our special delight. The monks as usual found out the friendly solitude, and this place of St. Märgen was originally nothing but an Augustinian monastery. About three miles off is another place of like origin, called St. Peter's, formerly a Benedictine monastery, and still used as a place of preparation for the Catholic priesthood. The Monks have all vanished, but the people are devout Catholics. At every half mile by the roadside is a carefully kept crucifix, and last night as

> we were having our supper in the common room of the inn we suddenly heard sounds that seemed to me like those of an accordion. 'Is that a zittern?' said Mr. Lewes to the German lady by his side. 'No, it is prayer.' The servants, by themselves – the host and hostess were in the same room with us – were saying their evening prayers, men's and women's voices blending in unusually correct harmony. The same loud prayer is heard at morning noon and evening from the shepherds and workers in the fields ... The land is cultivated by rich peasant proprietors, and the people here as in Petersthal look healthy and contented. This really adds to one's pleasure in seeing natural beauties. (*Letters*, Vol. IV, p. 457)

Three years later, Eliot remembered those 'peaceful mountain tops' and the 'friendly solitude' again when writing to Anne Gilchrist on 19 April 1871, thanking her for 'hints about points of beauty to be sought for in our walks' around Shottermill, near Hastlemere, Surrey: 'That "sense of standing on a round world" which you speak of, is precisely what I most care for among out-of-door delights. The last time I had it fully was at St. Märgen near Freiberg, on green hill-tops whence we could see the Rhine and poor France' (*Letters*, Vol. V, p. 140). (She referred again to 'the sorrows of poor France' when the Prussians laid siege of Paris in the Franco-Prussian War, following the defeat and capture of Napoleon III in September 1870 (*Letters*, Vol. V, p. 125; *Biography*, p. 430).)

In his journal, Lewes wrote on 13 July 1868:

> From Freiberg we took a carriage and drove to St. Märgen (four hours). The first evening ravished us with the beauty of the place, but the next

day Polly was ill in bed, and the day after it was cold so that we could not sit about in the open air. Walked to St. Peter however, and made other charming rambles, especially to a peasant's house – a memorable visit – in company with the Gräfin Baudisin and her daughter. (*Letters*, Vol. IV, p. 459)

Haight adds the following note: 'Ida, Gräfin von Baudissin [1814–88], 2nd wife of Hermann Wilhelm, Graf von Baudissin [1798–1891] … lived at Freiberg im Breisgau. The visit to the peasant's cottage was the inspiration of GE's poem *Agatha*, in which she figures as the Countess Linda …' (*Letters*, Vol. IV, p. 459 n.). So much enamoured were the Leweses with this particular visit that Lewes wrote to Gräfin Baudissin on 4 February 1869 to introduce a family to her, adding that she might 'perhaps persuade them to go to St. Märgen and see Agatha! … Mrs. Lewes often recurs to our delightful expedition to Agatha's cottage' (*Letters*, Vol. V, p. 11).

The exact dating of 'Agatha' is somewhat confused, since Eliot herself gave two dates. The 1878 edition of *Jubal* dates the poem 1868; the Jubal M.S. (Add. 34,038), ff. 36–50 – with the title page reading 'Agatha (First draught [*sic*])' – bears no date. On 23 January 1869, in her 1861–77 Diary, Eliot recorded, 'Since I wrote last [January 1] I have finished a little poem on Old Agatha', and she repeated that date in her 'Order of Writings': 'Agatha, finished, January 23, 1869' (*Letters*, Vol. V, p. 6; *Journals*, pp. 96, 134). Margaret Harris and Judith Johnston, however, argue that the latter 'is written in the purple ink which GE first uses in this volume in 1873, and was presumably made after June 1876' (*Journals*, pp. 96, 96 n.). It is likely, therefore, that this mention of 'Agatha' and its completion date is simply based on the Diary entry. The title also appears in her Notebook (Folger M.a.13) for 1868–*c.* 70 under 'Themes for Poems' (cf. Pratt and Neufeldt, pp. 72, 155).

On 24 May 1869, Eliot wrote in her Diary, 'Sold "Agatha" to Fields and Osgood [Boston], for the "Atlantic Monthly", for £300' (*Journals*, p. 136), Lewes already having written to Mr and Mrs Charles Lee Lewes on 19 May 1869 that Fields 'offered £300 for the right of printing "Agatha" in the *Atlantic Monthly*' (*Letters*, Vol. V, pp. 34, 36–7; Vol. VIII, pp. 451–2). Fields took with him a fair copy of the original MS on 24 May, which is now in Harvard University and was probably used to print the *Atlantic Monthly* edition. That fair copy is dated January 1869. Meanwhile, it is assumed, the original MS was used at about the same time (May 1869) to print the Trübner & Co. edition of 'Agatha', for copyright purposes, before the poem appeared in the *Atlantic Monthly.* Mr and Mrs Trübner were Sunday visitors at the Priory, the Leweses' home, on 23 and 30 May; they called again on 26 May (*Letters*, Vol. V, pp. 36–7 n.). The British Museum received its copy of that first edition on 4 July 1869 (cf. copy in British Library, shelf number C.59.b.17: it contains the British Museum's stamp on p. 16).

Another copy of that first edition, together with a separate printing of 'How Lisa Loved the King', was given by Eliot to Mrs Cross in January 1874, and is dated Christmas 1868. However, since Eliot dated that particular copy years later, it is safe to assume that 'Agatha' was probably completed in January 1869 (Secor, p. 172; *Letters*, Vol. V, pp. 36–7 n., and Vol. VI, p. 5).

Besides the five genuine versions of 'Agatha', there are also two forgeries. T. J. Wise perpetrated one and the other apparently originated in America. These forged editions are now known as 1869b and 1869c respectively. For discussions on them, see John Carter and Graham Pollard, *An Enquiry into the Nature of Certain Nineteenth Century Pamphlets* (London, Constable, 1934), pp. 194–7; J. Carter and G. Pollard, 'T. J. Wise and H. Buxton Forman', *Times Literary Supplement* (1 June 1946), p. 264; and John Carter, 'George Eliot's Agatha 1869 and after', *Book Collector* (1957), pp. 244–52 (*Letters*, Vol. V, p. 37). The copy-text is the version in the 1878 *Jubal*.

Notes to the Jubal M.S. (Add. 34,038)

- f. 36: title page reads 'Agatha (First draught [*sic*])'
- f. 37: Eliot numbered this '1', later changed to '37', in line with Jubal M.S. numbering
- on ff. 37–50, Eliot wrote lines in the right half of pages, using the left half for corrections and notes to printers; on ff. 51–2, she wrote lines in the left half, using the right half for corrections and notes
- MS written in black ink on lined paper with no watermarks

Agatha

Come with me to the mountain, not where rocks
Soar harsh above the troops of hurrying pines,
But where the earth spreads soft and rounded breasts
To feed her children; where the generous hills
Lift a green isle betwixt the sky and plain
To keep some Old World[a] things aloof from change.
Here too 'tis hill and hollow:[b] new-born streams
With sweet enforcement, joyously compelled
Like laughing children, hurry down the steeps,[c]
And make a dimpled chase athwart the stones;
Pine woods[d] are black upon the heights, the slopes
Are green with pasture, and the bearded corn
Fringes the blue above the sudden ridge:
A little world whose round horizon cuts
This isle of hills with heaven for a sea,
Save in clear moments when southwestward[e] gleams
France by the Rhine,[f] melting anon to haze.
The monks[g] of old chose here their[h] still retreat,
And called it by the Blessed Virgin's name,
Sancta Maria,[i] which the peasant's tongue,
Speaking from out the parent's heart that turns
All loved things into little things, has made
Sanct Märgen, –[j] Holy little Mary, dear
As all the sweet home things she smiles upon,
The children and the cows, the apple-trees,
The cart, the plough, all named with that caress
Which feigns them little, easy to be held,

Familiar to the eyes[a] and hand and heart.
What though a Queen? She puts her crown away
And with her little Boy wears common clothes,
Caring for common wants, remembering
That day when good Saint Joseph left his work
To marry her[b] with humble trust sublime.

The monks are gone, their shadows fall no more
Tall-frocked and cowled athwart the evening fields
At milking-time; their silent corridors
Are turned to homes of bare-armed, aproned men,
Who toil for wife and children. But the bells,
Pealing on high from two quaint convent towers,
Still ring the Catholic signals, summoning
To grave remembrance of the larger life
That bears our own,[c] like perishable fruit[d]
Upon its heaven-wide branches. At their sound
The shepherd boy far off upon the hill,[e]
The workers with the saw and at the forge,
The triple generation round the hearth, –[f]
Grandames and mothers and the flute-voiced girls, –[g]
Fall on their knees and send forth prayerful cries
To the kind Mother with the little Boy,[h]
Who pleads for helpless men against the storm,[i]
Lightning and plagues[j] and all terrific shapes
Of power supreme.
Within the prettiest hollow of these hills,
Just as you enter it, upon the slope
Stands a low cottage[k] neighboured cheerily
By running water, which,[l] at farthest end
Of the same hollow, turns a heavy mill,
And feeds the pasture for the miller's cows,[m]
Blanchi and Nägeli, Veilchen and the rest,
Matrons with faces as Griselda mild,[1]

Coming at call. And on the farthest height
A little tower looks out above the pines
Where mounting you will find a sanctuary
Open[a] and still; without, the silent crowd
Of heaven-planted, incense-mingling flowers;
Within, the altar where the Mother sits
'Mid votive tablets hung from far-off years
By peasants succoured in the peril of fire,
Fever,[b] or flood, who thought that Mary's love,[c]
Willing but not omnipotent,[d] had stood
Between their lives and that dread power which slew
Their neighbour at their side. The chapel bell
Will melt to gentlest music ere it reach
That cottage on the slope,[e] whose garden gate
Has caught the rose-tree[f] boughs and stands ajar;[g]
So does the door, to let the sunbeams in;
For in the slanting sunbeams angels come
And visit Agatha who dwells within, –[h]
Old Agatha, whose cousins Kate and Nell
Are housed by her in Love and Duty's[i] name,
They being feeble, with small withered wits,
And she believing that the higher gift
Was given to be shared. So Agatha
Shares her one room, all neat on afternoons,
As if some memory were sacred there
And everything within the four low walls
An honoured relic.[j]
                                One long summer's day
An angel entered at the rose-hung gate,[k]
With skirts[l] pale blue, a brow to quench the pearl,[m]
Hair soft and blonde as infants',[n] plenteous
As hers who made the wavy lengths once speak
The grateful worship of a rescued soul.
The angel paused before the open door

To give good day.[a] "Come in," said Agatha.
I followed close, and watched and listened there.[b]
The angel was a lady, noble, young,
Taught in all seemliness that fits a court,[c]
All lore that shapes[d] the mind to delicate use,
Yet quiet, lowly, as a meek white dove[e]
That with its presence teaches gentleness.
Men called her Countess Linda;[f] little girls
In Freiburg town, orphans whom she caressed,
Said Mamma[g] Linda:[h] yet her years were few,[i]
Her outward beauties all in budding[j] time,
Her virtues the aroma of the plant
That dwells in all its being, root, stem, leaf,
And waits not ripeness.
"Sit," said Agatha.
Her cousins were at work in neighbouring homes[k]
But yet she was not lonely;[l] all things round
Seemed filled with noiseless yet responsive[m] life,
As of a child at breast that[n] gently clings:
Not sunlight only or[o] the breathing flowers
Or the swift shadows of the birds and[p] bees,[q]
But all the household goods, which,[r] polished fair
By hands that cherished them for service done,
Shone as with glad content. The wooden beams[s]
Dark and yet friendly, easy to be reached,[t]
Bore three white crosses for a speaking sign;[u]
The walls had little pictures hung a-row,
Telling the stories of Saint Ursula,[v]
And Saint Elizabeth,[2] the lowly queen;
And on the bench that served for table too,
Skirting the wall to save the narrow space,
There lay the Catholic books,[w] inherited
From those old times when printing still was young
With stout-limbed promise, like a sturdy boy.

And in the farthest[a] corner stood the bed
Where o'er the pillow hung two pictures wreathed
With fresh-plucked ivy: one the Virgin's death,
And one her flowering tomb, while high above
She smiling bends and lets her girdle down
For ladder to the soul that cannot trust[b]
In life which[c] outlasts burial.[3] Agatha
Sat at her knitting, aged, upright, slim,
And spoke her welcome with mild dignity.
She kept the company of kings and queens
And mitred saints who sat below the feet
Of Francis with the ragged frock and wounds;[4]
And Rank for her meant Duty,[d] various,[e]
Yet equal in its worth, done worthily.
Command was service;[f] humblest service done
By willing and discerning souls[g] was glory.
    Fair Countess Linda[h] sat upon the bench,
Close fronting the old knitter, and they talked[i]
With sweet antiphony of young and old.[j]

AGATHA.[k]

You[l] like our valley, lady?[m] I am glad
You thought it well to come again. But rest –
The walk is long from Master Michael's inn.

COUNTESS LINDA.

Yes, but no walk is prettier.

AGATHA.

                        It is true:
There lacks no blessing here, the waters all[n]
Have virtues[o] like the garments of the Lord,
And heal much sickness; then, the crops and cows
Flourish past speaking, and the garden[p] flowers,
Pink, blue, and purple, 'tis a joy to see

How they yield honey for the singing bees.
I would the whole world were as good a home.

COUNTESS LINDA.

And you are well off,[a] Agatha? – your friends
Left you a certain bread:[b] is it not so?

AGATHA.

Not so at all, dear lady.[c] I had nought,[d]
Was a poor orphan; but I came to tend
Here in this house,[e] an old afflicted pair,[f]
Who wore out slowly;[g] and the last who died,[h]
Full thirty years ago, left me this roof[i]
And all the household stuff.[j] It was great wealth;[k]
And so[l] I had a home for Kate and Nell.

COUNTESS LINDA.[m]

But how, then,[n] have you earned your daily bread
These thirty years?

AGATHA.

O,[o] that is easy earning.
We help the neighbours, and our bit and sup
Is never failing: they have work for us
In house and field, all[p] sorts of odds and ends,
Patching and mending, turning o'er the hay,
Holding sick children,[q] – there is always work;[r]
And they are very good, –[s] the neighbours are:
Weigh not our bits of work with weight and scale,[t]
But glad themselves with giving us good shares
Of meat and drink;[u] and in the big farm-house[v]
When cloth[w] comes home from weaving, the good wife
Cuts me a piece, – this very gown, –[x] and says:
"Here, Agatha,[y] you old maid, you have time[z]
To pray for Hans who is gone soldiering:

The saints might help him, and they have much to do,[a]
'Twere well they were besought[b] to think of him."[c]
She[d] spoke[e] half jesting,[f] but I pray, I pray
For poor young Hans. I take it much to heart
That other people are worse off than I, –[g]
I ease my soul with praying for them all.

COUNTESS LINDA.[h]

That is your way of singing, Agatha;[i]
Just as the nightingales pour forth sad songs,
And[j] when they reach men's ears they make men's hearts
Feel the more kindly.[k]

AGATHA.

Nay, I cannot sing:[l]
My voice is hoarse, and oft I think my prayers
Are foolish, feeble things; for Christ is good
Whether I pray or not, –[m] the Virgin's heart[n]
Is kinder[o] far than mine; and then I stop
And feel I can do nought[p] towards helping men,[q]
Till out it comes, like tears that will not hold,[r]
And I must pray again for all the world.
'Tis good to me, –[s] I mean the neighbours are:
To Kate and Nell too. I have money saved
To go on pilgrimage the second time.

COUNTESS LINDA.[t]

And do you mean to go on pilgrimage
With all your years to carry, Agatha?

AGATHA.

The years are light, dear lady:[u] 'tis my sins
Are heavier than I would. And I shall go
All the way to Einsiedeln[5v] with that load:
I need to work it off.

COUNTESS LINDA.
What sort of sins,
Dear Agatha? I think they must be small.

AGATHA.
Nay, but they may be greater than I know;[a]
'Tis but dim light[b] I see by. So I try
All ways I know of to be cleansed and pure.[c]
I would not sink where evil spirits are.
There's perfect goodness somewhere:[d] so I strive.

COUNTESS LINDA.[e]
You were the better for that pilgrimage
You made before? The shrine is beautiful;[f]
And then you saw fresh country all the way.[g]

AGATHA.
Yes,[h] that is true. And ever since that time
The world seems greater,[i] and the Holy Church[j]
More wonderful. The blessed pictures all,[k]
The heavenly images with books and wings,
Are company to me through[l] the day and night.
The time![m] the time! It never seemed far back,[n]
Only to father's father and his kin
That lived before him. But the time stretched out
After that pilgrimage: I[o] seemed to see
Far back, and yet I knew[p] time lay behind,[q]
As there are countries lying still behind
The highest[r] mountains, there in Switzerland.
O,[s] it is great to go on pilgrimage!

COUNTESS LINDA.[t]
Perhaps some neighbours will be pilgrims too,
And you can start together in a band.[u]

AGATHA.

Not from these hills: people are busy here,[a]
The beasts want tendance. One who is not missed[b]
Can go and pray for others who must work.
I owe it to all[c] neighbours, young and old;[d]
For they are good past thinking, –[e] lads and girls
Given[f] to mischief, merry[g] naughtiness,
Quiet it, as the[h] hedgehogs smooth their spines,
For fear of hurting poor old Agatha.
'Tis pretty: why,[i] the cherubs in the sky
Look young and merry, and the angels play
On citherns,[j] lutes,[k] and all sweet instruments.
I would have young[l] things merry. See the Lord!
A little baby[m] playing with the birds;
And how the Blessed Mother smiles at him.[n]

COUNTESS LINDA.[o]

I think you are too happy, Agatha,
To care[p] for heaven. Earth contents you well.[q]

AGATHA.

Nay, nay, I shall be called, and I shall go
Right willingly. I shall get helpless, blind,
Be like an old stalk to be plucked away:[r]
The garden must be cleared for young spring plants.
'Tis[s] home[t] beyond the grave,[u] the most are there,
All those we pray to, all the Church's lights, –[v]
And poor old souls are welcome in their rags:[w]
One sees it by the pictures.[x] Good Saint Ann,
The Virgin's mother, she is[y] very old,
And had[z] her troubles with her husband too.[6]
Poor Kate and Nell are younger[aa] far than I,
But they will have this roof to cover them.
I shall go willingly; and willingness[ab]
Makes the yoke easy and the burden[ac] light.

COUNTESS LINDA.

When you go southward in[a] your pilgrimage,[b]
Come[c] to see me in Freiburg, Agatha.
Where you have friends[d] you should not go to inns.

AGATHA.

Yes, I will gladly come to see you, lady.[e]
And you will give me sweet hay for a bed,
And in the morning I shall wake betimes
And start when all the birds begin to sing.

COUNTESS LINDA.[f]

You wear your smart clothes on the pilgrimage,
Such pretty clothes as all the women here
Keep by them for their best:[g] a velvet[h] cap
And collar golden-broidered? They look well
On old and young alike.

AGATHA.

Nay, I have none, –[i]
Never[j] had better clothes than these you see.
Good clothes[k] are pretty, but one sees them best
When others wear them, and I somehow thought
'Twas not worth while. I had so many things[l]
More[m] than some[n] neighbours, I was partly shy
Of wearing better clothes than they,[o] and now
I am so old and custom is so strong
'Twould hurt me sore to put on finery.

COUNTESS LINDA.

Your grey hair is a crown, dear Agatha.
Shake hands;[p] good-bye.[q] The sun is going down,
And I must see the glory from the hill.

I stayed among those hills;[a] and oft heard more
Of Agatha. I liked to hear her name,
As that of one half grandame and half saint,[b]
Uttered with reverent playfulness. The lads
And younger men all called her mother, aunt,
Or granny, with[c] their pet diminutives,
And bade their lasses and their brides behave[d]
Right well to one who surely made a link
'Twixt faulty folk[e] and God[f] by loving both:
Not one[g] but counted service done by her,[h]
Asking no pay save just her daily bread.
At feasts and weddings, when they passed in groups
Along the vale,[i] and the good country[j] wine,[k]
Being[l] vocal in them, made them quire along[m]
In quaintly mingled mirth and piety,[n]
They fain must jest and play some friendly trick
On three old maids;[o] but when the moment came
Always they bated breath and made their sport[p]
Gentle as feather-stroke, that Agatha
Might like the waking for the love it showed.
Their song made happy music 'mid the hills,
For nature[q] tuned their race to harmony,
And poet Hans, the tailor,[r] wrote them songs
That grew[s] from out their life, as crocuses[t]
From out the meadow's moistness. 'Twas his song[u]
They oft sang, wending homeward from a feast, –[v]
The song I give you. It brings in, you see,[w]
Their gentle jesting with the three old maids.[x]

Midnight[y] by the chapel bell!
Homeward, homeward all, farewell!
I with you, and you with me,
Miles are short with company.
Heart of Mary, bless the way,
Keep us all by night and day!

Moon and stars at feast with night[a]
Now have drunk their fill of light.
Home they hurry, making time[b]
Trot apace, like merry rhyme.
Heart of Mary, mystic rose,
Send us all a sweet repose!

Swiftly through the wood down hill,
Run till you can hear the mill.
Toni's ghost is wandering now,
Shaped just like a snow-white cow.
Heart of Mary, morning star,[c]
Ward off danger, near or far!

Toni's waggon with its load
Fell and crushed him in the road
'Twixt these pine-trees. Never fear!
Give a neighbour's ghost good cheer.
Holy Babe, our God and Brother,[d]
Bind us fast to one another!

Hark! the mill is at its work,
Now we pass beyond the murk[e]
To the hollow, where the moon
Makes her silvery afternoon.
Good Saint Joseph, faithful spouse,
Help us all to keep our vows!

Here the three old maidens dwell,
Agatha and Kate and Nell;[f]
See, the moon shines on the thatch,
We will go and shake the latch.
Heart of Mary, cup of joy,[g]
Give us mirth without alloy!

Hush 'tis here, no noise, sing low,
Rap with gentle knuckles – so!
Like the little tapping birds,
On the door; then sing good words.
Meek[a] *Saint Anna, old and fair,*
Hallow all the snow-white hair!

Little maidens old, sweet dreams![b]
Sleep one sleep till morning beams.[c]
Mothers ye, who help us all,
Quick at hand, if ill befall.
Holy Gabriel, lily-laden,[7d]
Bless the aged mother-maiden![e]

Forward, mount the broad hillside[f]
Swift as soldiers when they ride.[g]
See the two towers how they peep,
Round-capped giants, o'er the steep.
Heart of Mary, by thy sorrow,[h]
Keep us upright through[i] *the morrow!*[j]

Now they rise quite suddenly[k]
Like a man from bended knee,[l]
Now Saint Märgen is in sight,
Here the roads branch off – good night![m]
Heart of Mary,[n] *by thy grace,*
Give us with the saints a place![o]

ARMGART

This dramatic poem is essential reading for anyone interested in Eliot's views on the position of women. Armgart is like Antigone, insofar as she is caught up in what Eliot once called an 'antagonism between valid claims' ('The *Antigone* and Its Moral', *Leader*, VII (29 March 1856), p. 306; reprinted in Pinney, pp. 261–5); *George Eliot: Selected Essays, Poems and Other Writings*, eds A. S. Byatt and Nicholas Warren (London, Penguin Books, 1990), p. 365). Armgart's particular conflict arises when she is made to choose between pursuing her highly successful singing career and becoming a wife and mother. Ambitious to fulfil her artistic destiny, she foregoes marriage, only to lose her voice, following a throat disorder, and 'take humble work and do it well – / Teach music, singing – what I can – not here, / But in some smaller town' (ll. 889–91). Eliot greatly admired Sophocles's tragedy and argued that the play's central interest and particular power are found in the conflict between the protagonists:

> It is a very superficial criticism which interprets the character of Creon as that of a hypercritical tyrant, and regards Antigone as a blameless victim. Coarse contrasts like this are not the materials handled by great dramatists. The exquisite art of Sophocles is shown in the touches by which he makes us feel that Creon, as well as

> Antigone, is contending for what he believes to be right, while both are also conscious that, in following out one principle, they are laying themselves open to just blame for transgressing another; and it is this consciousness which secretly heightens the exasperation of Creon and the defiant hardness of Antigone. The best critics have agreed with Böckh [Philip August Boeckh (1785–1867)] in recognizing this balance of principles, this antagonism between valid claims; they generally regard it, however, as dependent entirely on the Greek point of view, as springing simply from the polytheistic conception, according to which the requirements of the Gods often clashed with the duties of man. (Pinney, p. 264)

To see Antigone's story as only relevant to the ancient Greeks, however, Eliot went on to say, is wrong: 'the struggle between Antigone and Creon represents that struggle between elemental tendencies and established laws by which the outer life of man is gradually and painfully being brought into harmony with his inward needs'. Armgart's concerns follow a similar pattern, because initially she is asked to choose between her art and the needs, or, more accurately, the demands, of others. Insofar as Armgart's artistic talents are undisputed, she both resembles the Princess Leonora Halm-Eberstein in *Daniel Deronda* and stands apart from Eliot's other great heroines, Maggie Tulliver, Romola and Dorothea Brooke; however, insofar as she is left to reconcile herself to a 'widening retrospect that [breeds] despair' ('The Choir Invisible', l. 15), she inherits the common lot of Eliot's women.

The period immediately before the composition of 'Armgart' was particularly dark for Eliot. The death of

Lewes's son, Thornie, on 19 October 1869, left the Leweses 'shaken', 'crushed', 'shattered' (*Letters*, Vol. V, pp. 60ff) and slow to recover. In the spring of 1870 (14 March–6 May) they again travelled to Germany and Austria, hoping that relaxation would restore Lewes (*Letters*, Vol. V, p. 79). While in Berlin, they saw 'Gluck's *Armida*, Mozart's *Figaro*, and Wagner's *Tannhäuser*, besides hearing delightful instrumental concerts at 6d a head' (*Letters*, Vol. V, p. 84). It was at this time that Lewes famously wrote to his son, Charles, 'The Mutter and I have come to the conclusion that the Music of the future is not for us – Schubert, Beethoven, Mozart, Gluck or even Verdi – but not Wagner – is what we are made to respond to. Lucca as Cherubino is enchanting and if she plays it while you are in London don't miss the chance' (*Letters*, Vol. V, p. 85). Haight notes that many of Eliot's contemporaries felt the same way about Wagner (*Letters*, Vol. V, p. 85 n.), although Beryl Gray points out that Eliot was 'generally more tolerant' of him (*George Eliot and Music* (London, Macmillan, 1989), p. 127).

They came back from their trip, Eliot's head 'still swimming from the journey' (*Letters*, Vol. V, p. 93), but not much restored, especially Lewes. Consequently, on the advice of a doctor, the Leweses set off again on 15 June 1870, this time for the 'bracing air of the Yorkshire coast' (*Letters*, Vol. V, p. 102), specifically, Cromer, Harrogate and Whitby. While in Harrogate on 13 July 1870, Lewes wrote in his diary about Eliot's plan for 'Armgart': 'Woman's triumph – losing her voice & obliged to sink into insignificance' (Secor, p. 328; Rosemary Ashton, *George Eliot. A Life* (London, Penguin, 1997), pp. 309–10). A few days before, 8 July 1870, Eliot had written a consoling letter to Edith Lytton, whose much loved uncle had died, which helps to shed light on her state of mind while planning 'Armgart'. In it she said that death had also been her 'most intimate daily companion' for 'nearly a year':

> I mingle the thought of it with every other, not sadly, but as one mingles the thought of some one who is nearest in love and duty with all one's motives. I try to delight in the sunshine that will be when I shall never see it any more. And I think it is possible for this sort of impersonal life to attain great intensity, – possibly for us to gain much more independence, than is usually believed, of the small bundle of facts that make our own personality.
>
> I don't know why I should say this to you, except that my pen is chatting as my tongue would if you were here. We women are always in danger of living too exclusively in the affections; and though our affections are perhaps the best gifts we have, we ought also to have our share of the more independent life – some joy in things for their own sake. It is piteous to see the helplessness of some sweet women when their affections are disappointed – because all their teaching had been, that they can only delight in study of any kind for the sake of personal love. They have never contemplated an independent delight in ideas as an experience which they could confess without being laughed at. Yet surely women need this sort of defence against passionate affliction even more than men.
>
> Just under the pressure of grief, I do not believe there is any consolation. The word seems to me to be drapery for falsities. Sorrow must be

> sorrow, ill must be ill, till duty and love towards all who remain recover their rightful predominance. (*Letters*, Vol. V, p. 107)

Armgart's situation, of course, is quite different from that of most women: she has 'contemplated an independent delight in ideas as an experience ... [though] without being laughed at'. Nevertheless, she, too, becomes 'piteous to see' when she loses her voice and is made to suffer 'till duty and love towards all who remain recover their rightful predominance'.

The Leweses returned to London on 1 August 1870, and on 4 August Eliot wrote in her Diary 1861–77, 'Today, under much depression, I begin a little dramatic poem the subject of which engaged my interest at Harrogate' (*Journals*, p. 141). From 8–29 August the Leweses were at Limpsfield, Surrey, and, on 27 October 1870, Eliot wrote in her Diary 1861–77:

> During our stay at Limpsfield I wrote the greater part of 'Armgart', and finished it at intervals during September. Since then I have been continually suffering from headache and depression, with almost total despair of future work. I look into this little book now to assure myself that this is not unprecedented. (*Journals*, p. 141)

By November 1870 she began 'Miss Brooke', which was later incorporated into *Middlemarch*.

'Armgart' was sold to *Macmillan's Magazine* for £200 and the *Atlantic Monthly* for £100, appearing in both in July 1871 (*Letters*, Vol. V, p. 139). In the former, it appeared as 'Armgart: A Tragic Poem'. The MS is signed 'George Eliot' and dated 'August 1870', although in Eliot's Diary 1861–77 it is listed under 'Order of Writings' as 'Armgart finished, September

1870' (*Journals*, p. 96). Evidently, she continued revising the work, because, as Secor notes, 'the MS indicates a play of seven scenes, the *Atlantic Monthly*, six scenes, and *Macmillan's* and the two subsequent editions, five scenes … the implication [being] that this final scene division was arrived at after the early sheets had been dispatched to America' (Secor, p. 331). The 1874 edition of the poem in *The Legend of Jubal and Other Poems* has further substantive changes, but the 1878 version has only two more. The latter is the copy-text.

Notes to the Jubal M.S. (Add. 34,038)

- MS pagination, ff. 91–117, added in pencil; original is 1–26
- pages of original, loose MS were cropped to match rest of bound MS
- MS written in black ink on unlined, shiny (thicker) paper, with watermark 'Parkins & Gotto London', also used for 'Two Lovers'
- MS title page reads

  'Armgart:
a poem
by
George Eliot'
- MS signed 'George Eliot', dated 'August 1870' (f. 117)

Armgart

SCENE I.[a]

A Salon lit with lamps and ornamented with green plants. An open piano with many scattered sheets of music. Bronze busts of Beethoven and Gluck on pillars opposite each other. A small table spread with supper. To FRÄULEIN WALPURGA, *who advances with a slight lameness of gait from an adjoining room, enters* GRAF DORNBERG *at the opposite door in a travelling dress.*

GRAF.

Good morning,[b] Fräulein!

WALPURGA.[c]

What, so soon returned?[d]
I feared your mission kept you still at Prague.

GRAF.

But now arrived! You see my travelling dress.
I hurried from the panting, roaring steam
Like any courier of embassy
Who hides the fiends of war within his bag.

WALPURGA.[e]

You know that Armgart sings to-night?[f]

GRAF.

Has sung!
'Tis close on half-past[a] nine. The *Orpheus*[1b]
Lasts not so long. Her spirits – were they high?
Was Leo confident?

WALPURGA.

He only feared
Some tameness at beginning. Let the house
Once ring, he said, with plaudits, she is safe.

GRAF.

And Armgart?

WALPURGA.

She was stiller than her wont.
But once, at some such trivial word of mine,
As[c] that the highest prize might yet be won
By her who took the second – she was roused.
"For me," she said, "I triumph or I fail.
I never strove for any second prize."

GRAF.

Poor human-hearted singing-bird! She bears
Caesar's ambition in her delicate breast,[d]
And nought to still it with but quivering song!

WALPURGA.

I had not for the world been there to-night:
Unreasonable dread oft chills me more
Than any reasonable hope can warm.

GRAF.

You have a rare affection for your cousin;
As tender as a sister's.

WALPURGA.

Nay, I fear
My love is little more than what I felt
For happy stories when I was a child.
She fills my life that would be empty else,
And lifts my nought to value by her side.

GRAF.

She is reason good enough, or seems to be,[a]
Why all were born whose being ministers
To her completeness. Is it most her voice
Subdues us? or her instinct exquisite,[b]
Informing each old strain with some new grace
Which takes our sense like any natural good?
Or most her spiritual energy
That sweeps us in the current of her song?

WALPURGA.

I know not. Losing either, we should lose
That whole we call our Armgart. For herself,
She often wonders what her life had been
Without that voice for channel to her soul.
She says, it must have leaped through all her limbs –[c]
Made her a Mænad[2] – made her snatch a brand
And fire some forest, that her rage might mount
In crashing roaring flames through half a land,
Leaving her still and patient for a while.
"Poor wretch !" she says, of any murderess –
"The world was cruel, and she could not sing:
I carry my revenges in my throat;
I love in singing,[d] and am loved again."

GRAF.

Mere mood! I cannot yet believe it more.
Too much ambition has unwomaned her;

But only for a while. Her nature hides
One half its treasures by its very wealth,
Taxing the hours to show it.

WALPURGA.

Hark ! she comes.[a]

Enter LEO *with a wreath in his hand, holding the door open for* ARMGART,[b] *who wears a furred mantle and hood. She is followed by her maid, carrying an armful of bouquets.*[3]

LEO.

Place for the queen of song!

GRAF (*advancing towards* ARMGART, *who throws off her hood and mantle,*[c] *and shows a star of brilliants in her hair*).[d]

A triumph, then.
You will not be a niggard of your joy
And chide the eagerness that came to share it.

ARMGART.[e]

O kind! you hastened your return for me.
I would you had been there to hear me sing!
Walpurga, kiss me: never tremble more
Lest Armgart's wing should fail her. She has found
This night the region where her rapture breathes –
Pouring her passion on the air made live
With human heart-throbs. Tell them, Leo, tell them
How I outsang your hope and made you cry
Because Gluck could not hear me. That was folly!
He sang, not listened: every linkèd[f] note
Was his immortal pulse that stirred in mine,
And all my gladness is but part of him.
Give me the wreath.

(*She crowns the bust of* GLUCK.)[a]

LEO (*sardonically*).

Ay, ay, but mark you this:
It was not part of him – that trill you made
In spite of me and reason!

ARMGART.

You were wrong –
Dear Leo, you were wrong:[b] the house was held
As if a storm were listening with delight
And hushed its thunder.

LEO.

Will you ask the house
To teach you singing? Quit your *Orpheus*[c] then,
And sing in farces grown to operas,
Where all the prurience of the full-fed[d] mob
Is tickled with melodic impudence:
Jerk forth burlesque bravuras, square your arms
Akimbo with a tavern wench's grace,
And set the splendid compass of your voice
To lyric jigs. Go to! I thought you meant
To be an artist – lift your audience
To see your vision, not trick forth a show
To please the grossest taste of grossest numbers.

ARMGART

(*taking*[e] *up* LEO'S *hand, and kissing it*).

Pardon, good Leo, I am penitent.
I will do penance: sing a hundred trills
Into a deep-dug[f] grave, then burying them
As one did Midas' secret,[4] rid myself
Of naughty exultation. O I trilled

At nature's prompting, like the nightingales.
Go scold them, dearest Leo.

LEO.

I stop my ears.
Nature in Gluck inspiring Orpheus,
Has done with nightingales. Are bird-beaks lips?

GRAF.

Truce to rebukes! Tell us – who were not there –
The double drama: how the expectant house
Took the first notes.

WALPURGA (*turning*[a] *from her occupation of decking the room with the flowers*).

Yes, tell us all, dear Armgart.[b]
Did you feel[c] tremors? Leo, how did she look?
Was there a cheer to greet her?

LEO.

Not a sound.
She walked like Orpheus in his solitude,
And seemed to see nought but what no man[d] saw.
'Twas famous. Not the Schroeder-Devrient[5]
Had done it better. But your blessed public
Had never any judgment in cold blood –
Thinks all perhaps were better otherwise,
Till rapture brings a reason.

ARMGART (*scornfully*).

I knew that![e]
The women whispered, "Not a pretty face!"
The men, "Well, well, a goodly length of limb:
She beats the chiton."[6] – It were all the same
Were I the Virgin Mother and my stage

The opening heavens at the Judgment-day:[a]
Gossips would peep, jog elbows, rate the price
Of such a woman in the social mart.
What were the drama of the world to them,
Unless they felt the hell-prong?

LEO.

Peace, now, peace!
I hate my phrases to be smothered o'er
With sauce of paraphrase,[b] my sober tune
Made bass to rambling trebles, showering down
In endless demi-semi-quavers.[c]

ARMGART (*taking a bon-bon from the table, uplifting*[d] *it before putting it into her mouth, and turning away*).

Mum![e]

GRAF.

Yes, tell us all the glory, leave the blame.

WALPURGA.

You first, dear Leo – what you saw and heard;[f]
Then Armgart –[g] she must tell us what she felt.

LEO.

Well! The first notes came clearly firmly forth.[h]
And I was easy, for behind those rills
I knew there was a fountain. I could see
The house was breathing gently, heads were still;
Parrot opinion was struck meekly mute,[i]
And human hearts were swelling. Armgart stood
As if she had been new-created[j] there
And found her voice which found a melody.
The minx! Gluck had not written, nor I taught:[k]

Orpheus was Armgart, Armgart Orpheus.
Well, well, all through the *scena* I could feel
The silence tremble now, now poise itself
With added weight of feeling, till at last
Delight o'er toppled it. The final note
Had happy drowning in the unloosed roar
That surged and ebbed and ever surged again,
Till expectation kept it pent awhile
Ere Orpheus returned. Pfui! He was changed:[a]
My demi-god[b] was pale, had downcast eyes
That quivered like a bride's who fain would send
Backward the rising tear.

ARMGART (*advancing,*[c] *but then turning*[d] *away, as if to check her speech*).

I *was* a bride,[e]
As nuns are at their spousals.

LEO.

Ay, my lady,[f]
That moment will not come again: applause
May come and plenty; but the first, first draught![g]
(*Snaps his fingers.*)[h]
Music has sounds for it –[i] I know no words.
I felt it once myself when they performed
My overture to Sintram.[7] Well![j] 'tis strange,
We know not pain from pleasure in such joy.

ARMGART (*turning quickly*).

Oh,[k] pleasure has cramped dwelling in our souls,[l]
And when full Being[m] comes must call on pain
To lend it liberal space.

WALPURGA.
I hope the house
Kept a reserve of plaudits: I am jealous
Lest they had dulled themselves for coming good
That should have seemed the better and the best.

LEO.
No, 'twas a revel where they had but quaffed
Their opening cup. I thank the artist's star,
His audience keeps not sober: once afire,[a]
They flame towards climax, though his merit hold
But fairly even.

ARMGART (*her hand on* LEO'S *arm*).
Now, now, confess the truth:[b]
I sang still better to the very end –[c]
Ah save the trill; I give that up to you,
To bite and growl at. Why, you said yourself,
Each time I sang, it seemed new doors were oped
That you might hear heaven clearer.

LEO (*shaking his finger*).
I was raving.[d]

ARMGART.
I am not glad with that mean vanity
Which knows no good beyond its appetite
Full feasting upon praise! I am only glad,[e]
Being praised for what I know is worth the praise;
Glad of the proof that I myself have part
In what I worship! At the last applause –[f]
Seeming a roar of tropic winds that tossed
The handkerchiefs and many-coloured[g] flowers,
Falling like shattered rainbows all around –[h]
Think you I felt myself a *prima donna*?

No, but a happy spiritual star
Such as old Dante saw, wrought in a rose
Of light in Paradise,[a] whose only self
Was consciousness of glory wide-diffused,
Music, life, power –[b] I moving in the midst
With a sublime necessity of good.

LEO (*with a shrug*).

I thought it was a *prima donna* came[c]
Within the side-scenes; ay, and she was proud
To find the bouquet from the royal box
Enclosed a jewel-case, and proud to wear
A star of brilliants, quite an earthly star,
Valued by thalers.[8] Come, my lady, own
Ambition has five senses, and a self
That gives it good warm lodging when it sinks
Plump down from ecstasy.

ARMGART.

Own it? why not?
Am I a sage whose words must fall like seed
Silently buried toward a far-off spring?
I sing to living men and my effect
Is like the summer's sun,[d] that ripens[e] corn
Or now or never. If the world brings me gifts,
Gold, incense, myrrh –[f] 'twill be the needful sign
That I have stirred it as the high year stirs
Before I sink to winter.

GRAF.

Ecstasies
Are short – most happily! We should but lose
Were Armgart borne too commonly and long
Out of the self that charms us. Could I choose,
She were less apt to soar beyond the reach

Of woman's foibles, innocent vanities,
Fondness for trifles like that pretty star
Twinkling beside her cloud of ebon hair.

ARMGART (*taking out the gem and looking at it*).[a]
This little star! I would it were the seed
Of a whole Milky Way,[b] if such bright shimmer
Were the sole speech men told their rapture with
At Armgart's music. Shall I turn aside
From splendours[c] which flash out the glow I make,
And live to make, in all the chosen breasts
Of half a Continent? No, may it come,
That splendour![d] May the day be near when men
Think much to let my horses draw me home,
And new lands welcome me upon their beach,
Loving me for my fame. That is the truth
Of what I wish, nay, yearn for. Shall I lie?[e]
Pretend to seek obscurity –[f] to sing
In hope of disregard? A vile pretence!
And blasphemy besides. For what is fame
But the benignant strength of One[g] transformed
To joy of Many?[h] Tributes, plaudits come
As necessary breathing of such joy;[i]
And may they come to me!

GRAF.
The auguries
Point clearly that way. Is it no offence
To wish the eagle's wing may find repose,
As feebler wings do, in a quiet nest?
Or has the taste of fame already turned
The Woman to a Muse . . .[j]

LEO (*going to the table*).
Who needs supper.[a]
I am her priest, ready to eat her share
Of good Walpurga's offerings.

WALPURGA.
Armgart, come.
Graf, will you come?[b]

GRAF.
Thanks, I play truant here,
And must retrieve my self-indulged delay.
But will the Muse receive a votary
At any hour tomorrow!

ARMGART.
Any hour
After rehearsal, after twelve at noon.

SCENE II.[c]

The same Salon, morning. ARMGART[d] *seated, in her bonnet and walking dress. The* GRAF[e] *standing near her against the piano.*

GRAF.
Armgart, to many minds the first success
Is reason for desisting. I have known
A man so versatile,[f] he tried all arts,
But when in each by turns he had achieved
Just so much mastery as made men say,
"He could be king here if he would," he threw
The lauded skill aside. He hates, said one,

The level of achieved pre-eminence,
He must be conquering still; but others[a] said –

ARMGART.
The truth, I hope: he[b] had a meagre soul,
Holding no depth where love could root itself.
"Could if he would?"[c] True greatness ever wills –
It lives in wholeness if it live at all,[d]
And all its strength is knit with constancy.

GRAF.
He used to say himself he was too sane
To give his life away for excellence
Which yet must stand,[e] an ivory statuette
Wrought to perfection through long lonely years,
Huddled in the mart[f] of mediocrities.
He said, the very finest doing wins
The admiring only; but to leave undone,
Promise and not fulfil, like buried youth,
Wins all the envious, makes them sigh your name
As that fair Absent, blameless Possible,[g]
Which could alone impassion them; and thus,
Serene negation has free gift of all,[h]
Panting[i] achievement struggles, is denied,
Or wins to lose again. What say you, Armgart?
Truth has rough flavours[j] if we bite it through;[k]
I think this sarcasm came from out its[l] core
Of bitter irony.

ARMGART.
It is the truth
Mean souls select to feed upon.[m] What then?
Their meanness is a truth, which I will spurn.
The praise I seek lives not in envious breath
Using my name to blight another's deed.

I sing for love of song and that renown
Which is the spreading act, the world-wide share,
Of good that I was born with. Had I failed –[a]
Well, that had been a truth most pitiable.[b]
I cannot bear to think what life would be
With high hope shrunk to endurance, stunted aims
Like broken lances ground to eating-knives,
A self sunk down to look with level eyes
At low achievement, doomed from day to day
To distaste of its consciousness. But I —

GRAF.

Have won, not lost, in your decisive throw.[c]
And I too glory in this issue; yet,
The public verdict has no potency
To sway my judgment of what Armgart is:
My pure delight in her would be but sullied,
If it o'erflowed with mixture of men's praise.
And had she failed, I should have said, "The pearl
Remains a pearl for me, reflects the light
With the same fitness that first charmed my gaze –[d]
Is worth as fine a setting now as then."[e]

ARMGART (*rising*).[f]

Oh,[g] you are good! But why will you rehearse
The talk of cynics, who with insect eyes[h]
Explore[i] the secrets of the rubbish-heap?[j]
I hate your epigrams and pointed saws
Whose narrow truth is but broad falsity.
Confess[k] your friend was shallow.

GRAF.

I confess
Life is not rounded in an epigram,
And saying aught, we leave a world unsaid.

I quoted, merely[a] to shape forth my thought
That high success has terrors when achieved –[b]
Like preternatural spouses whose dire love
Hangs perilous on slight observances:
Whence it were possible that Armgart crowned
Might turn and listen to a pleading voice,
Though Armgart striving in the race was deaf.[c]
You said you dared not think what life had been
Without the stamp of eminence; have you thought
How you will bear the poise of eminence
With dread of sliding? Paint the future out
As an unchecked and glorious career,
'Twill grow more strenuous by the very love
You bear to excellence, the[d] very fate
Of human powers, which tread at every step
On possible verges.

ARMGART.

I accept the peril.
I choose to walk high with sublimer dread
Rather than crawl in safety. And, besides,
I am an artist as you are a noble:
I ought to bear[e] the burthen of my rank.

GRAF.

Such parallels, dear Armgart, are but snares
To catch the mind with seeming argument –
Small baits of likeness 'mid disparity.
Men rise the higher as their task is high,
The task being well achieved. A woman's rank
Lies in the fulness of her womanhood:[f]
Therein alone she is royal.

ARMGART.

Yes, I know
The oft-taught Gospel: "Woman, thy desire
Shall be that all superlatives on earth
Belong to men, save the one highest kind –[a]
To be a mother. Thou shalt not desire
To do aught best save pure subservience:
Nature has willed it so!"[b] O blessed Nature!
Let her be arbitress; she gave me voice
Such as she only gives a woman child,
Best of its kind, gave me ambition too,
That sense transcendent which can taste the joy
Of swaying multitudes, of being adored
For such achievement, needed excellence,
As man's best art must wait for, or be dumb.
Men did not say, when I had sung last night,[c]
"'Twas good, nay, wonderful, considering
She is a woman" – and then turn to add,[d]
"Tenor or baritone had sung her songs
Better, of course: she's but a woman spoiled."
I beg your pardon, Graf, you said it.

GRAF.

No![e]
How should I say it, Armgart? I who own
The magic of your nature-given art
As sweetest effluence of your womanhood
Which, being to my choice the best, must find
The best of utterance. But this I say:
Your fervid youth beguiles you; you mistake
A strain of lyric passion for a life
Which in the spending is a chronicle
With ugly pages. Trust me, Armgart, trust me;[f]
Ambition exquisite as yours which soars

Toward something quintessential you call fame,
Is not robust enough for this gross world
Whose fame is dense with false and foolish breath.
Ardour, a-twin with nice refining thought,[a]
Prepares a double pain. Pain had been saved,
Nay, purer glory reached, had you been throned
As woman only, holding all your art
As attribute to that dear sovereignty –[b]
Concentering your power in home delights
Which penetrate and purify the world.

ARMGART.

What![c] leave the opera with my part ill-sung[d]
While I was warbling in a drawing-room?
Sing in the chimney-corner to inspire
My husband reading news? Let the world hear
My music only in his morning speech
Less stammering than most honourable[e] men's?
No! tell me that my song is poor, my art
The piteous feat of weakness aping strength –[f]
That were fit proem to your argument.
Till then, I am an artist by my birth –[g]
By the same warrant that I am a woman:
Nay, in the added rarer gift I see
Supreme vocation: if a conflict comes,[h]
Perish –[i] no, not the woman, but the joys
Which men make narrow by their narrowness.
Oh,[j] I am happy! The great masters write
For women's voices, and great Music wants me!
I need not crush myself within a mould
Of theory called Nature: I have room
To breathe and grow unstunted.

GRAF.

Armgart, hear me.[a]
I meant not that our talk should hurry on
To such collision. Foresight of the ills
Thick shadowing your path, drew on my speech
Beyond intention. True, I came to ask
A great renunciation, but not this
Towards which my words at first perversely
strayed,
As if in memory of their earlier suit,
Forgetful . . . .
Armgart, do you remember too ? the suit[b]
Had but postponement, was not quite disdained –[c]
Was told to wait and learn – what it has learned –
A more submissive speech.

ARMGART (*with some agitation*).

Then it forgot
Its lesson cruelly. As I remember,
'Twas not to speak save[d] to the artist crowned,
Nor speak to her of casting off her crown.

GRAF.

Nor will it, Armgart. I come not to seek
Any[e] renunciation save the wife's,
Which turns away from other[f] possible love
Future and worthier, to take his love
Who asks the name of husband. He who sought
Armgart obscure, and heard her answer, "Wait" –[g]
May come without suspicion now to seek
Armgart applauded.

ARMGART (*turning towards him*).

Yes, without suspicion
Of aught save what consists with faithfulness

In all expressed intent. Forgive me, Graf –[a]
I am ungrateful to no soul that loves me –[b]
To you most grateful. Yet the best intent
Grasps but a living present which may grow
Like any unfledged bird. You are a noble,
And have a high career; just[c] now you said
'Twas higher far than aught a woman seeks
Beyond mere womanhood. You claim to be
More than a husband, but could not rejoice
That I were more than wife. What follows, then?
You choosing me with such persistency
As is but stretched-out rashness, soon must find
Our marriage asks concessions, asks resolve
To share renunciation or demand it.
Either we both renounce a mutual ease,
As in a nation's need both man and wife
Do public services, or one of us
Must yield that something else for which each lives
Besides the other. Men are reasoners:[d]
That premiss of superior claims perforce
Urges conclusion –[e] "Armgart, it is you."

GRAF.

But if I say I have considered this
With strict prevision, counted all the cost
Which that great good of loving you demands –
Questioned my stores of patience, half resolved
To live resigned without a bliss whose threat
Touched you as well as me –[f] and finally,
With impetus of undivided will
Returned to say, "You shall be free as now;
Only accept the refuge, shelter, guard,
My love will give your freedom" –[g] then your words
Are hard accusal.

ARMGART.

Well, I accuse myself.
My love would be accomplice of your will.

GRAF.

Again –[a] my will?

ARMGART.

Oh,[b] your unspoken will.
Your silent tolerance would torture me,
And on that rack I should deny the good
I yet believed in.

GRAF.

Then I am the man
Whom you would love?

ARMGART.

Whom I refuse to love!
No;[c] I will live alone and pour my pain
With passion into music,[d] where it turns
To what is best within my better self.
I will not take for husband one who deems
The thing my soul acknowledges as good –[e]
The thing I hold worth striving, suffering for,
To be a thing dispensed with easily,
Or else the idol of a mind infirm.

GRAF.

Armgart, you are ungenerous; you strain
My thought beyond its mark. Our difference
Lies not so deep as love –[f] as union
Through a mysterious fitness that transcends
Formal agreement.

ARMGART.

It lies deep enough
To chafe the union.[a] If many a man
Refrains, degraded, from the utmost right,
Because the pleadings of his wife's small fears
Are little serpents biting at his heel, –
How shall a woman keep her steadfastness[b]
Beneath a frost within her husband's eyes
Where coldness scorches? Graf, it is your sorrow
That you love Armgart. Nay, it is her sorrow
That she may not love you.

GRAF.

Woman, it seems,
Has enviable power to love or not
According to her will.

ARMGART.

She has the will[c] –
I have – who am one woman – not to take
Disloyal pledges that divide her will.
The man who marries me must wed[d] my Art –[e]
Honour and cherish it, not tolerate.

GRAF.

The man is yet to come whose theory
Will weigh as nought with you against his love.

ARMGART.

Whose theory will plead beside his love.

GRAF.

Himself a singer, then? who knows no life
Out of the opera books, where tenor parts
Are found to suit him?

ARMGART.

You are bitter, Graf.
Forgive me; seek the woman you deserve,
All grace, all goodness, who has not yet found
A meaning in her life, nor any end
Beyond fulfilling yours. The type abounds.

GRAF.

And[a] happily, for the world.

ARMGART.

Yes, happily.
Let it excuse me that my kind is rare:
Commonness is its own security.

GRAF.

Armgart, I would with all my soul I knew
The man so rare that he could make your life
As woman sweet to you, as artist safe.

ARMGART.

Oh,[b] I can live unmated, but not live
Without the bliss of singing to the world,
And feeling all my world respond to me.

GRAF.

May it be lasting. Then, we two must part?

ARMGART.

I thank you from my heart for all. Farewell!

SCENE III.[a]

A YEAR LATER.

The same Salon. WALPURGA *is standing looking towards the window with an air of uneasiness.* DOCTOR GRAHN.[b]

DOCTOR.

Where is my patient, Fräulein?

WALPURGA.

Fled! escaped!
Gone to rehearsal. Is it dangerous?

DOCTOR.

No, no; her throat is cured. I only came
To hear her try her voice. Has she yet sung?

WALPURGA.

No; she had meant to wait for you. She said,
"The Doctor has a right to my first song."
Her gratitude was full of little plans,
But all were swept[c] away like gathered flowers
By sudden storm. She saw this opera bill –[d]
It was a wasp to sting her: she turned pale,
Snatched up her hat and mufflers, said in haste,
"I go to Leo – to rehearsal – none
Shall sing Fidelio[9] to-night but me!"
Then rushed down-stairs.[e]

DOCTOR (*looking at his watch*).

And this, not long ago?

WALPURGA.

Barely an hour.

DOCTOR.

I will come again,[a]
Returning from Charlottenburg at one.

WALPURGA.

Doctor, I feel a strange presentiment.
Are you quite easy?

DOCTOR.

She can take no harm.
'Twas time for her to sing: her throat is well.
It was a fierce attack and dangerous;
I had to use strong remedies, but – well!
At one, dear Fräulein, we shall meet again.[b]

SCENE IV.

TWO HOURS LATER.[c]

WALPURGA *starts up, looking towards the door.* ARMGART *enters, followed by* LEO. *She throws herself on a chair which stands with its back towards the door,*[d] *speechless, not seeming to see anything.* WALPURGA *casts a questioning terrified look at Leo. He shrugs his shoulders, and lifts up his hands behind* ARMGART, *who sits like a helpless image while* WALPURGA *takes off her hat and mantle.*[e]

WALPURGA.

Armgart, dear Armgart (*kneeling and taking her hands)*, only speak to me,
Your poor Walpurga. Oh,[f] your hands are cold.
Clasp mine, and warm them! I will kiss them warm.

(ARMGART *looks at her an instant, then draws away her hands, and, turning aside, buries her face against the back of the chair,* WALPURGA *rising and standing near.*)

(DOCTOR GRAHN *enters.*)[a]

DOCTOR.

News! stirring news to-day! wonders come thick.[b]

ARMGART (*starting*[c] *up at the first sound of his voice, and speaking vehemently*).

Yes, thick, thick, thick! and you have murdered it!
Murdered my voice –[d] poisoned the soul in me,[e]
And kept me living.
You never told me that your cruel cures
Were clogging films –[f] a mouldy, dead'ning[g] blight –[h]
A lava-mud to crust and bury me,[i]
Yet hold me living in a deep, deep tomb,
Crying unheard for ever! Oh,[j] your cures
Are devil's[k] triumphs: you can rob, maim, slay,
And keep a hell on the other side your cure
Where you can see your victim quivering
Between the teeth of torture –[l] see a soul
Made keen by loss –[m] all anguish with a good
Once known and gone! (*Turns and sinks back on her chair.*)[n]
O misery, misery!
You might have killed me, might have let me sleep
After my happy day and wake –[o] not here!
In some new unremembered world, – not here,
Where all is faded, flat – a feast broke off –
Banners all meaningless – exulting words[p]
Dull, dull – a drum that lingers in the air
Beating to melody which no man hears.

DOCTOR (*after a moment's silence*).
A sudden check has shaken you, poor child!
All things seem livid, tottering to your sense,[a]
From inward tumult. Stricken by a threat
You see your terrors only. Tell me, Leo:
'Tis not such utter loss.

(LEO, *with a shrug goes quietly out.*)

The freshest bloom
Merely, has left the fruit; the fruit itself . . .

ARMGART.
Is ruined, withered, is a thing to hide
Away from scorn or pity. Oh,[b] you stand
And look compassionate now, but when Death came
With mercy in his hands, you hindered him.
I did not choose to live and have your pity.
You never told me, never gave me choice
To die a singer, lightning-struck, unmaimed,
Or live what you would make me with your cures –[c]
A self accursed with consciousness of change,
A mind that lives in nought but members lopped,
A power turned to pain –[d] as meaningless
As letters fallen asunder that once made
A hymn of rapture. Oh,[e] I had meaning once,[f]
Like day and sweetest air.[g] What am I now?
The millionth woman in superfluous herds.
Why should I be, do, think? 'tis thistle-seed,[h]
That grows and grows to feed the rubbish-heap.
Leave me alone!

DOCTOR.
Well, I will come again;
Send for me when you will, though but to rate me.
That is medicinal – a letting blood.

ARMGART.
Oh,[a] there is one physician, only one,
Who cures and never spoils. Him I shall send for;[b]
He comes readily.

DOCTOR (*to* WALPURGA)
One word, dear Fräulein.

SCENE V.

ARMGART, WALPURGA.[c]

ARMGART.
Walpurga, have you walked this morning?

WALPURGA.
No.

ARMGART.
Go, then, and walk; I wish to be alone.

WALPURGA.
I will not leave you.

ARMGART.
Will not, at my wish?

WALPURGA.
Will not, because you wish it. Say no more,
But take this draught.

ARMGART.
The Doctor gave it you?
It is anodyne. Put it away.

He cured me of my voice, and now he wants
To cure me of my vision and resolve –[a]
Drug me to sleep that I may wake again
Without a purpose, abject as the rest
To bear the yoke of life. He shall not cheat me
Of that fresh strength which anguish gives the soul,
The inspiration of revolt, ere rage
Slackens to faltering. Now I see the truth.

WALPURGA (*setting down the glass*).
Then you must see a future in your reach,
With happiness enough to make a dower
For two of modest claims.

ARMGART.
Oh,[b] you intone
That chant of consolation wherewith ease
Makes itself easier in the sight of pain.

WALPURGA.
No;[c] I would not console you, but rebuke.

ARMGART.
That is more bearable.[d] Forgive me, dear.
Say what you will. But now I want to write.

(*She rises and moves towards the table.*)

WALPURGA.
I say then, you are simply fevered, mad;
You cry aloud at horrors that would vanish
If you would change the light, throw into[e] shade
The loss you aggrandise, and let day fall
On good remaining, nay[f] on good refused
Which may be gain now. Did you not reject
A woman's lot more brilliant, as some held,

Than any singer's? It may still be yours.
Graf Dornberg loved you well.

ARMGART.

Not me, not me.
He loved one well who was like me in all
Save in a voice which made that All[a] unlike
As diamond is to charcoal. Oh,[b] a man's love!
Think you he loves a woman's inner self
Aching with loss of loveliness? – as mothers[c]
Cleave to the palpitating pain that dwells
Within their misformed offspring?

WALPURGA.

But let Graf
Chose you as simple Armgart –[d] had preferred
That you should never seek for any fame
But such as matrons have who rear great sons.
And therefore you rejected him; but now –

ARMGART.

Ay, now – now he would see me as I am,
(*She takes up a hand-mirror.*)
Russet and songless as a missel-thrush.
An ordinary girl –[e] a plain[f] brown girl,
Who, if some meaning flash from out her words,[g]
Shocks as a disproportioned thing –[h] a Will[i]
That,[j] like an arm astretch and broken off,[k]
Has nought to hurl –[l] the torso of a soul.
I sang him into love of me: my song
Was consecration, lifted me apart
From the crowd chiselled like me, sister forms,[m]
But empty of divineness. Nay, my charm
Was half that I could win fame yet renounce![n]

A wife with glory possible absorbed
Into her husband's actual.

WALPURGA.

For shame!
Armgart, you slander him. What would you say
If now he came to you and asked again
That you would be his wife?

ARMGART.

No, and thrice no!
It would be pitying constancy, not love,
That brought him to me now. I will not be
A pensioner in marriage. Sacraments
Are not to feed the paupers of the world.
If he were generous –[a] I am generous too.

WALPURGA.

Proud, Armgart, but not generous.

ARMGART.

Say no more.
He will not know until –[b]

WALPURGA.

He knows already.

ARMGART. (*quickly*)

Is he come back?

WALPURGA.

Yes, and will soon be here.
The Doctor had twice seen him and would go
From hence again to see him.

ARMGART.
Well, he knows.
It is all one.

WALPURGA.
What if he were outside?
I hear a footstep in the ante-room.

ARMGART (*raising herself and assuming calmness*).
Why let him come, of course. I shall behave
Like what I am, a common personage
Who looks for nothing but civility.
I shall not play the fallen heroine,
Assume a tragic part and throw out cues
For a beseeching lover.[a]

WALPURGA.
Some one raps.
(*Goes to the door*).
A letter – from the Graf.

ARMGART.
Then open it.
(WALPURGA *still offers it*.)
Nay, my head swims. Read it. I cannot see.
(WALPURGA *opens it, reads and pauses*.)
Read it. Have done! No matter what it is.

WALPURGA (*reads in a low, hesitating voice*).
"I am deeply moved – my heart is rent, to hear of your illness and its cruel result, just now communicated to me by Dr Grahn. But surely it is possible that this result may not be permanent. For youth

such as yours, Time may hold in store something more than resignation: who shall say that it does not hold renewal? I have not dared to ask admission to you in the hours of a recent shock, but I cannot depart on a long mission without tendering my sympathy and my farewell. I start this evening for the Caucasus, and thence[a] I proceed to India, where I am intrusted by the Government with business which may be of long duration."

(WALPURGA *sits down dejectedly.*)

ARMGART (*after a slight shudder, bitterly*).

The Graf has much discretion. I am glad.
He spares us both a pain, not seeing me.
What I like least is that consoling hope –[b]
That empty cup, so neatly ciphered "Time,"
Handed me as a cordial for despair.
(*Slowly and dreamily*) Time –[c] what a word to fling as charity!
Bland neutral word for slow, dull-beating pain –[d]
Days, months, and years! – If[e] I would wait for them[f]

(*She takes up her hat and puts it on, then wraps her mantle round her.* WALPURGA *leaves the room.*)

Why, this is but beginning. (WALP. *re-enters.*) Kiss me, dear.[g]
I am going now – alone – out – for a walk.[h]
Say you will never wound me any more
With such cajolery as nurses use
To patients amorous of a crippled life.
Flatter the blind: I see.

WALPURGA.

Well, I was wrong.

In haste to soothe, I snatched at flickers merely.
Believe me, I will flatter you no more.

ARMGART.

Bear witness, I am calm. I read my lot
As soberly as if it were a tale
Writ by a creeping feuilletonist[10] and called
"The Woman's Lot: a Tale of Everyday:"[a]
A middling woman's, to impress the world
With high superfluousness; her thoughts a crop
Of chick-weed[b] errors or of pot-herb[c] facts,
Smiled at like some child's drawing on a slate.[d]
"Genteel?" "O yes, gives lessons; not so good
As any man's would be, but cheaper far."
"Pretty?" "No; yet she makes a figure fit
For good society. Poor thing, she sews
Both late and early, turns and alters all
To suit the changing mode. Some widower
Might do well, marrying her; but in these days! . . .
Well, she can somewhat eke her narrow gains
By writing, just to furnish her with gloves
And droschkies[11e] in the rain. They print her things
Often for charity."[f]– Oh, a dog's life!
A harnessed dog's, that draws a little cart
Voted a nuisance! I am going now.

WALPURGA.

Not now, the door is locked.

ARMGART.

Give me the key!

WALPURGA.

Locked on the outside. Gretchen has the key:
She is gone on errands.

ARMGART.

What, you dare to keep me
Your prisoner?

WALPURGA.

And have I not been yours?
Your wish has been a bolt to keep me in.
Perhaps that middling woman whom you paint
With far-off scorn . . . . .

ARMGART.

I paint what I must be!
What is my soul to me without the voice
That gave it freedom? – gave it one grand touch
And made it nobly human! – Prisoned now,
Prisoned in all the petty mimicries
Called woman's knowledge, that will fit the world
As[a] doll-clothes[b] fit a man. I can do nought
Better than what a million women do –[c]
Must drudge among the crowd and feel my life
Beating upon the world without response,
Beating with passion through an insect's horn
That moves a miller-seed laboriously.
If I *would* do it!

WALPURGA (*coldly*).

And why should you not?

ARMGART (*turning quickly*).

Because Heaven made me royal –[d] wrought me out
With subtle finish towards pre-eminence,
Made every channel of my soul converge
To one high function, and then flung me down,
That breaking I might turn to subtlest pain.
An inborn passion gives a rebel's right:

I would rebel and die in twenty worlds
Sooner than bear the yoke of thwarted life,
Each keenest sense turned into keen distaste,
Hunger not satisfied but kept alive
Breathing in languor half a century.
All the world now is but a rack of threads
To twist and dwarf me into pettiness
And basely feigned content, the placid mask
Of women's misery.

WALPURGA (*indignantly*).
Ay, such a mask
As the few born like you to easy joy,
Cradled in privilege, take for natural
On all the lowly faces that must look
Upward to you! What revelation now
Shows you the mask or gives presentiment
Of sadness hidden? You who[a] every day
These five years saw me limp to wait on you,[b]
And thought the order perfect which gave *me*,
The girl without pretension to be aught,
A splendid cousin for my happiness:
To watch the night through when her brain was fired
With too much gladness –[c] listen, always listen
To what *she* felt, who having power had right
To feel exorbitantly, and submerge
The souls around her with the poured-out flood
Of what must be ere she were satisfied!
That was feigned patience, was it? Why not love,[d]
Love nurtured even with that strength of self[e]
Which found no room save in another's life?
Oh,[f] such as I know joy by negatives,
And all their deepest passion is a pang
Till they accept their pauper's heritage,

And meekly live from out the general store
Of joy they were born stripped of. I accept –[a]
Nay, now would sooner choose it than the wealth
Of natures you call royal, who can live
In mere mock knowledge of their fellows' woe,
Thinking their smiles may heal it.

ARMGART (*tremulously*).

Nay, Walpurga,
I did not make a palace of my joy
To shut the world's truth from me. All my good
Was that I touched the world and made a part
In the world's dower of beauty, strength, and bliss;
It was the glimpse of consciousness divine
Which pours out day and sees the day is good.
Now I am fallen dark; I sit in gloom,
Remembering bitterly. Yet you speak truth;
I wearied you, it seems; took all your help
As cushioned nobles use a weary serf,
Not looking at his face.

WALPURGA.

Oh,[b] but I stand
As a small symbol for the mighty sum[c]
Of claims unpaid to needy myriads;[d]
I think you never set your loss beside
That mighty deficit. Is your work gone –[e]
The prouder queenly work that paid itself
And yet was overpaid with men's applause?
Are you no longer chartered, privileged,
But sunk to simple woman's penury,
To ruthless Nature's chary average –
Where is the rebel's right for you alone?
Noble rebellion lifts a common load;
But what is he who flings his own load off

And leaves his fellows toiling? Rebel's right?
Say rather, the deserter's. Oh, you smiled
From your clear height on all the million lots
Which yet you brand as abject.

ARMGART.

I was blind
With too much happiness: true vision comes
Only, it seems, with sorrow. Were there one
This moment near me, suffering what I feel,
And needing me for comfort in her pang –[a]
Then it were worth the while to live; not else.

WALPURGA.

One – near you – why, they throng! you hardly stir
But your act touches them. We touch afar.
For did[b] not swarthy slaves of yesterday
Leap[c] in their bondage at the Hebrews' flight,[d]
Which touched them through the thrice millennial dark?
But you can find the sufferer you need
With touch less subtle.

ARMGART.

Who has need of me?

WALPURGA.

Love finds the need it fills. But you are hard.

ARMGART.

Is it not you, Walpurga, who are hard?
You humoured all my wishes till to-day,[e]
When fate has blighted me.

WALPURGA.

You would not hear
The "chant of consolation:"[a] words of hope
Only embittered you. Then hear the truth –[b]
A lame girl's truth, whom no one ever praised
For being cheerful. "It is well," they said:[c]
"Were she cross-grained[d] she could not be endured."
A word of truth from her had startled you;
But you –[e] you claimed the universe; nought less
Than all existence working in sure tracks
Towards your supremacy. The wheels might scathe
A myriad destinies –[f] nay, must perforce;
But yours they must keep clear of; just for you
The seething atoms through the firmament
Must bear a human heart –[g] which you had not!
For what is it to you that women, men,
Plod, faint, are weary, and espouse despair
Of aught but fellowship?[h] Save that you spurn
To be among them? Now, then, you are lame –[i]
Maimed, as you said, and levelled with the crowd:
Call it new birth –[j] birth from that monstrous Self[k]
Which, smiling down upon a race oppressed,
Says, "All is good, for I am throned at ease."
Dear Armgart –[l] nay, you tremble –[m] I am cruel.

ARMGART.

O no! hark! Some one knocks. Come in! – come in![n]
(*Enter* LEO.)

LEO.

See, Gretchen let me in. I could not rest
Longer away from you.

ARMGART.

Sit down, dear Leo.
Walpurga, I would speak with him alone.

(WALPURGA *goes out*.)

LEO (*hesitatingly*).

You mean[a] to walk?

ARMGART.

No, I shall stay within.

(*She takes off her hat and mantle, and sits down immediately.*[b] *After a pause, speaking*[c] *in a subdued tone to* LEO.)

How old are you?

LEO.

Threescore and five.

ARMGART.

That's old.
I never thought till now how you have lived.
They hardly ever play your music?

LEO (*raising his eyebrows and throwing out his lip*).

No!
Schubert too wrote for silence: half his work
Lay like a frozen Rhine till summers came[d]
That warmed the grass above him. Even so!
His music lives now with a mighty youth.

ARMGART.

Do you think yours will live when you are dead?

LEO.

Pfui! The time was, I drank that home-brewed wine
And found it heady, while my blood was young:
Now it scarce warms me. Tipple it as I may,
I am sober still, and say: "My old[a] friend Leo,
Much grain is wasted in the world and rots;
Why not thy handful?"

ARMGART.

Strange! since I have known you
Till now I never wondered how you lived.
When I sang well – that was your jubilee.
But you were old already.

LEO.

Yes, child, yes:
Youth thinks itself the goal of each old life;
Age has but travelled from a far-off time
Just to be ready for youth's service. Well!
It was my chief delight to perfect you.

ARMGART.

Good Leo! You have lived on little joys.
But your delight in me is crushed for ever
Your pains, where are they now? They shaped intent
Which action frustrates; shaped an inward sense
Which is but keen despair, the agony
Of highest vision in the lowest pit.

LEO.

Nay, nay, I have a thought: keep to the stage,
To drama without song; for you can act –[b]
Who knows how well, when all the soul is poured
Into that sluice alone?

ARMGART.

I know, and you:
The second or third best in tragedies
That cease to touch the fibre of the time.
No; song is gone, but nature's other gift,
Self-judgment, is not gone. Song was my speech,
And with its impulse only, action came:
Song was the battle's onset, when cool purpose
Glows into rage, becomes a warring god
And moves the limbs with miracle. But now –
Oh,[a] I should stand hemmed in with thoughts and rules –
Say, "This[b] way passion acts," yet never feel
The might of passion. How should I declaim?
As monsters write with feet instead of hands.
I will not feed on doing great tasks ill,
Dull the world's sense with mediocrity,
And live by trash that smothers excellence.
One gift I had that ranked me with the best –
The secret of my frame – and that is gone.
For all life now I am a broken thing.
But silence there! Good Leo, advise me now.
I would take humble work and do it well –[c]
Teach music, singing –[d] what I can – not here,[e]
But in some smaller town where I may bring
The method you have taught me, pass your gift
To others who can use it for delight.
You think I can do that?

(*She pauses with a sob in her voice.*)

LEO.

Yes, yes, dear child!
And it were well, perhaps, to change the place –[f]

Begin afresh as I did when I left
Vienna with a heart half broken.

ARMGART (*roused by surprise*).[a]
You?

LEO.
Well, it is long ago. But I had lost –
No matter! We must bury our dead joys
And live above them with a living world.
But whither, think you, you would like to go?

ARMGART.
To Freiburg.

LEO.
In the Breisgau?[12] And why there?
It is too small.

ARMGART.
Walpurga was born there,
And loves the place. She quitted it for me
These five years past. Now I will take her there.
Dear Leo, I will bury my dead joy.

LEO.
Mothers do so, bereaved; then learn to love
Another's living child.

ARMGART.
Oh,[b] it is hard
To take the little corpse, and lay it low,
And say, "None misses it but me."
She sings . . .[c]

I mean Paulina sings Fidelio,
And they will welcome her to-night.

LEO.

Well, well,
'Tis better that our griefs should not spread far.[a]

HOW LISA LOVED THE KING

'How Lisa Loved the King' is probably one of the minor poems Eliot contemplated writing on 1 January 1869 (see headnote to 'Brother and Sister'). Haight says that she read a good deal of Sicilian history in preparation for the poem on Timoleon (d. *c.* 337 BC), a Corinthean statesman and general vehemently opposed to tyranny. Typically, she collected an extraordinarily detailed history and chronology extending more than 500 years before Timoleon's death. Haight adds, 'Happily no more is heard of what might have been painful work for everyone' (*Biography*, p. 413). Eliot told Blackwood, 'When I began to write it ['Lisa'], it was simply with the longing to fulfil an old intention, and with no distinct thought of printing' (*Letters*, Vol. V, p. 16), but perhaps 'Lisa', also set in Sicily, was in some way the fruit or outcome of her Timoleon research.

Whatever the case, 'Lisa' is a more or less faithful rendering of Boccaccio's *Decameron*, X.7, notwithstanding a few name changes: Lisa not Lisana, Minuccio not Manutio and Perdicone not Perdicano (cf. Creel, p. 127 n.). According to the poem's L'Envoi, Boccaccio 'pleased [Eliot] long ago' (l. 643) – probably as early as 1840, when she began Italian and German lessons with Joseph Brezzi, a Coventry language teacher (*Biography*, pp. 24–5). She maintained her interest in Boccaccio and many other writers and things Italian throughout her life. She copied extracts from Boccaccio's *Life of Dante* in her notebook for 1854–79 and recorded her readings of Boccaccio in her Journal on 2 August and 27 October 1861, and 26 September and 14 November 1862 ('Finished reading Boccaccio through for the second time', Wiesenfarth, pp. 52, 179). These 1861–2 readings were all part of her enormous research for *Romola* (1862–3). Once again she read 'some Italian' on 23 January 1869, and on the 27 of that month, noting 'The last two days I have been writing a rhymed poem on Boccaccio's story of Lisa'. Part of her entry for 6 February 1869 reads, 'Yesterday I wrote the song of Minuccio in Lisa. Today at verse 404, "who meetly told that lovetale meet to know"' (l. 388 in the poem's final version). Her entries for 14 and 15 February 1869 record: 'Finished the poem from Boccaccio' and 'I prepared and sent off "How Lisa Loved the King" to Edinburgh' (*Journals*, pp. 96, 104, 113, 134, 135).

Blackwood enthusiastically accepted it for *Blackwood's Edinburgh Magazine*, writing on 18 February:

> I have read the simple tale of Lisa's love first in the M.S. and then in type with increased admiration. The complete story is told in beautifully clear and simple language. Such lines as 'Eyes that could see her on the summer's day might find it hard to turn another way' [ll. 75–6] have a wonderful effect … I beg to offer you £50 [for the poem] which I hope you will think handsome. (*Letters*, Vol. V, p. 15)

Pleased with Blackwood's response, Eliot nevertheless made a point of resisting some of his suggested corrections.

> Mr. Lewes wishes me not to have it published in the March number, for it is *absolutely* unrevised, and stands just as it came to me in the first writing, for when I copied some of the pages fairly to send to you, I did not alter. I do not know that I shall make much alteration anyhow, but it is best not to be in a hurry, and as I conclude that your wish to have it in time for the next number was in kind consideration of what was *my* wish, I do not return the proofs as you requested; though I have read it and made every correction that I see my way to now, except those lines about which you are doubtful and which I will reconsider. Mr. Lewes has not yet read the Proof. (*Letters*, Vol. V, p. 16)

Over the next few days, there was some confusion between the Leweses and Blackwood concerning the poem's publication date. Blackwood thought they wished to see 'Lisa' in print as soon as possible, knowing they planned to set off for Italy at the end of February (in the event, they left on 3 March). During an exchange of letters and a telegram – Lewes asking George Simpson, Blackwood's Edinburgh printer, to return the MS; Simpson asking Eliot to return the proofs – Eliot told Blackwood 'I have made various verbal corrections of importance, and have rewritten the passage you have marked' (*Letters*, Vol. V, p. 17). 'Lisa' was finally published in *Blackwood's* in May 1869. The galley proofs for this publishing are in Princeton University's Parrish Collection, dated March 1869, and include three more punctuation corrections in Eliot's hand (*BH*, p. 386). Eliot carried revises with her to Italy and, on 6 April, she wrote to Blackwood from Rome asking for three further changes (*Letters*, Vol. V, p. 23; see Textual Notes to ll. 34, 35, 560 below, pp. 225, 236).

Before leaving for Italy, Lewes wrote to Blackwood about the possibility of selling 'Lisa' for publication in America:

> Ticknor and Fields of Boston would give Mrs. Lewes a good sum for permission to print the poem in the *Atlantic Monthly* simultaneously with its appearance in Maga [*Blackwood's*] if you would not object to the entrance into England of the 250 copies which the *Atlantic* subscribers would receive in due course i.e. a fortnight or so *after* the appearance in Maga … I should like to be sure from you on the point before selling the proofs. (*Letters*, Vol. V, p. 18)

Blackwood responded that he had obligations regarding American reprints of his magazine: however, 'If you can get any material sum from the Americans do not consider me at all, as although I admire the Poem so much I shall not be in the least disappointed although it should be published elsewhere' (*Letters*, Vol. V, p. 20). It appears that Lewes came to a different arrangement with the American publisher Fields, Osgood and Co., Boston: on their return from Rome, Fields proposed a 'uniform edition of George Eliot – [and] also offered 300 £ for a poem (Agatha) to appear in *Atlantic*' (Lewes's Diary, Thursday, 13 May 1869; cited in *Letters*, Vol. V, p. 34). Apparently, negotiations between Lewes and Fields led to a plan to publish 'Agatha' and 'Lisa' in one volume, which was later changed because, on 6 July 1869, Lewes wrote to Barbara Bodichon, 'the Americans had reprinted 'Lisa' [post-May] separately in a little volume at 50 cents' (*Letters*, Vol. V, p. 46).

Separate copies of the Boston 1869 'Lisa' and 'Agatha' were bound by Joseph Langford, Blackwood's London manager, and presented by Eliot to Anna Cross in January 1874. This copy is now in the Beinecke Library, Yale University, and contains an inscription to Mrs Cross, including ll. 174–8 from 'Lisa' (*BH*, pp. 389, 393; *Letters*, Vol. V, p. 37 n. 2; Vol. VI, p. 5 n. 2). The presentation copy has five alterations to 'Lisa' in Eliot's hand, which are recorded in the Textual Variants below, pp. 224–38, and has many pencilled scansion markings throughout, which Haight claims were done by Eliot for 'reading aloud' (cited in *BH*, p. 393).

The copy-text is the poem in the 1878 *Jubal*.

Notes to the Jubal M.S. (Add. 34,038)

- Eliot's numbering of MS is 1–28: Jubal M.S. numbering is 53–79, altered when MS was bound
- ff. 53–79 are lined paper (no watermarks); MS written in black ink
- on ff. 53–61, Eliot wrote lines in the right half of each page, using the left half for corrections; on ff. 62–5, she wrote on the left side of the paper; on ff. 66–7, containing Minuccio's song, lines are centred; on f. 68 lines on the left of the page; on ff. 69–70, on right; on ff. 71–2 on left; on ff. 73–5 on right; on ff. 76–8, on left; and on f. 79 on right
- f. 53 has 'How Lisa loved the King' at the very top of the page; at right top corner, inside box drawn in by Eliot: 'From Boccaccio, [top of page cropped, so difficult to read: probably 'Giorn.'] X. Nov. 7.'
- MS signed 'George Eliot'

How Lisa Loved the King

Six hundred years ago, in Dante's time,
Before his cheek was furrowed by deep rhyme –[a]
When Europe, fed afresh from Eastern story,
Was like a garden tangled with the glory
Of flowers hand-planted and of flowers air-sown,[b]
Climbing and trailing, budding and full-blown, [c]
Where purple bells are tossed amid pink stars,
And springing blades, green troops in innocent wars,
Crowd every shady spot of teeming earth,[d]
Making invisible motion visible birth –
Six hundred years ago, Palermo town
Kept holiday. A deed of great renown,
A high revenge, had freed it from the yoke
Of hated Frenchmen, and from Calpe's rock[1]
To where the Bosporus[2] caught the earlier sun,
'Twas told that Pedro, King of Aragon,[3e]
Was welcomed master of all Sicily,
A royal knight, supreme as kings should be
In strength and gentleness that make high chivalry.[f]

Spain was the favourite home of knightly grace,
Where generous men rode steeds of generous race;[g]
Both Spanish, yet half Arab, both inspired
By mutual spirit,[h] that each motion fired
With beauteous response, like minstrelsy
Afresh fulfilling fresh expectancy.[i]
So when Palermo made high festival,[j]

The joy of matrons and of maidens all
Was the mock terror of the tournament,[a]
Where safety with the glimpse of danger blent,[b]
Took exaltation as from epic song,[c]
Which greatly tells the pains that to great life belong.

And in all eyes King Pedro was the king
Of cavaliers:[d] as in a full-gemmed ring
The largest ruby, or as that bright star
Whose shining shows[e] us where the Hyads[4] are.[f]
His the best jennet,[g] and he sat it best;
His weapon, whether tilting or in rest,[h]
Was worthiest watching,[i] and his face once seen
Gave to the promise of his royal mien
Such rich fulfilment as the opened eyes
Of a loved sleeper, or the long-watched[j] rise
Of vernal day, whose joy o'er stream and meadow flies.[k]

But of the maiden forms that thick enwreathed
The broad[l] piazza and sweet witchery breathed,
With innocent faces budding all arow
From balconies and windows high and low,
Who was it felt the deep mysterious glow,[m]
The impregnation with supernal fire[n]
Of young ideal love – transformed desire,[o]
Whose passion is but worship of that Best[p]
Taught by the many-mingled creed of each young
breast?

'Twas gentle Lisa, of no noble line,
Child of Bernardo, a rich Florentine,[q]
Who from his merchant-city[r] hither came
To trade in drugs; yet kept an honest fame,
And had the virtue not to try[s] and sell
Drugs that had none. He loved his riches well,[t]

But loved them chiefly for his Lisa's[a] sake,
Whom with a father's care he sought to make
The bride of some true honourable man: –
Of Perdicone (so the rumour ran),
Whose birth was higher than his fortunes were;
For still your trader likes a mixture fair
Of blood that hurries to some higher strain[b]
Than reckoning money's loss and money's gain.[c]
And of such mixture good may surely come:[d]
Lords'[e] scions so may learn to cast a sum,
A trader's grandson bear a well-set head,[f]
And have less conscious manners, better bred;[g]
Nor,[h] when he tries to be polite, be rude instead.[i]

'Twas Perdicone's friends made overtures
To good Bernardo: so one[j] dame assures
Her neighbour dame who notices the youth
Fixing his eyes on Lisa;[k] and in truth
Eyes that could see her on this summer day
Might find it hard to turn another way.
She had a pensive beauty, yet not sad;
Rather, like minor cadences that glad
The hearts of little birds[l] amid spring boughs;
And oft the trumpet or the joust would rouse[m]
Pulses that gave her cheek a finer glow,
Parting her[n] lips that seemed a mimic bow
By chiselling Love for play in coral wrought,
Then quickened by him with the passionate thought,
The soul that trembled in the lustrous night
Of slow long eyes. Her body was so slight,[o]
It seemed she could have floated in the sky,[p]
And with the angelic choir[q] made symphony;
But in her cheek's rich tinge, and in the dark[r]
Of darkest hair and eyes, she bore a[s] mark

Of kinship to her generous mother earth,[a]
The fervid land that gives the plumy palm-trees birth.[b]

She saw not Perdicone;[c] her young mind
Dreamed not that any man had ever pined
For such a little simple maid as she:
She had but dreamed how heavenly it would be
To love some hero noble, beauteous, great,
Who[d] would live stories worthy to narrate,
Like Roland, or the warriors of Troy,
The Cid,[e] or Amadis,[5] or that fair boy
Who conquered everything beneath the sun,[f]
And somehow,[g] some time, died at Babylon
Fighting the Moors.[6] For heroes all were good
And fair as that archangel who withstood
That Evil One, the author of all wrong –[h]
That Evil One who made the French so strong;[i]
And now the flower of heroes must be he[j]
Who drove those tyrants from dear Sicily,[k]
So that her maids might walk to vespers[l] tranquilly.[m]

Young Lisa saw this hero[n] in the king,
And as wood-lilies that sweet odours bring[o]
Might dream the light that opes their modest eyne
Was lily-odoured, – and as rites divine,
Round turf-laid altars, or 'neath roofs of stone,
Draw sanctity from out the heart alone
That loves and worships, so the miniature[p]
Perplexed of her soul's world, all virgin pure,
Filled with heroic virtues that bright form,[q]
Raona's royalty,[7] the finished norm
Of horsemanship – the half of chivalry:[r]
For how could generous men avengers be,[s]
Save as God's messengers on coursers fleet? –[t]
These, scouring earth,[u] made Spain with Syria meet

In one self world where the same right had sway,[a]
And good must grow as grew the blessed day.
No more;[b] great Love his essence had endued
With Pedro's form, and entering subdued
The soul of Lisa, fervid and intense,
Proud in its choice of proud obedience
To hardship glorified by perfect reverence.[c]

Sweet Lisa homeward carried that dire guest,[d]
And in her chamber through the hours of rest
The darkness was alight for her with sheen
Of arms, and plumèd helm,[e] and bright between
Their commoner gloss, like the pure living spring
'Twixt porphyry lips, or living bird's bright wing
'Twixt golden wires, the glances of the king[f]
Flashed on her soul,[g] and waked vibrations there
Of known delights love-mixed[h] to new and rare:
The impalpable dream was turned to breathing
flesh,
Chill thought of summer to the warm close mesh
Of sunbeams held between the citron-leaves,[i]
Clothing her life of life. Oh,[j] she believes
That she could be content if he but knew
(Her poor small self could claim no other due)
How Lisa's lowly love had highest reach
Of wingèd passion, whereto wingèd[k] speech
Would be scorched remnants left by mounting flame.
Though, had she such lame message, were it blame
To tell what greatness dwelt in her, what rank
She held in loving? Modest maidens shrank
From telling love that fed on selfish hope;[l]
But love,[m] as hopeless as the shattering song
Wailed for loved beings who have joined the throng[n]
Of mighty dead ones. . . . Nay, but she was weak –[o]

Knew only prayers and ballads –[a] could not speak
With eloquence save what dumb creatures have,[b]
That with small cries and touches small boons crave.

She watched all day that she might see him pass
With knights and ladies; but she said, "Alas![c]
Though he should see me, it were all as one
He saw a pigeon sitting on the stone
Of wall or balcony: some coloured spot
His eye just sees, his mind regardeth not.
I have no music-touch[d] that could bring nigh
My love to his soul's hearing.[e] I shall die,
And he will never know who Lisa was –[f]
The trader's child, whose soaring spirit rose
As hedge-born aloe-flowers that rarest years disclose.[g]

"For were I now a fair deep-breasted[h] queen
A-horseback, with blonde hair,[i] and tunic green
Gold-bordered, like Costanza,[8] I should need
No change within to make me queenly there;
For they the royal-hearted women are
Who nobly love the noblest, yet have grace[j]
For needy suffering lives in lowliest place,
Carrying a choicer sunlight in their smile,
The[k] heavenliest ray that pitieth the vile.
My love is such, it cannot choose but soar
Up to the highest; yet for evermore,[l]
Though I were happy, throned beside the king,
I should be tender to each little thing
With hurt warm breast, that had no speech to tell
Its inward pang, and I would soothe it well
With tender[m] touch and with a low soft moan
For company: my dumb love-pang is lone,[n]
Prisoned as topaz-beam within a rough-garbed stone."[o]

So, inward-wailing, Lisa passed her days.
Each night the August moon with changing phase
Looked broader, harder on her unchanged pain;[a]
Each noon the heat lay heavier again
On her despair; until her body frail
Shrank like the snow that watchers in the vale
See narrowed on the height each summer morn;[b]
While her dark glance burnt larger, more forlorn,
As if the soul within her all on fire
Made of her being one swift funeral pyre.
Father and mother saw with sad dismay
The meaning of their riches melt away:
For without Lisa what would sequins buy?
What wish were left if Lisa were to die?
Through her they cared for summers still to come,[c]
Else[d] they would be as ghosts without a home
In any flesh that could feel glad desire.
They pay the best physicians, never tire
Of seeking what will soothe her, promising
That aught she longed for,[e] though it were a thing
Hard to be come at[f] as the Indian snow,[g]
Or roses that on alpine summits blow –[h]
It should be hers. She answers with low voice,
She longs for death alone – death is her choice;
Death is the King who never did think scorn,
But rescues every meanest soul to sorrow born.

Yet one day,[i] as they bent above her bed
And watched her in brief sleep, her drooping head
Turned gently, as the thirsty flowers that feel
Some moist revival through their petals steal,
And little flutterings of her[j] lids and lips
Told of such dreamy joy as sometimes dips
A skyey[k] shadow in the mind's poor pool.

She oped her eyes, and turned their dark gems full
Upon her father, as in utterance dumb[a]
Of[b] some new prayer that in her sleep had come.
"What[c] is it, Lisa?" "Father, I would see
Minuccio, the great singer; bring him me."[d]
For always, night and day, her unstilled thought[e]
Wandering all o'er its little world, had sought
How she could reach, by some soft pleading touch,[f]
King Pedro's soul,[g] that she who loved so much
Dying, might have a place within his mind –
A little grave which he would sometimes find
And plant some flower on it – some thought, some
    memory kind.[h]
Till in her dream she saw Minuccio
Touching his viola, and chanting low
A strain that, falling on her brokenly,[i]
Seemed blossoms lightly blown from off a tree,[j]
Each burthened with a word that was[k] a scent –
Raona, Lisa, love, death, tournament;[l]
Then in her dream she said, "He sings of me –[m]
Might be my messenger;[n] ah, now I see
The king is listening —" Then she awoke,
And, missing her dear dream, that new-born longing
    spoke.

She longed for music: that was natural;
Physicians said it was medicinal;[o]
The humours might be schooled by true consent
Of a fine tenor and fine instrument;[p]
In brief, good[q] music, mixed with doctor's stuff,
Apollo with Asklepios[9] – enough![r]
Minuccio, entreated, gladly came.[s]
(He was a singer of most gentle fame –[t]
A noble, kindly spirit, not elate

That he was famous, but that song was great –[a]
Would sing as finely to this suffering child
As at the court where princes on him smiled.)
Gently he entered and sat down by her,
Asking what sort of strain she would prefer –
The voice alone,[b] or voice with viol wed;
Then, when she chose the last, he preluded
With magic hand, that summoned from the strings
Aerial spirits, rare yet vibrant[c] wings
That fanned the pulses of his listener,[d]
And waked each sleeping sense with blissful stir.
Her cheek already showed a slow faint blush,
But soon the voice, in pure full liquid rush,[e]
Made all the passion, that till now she felt,[f]
Seem but cool[g] waters that in warmer melt.[h]
Finished the song, she prayed to be alone
With kind Minuccio; for her faith had grown
To trust him as if missioned like a priest
With some high grace, that when his singing ceased
Still made him wiser, more magnanimous
Than common men who had no genius.

So laying her small hand within his palm,[i]
She told him how that secret glorious harm
Of loftiest loving had befallen her;
That death, her only hope,[j] most bitter were,
If when she died her love must perish too
As songs unsung and thoughts unspoken do,
Which[k] else might live within another breast.
She said, "Minuccio, the grave were rest,[l]
If I were sure, that lying cold and lone,[m]
My love, my best of life,[n] had safely flown
And nestled in the bosom of the king;
See, 'tis a small weak bird, with unfledged[o] wing.

But you will carry it for me secretly,[a]
And bear it to the king,[b] then come to me
And tell me it is safe,[c] and I shall go
Content, knowing that he I love my love doth know."[d]

Then she wept silently, but each large tear
Made pleading music to the inward ear
Of good Minuccio. "Lisa, trust in me,"
He said, and kissed her fingers loyally;[e]
"It is sweet law to me to do your[f] will,
And ere the sun his round shall thrice fulfil,[g]
I hope to bring you news of such rare skill
As amulets have, that aches in trusting bosoms still."[h]

He needed not to pause and first devise
How he should tell the king; for in nowise
Were such love-message worthily bested
Save in fine verse by music renderèd.
He sought a poet-friend, a Siennese,
And "Mico,[i] mine," he said, "full oft to please
Thy whim of sadness[j] I have sung thee strains
To make thee weep in verse: now pay my pains,
And write me a canzòn[10] divinely sad,
Sinlessly passionate and meekly mad
With young despair, speaking a maiden's heart
Of fifteen summers, who would fain depart
From ripening life's new-urgent mystery –
Love-choice of one too high her love to be –
But cannot yield her breath till she has poured
Her strength away in this hot-bleeding word
Telling the secret of her soul to her soul's lord."[k]

Said Mico, "Nay, that thought is poesy,
I need but listen as it sings to me.
Come thou again to-morrow." The third day,

When linkèd notes had perfected the lay,[a]
Minuccio had his summons to the court
To make, as he was wont, the moments[b] short
Of ceremonious dinner to the king.[c]
This was the time when he had meant to bring[d]
Melodious message of young Lisa's love:
He waited till the air had ceased to move
To ringing silver, till Falernian wine
Made quickened sense with quietude combine,
And then with passionate descant made each ear
incline.[e]

Love, thou didst see me, light as morning's breath,[f]
Roaming a garden in a joyous error,
Laughing at chases vain, a happy child,[g]
Till of thy countenance the alluring terror
In majesty from out the blossoms smiled,
From out their life seeming a beauteous Death.[h]

O Love, who so didst choose me for thine own,[i]
Taking this little isle to thy great sway,
See now, it is the honour of thy throne
That what thou gavest perish not away,[j]
Nor leave some sweet remembrance to atone
By life that will be for the brief life gone:
Hear, ere the shroud o'er these frail limbs be thrown –
Since every king is vassal unto thee,[k]
My heart's lord needs must listen loyally –
O tell him I am waiting for my Death![l]

Tell him, for that he hath such royal power
'Twere hard for him to think how small a thing,
How slight a sign, would make a wealthy dower
For one like me, the bride of that pale king[m]
Whose bed is mine at some swift-nearing hour.

Go to my lord,[a] *and to his memory bring*
That happy birthday of my sorrowing
When his large glance made meaner gazers glad,
Entering the bannered lists: 'twas then I had
The wound that laid me in the arms of Death.[b]

Tell him, O Love, I am a lowly maid,
No more than any little knot of thyme
That he with careless foot may often tread;
Yet lowest fragrance oft will mount sublime
And cleave to things most high and hallowèd,
As doth the fragrance of my life's springtime,[c]
My lowly love,[d] *that soaring seeks to climb*
Within his thought, and make a gentle bliss,
More blissful[e] *than if mine, in being his:*
So shall I live in him and rest in Death.[f]

The strain was new. It seemed a pleading cry,[g]
And yet a rounded perfect melody,
Making grief beauteous as the tear-filled[h] eyes
Of little child at little miseries.
Trembling at first, then swelling as it rose,[i]
Like rising light that broad and broader grows,[j]
It filled the hall,[k] and so possessed the air
That not one breathing soul was present there,[l]
Though dullest, slowest but was quivering
In music's grasp, and forced to hear her sing.
But most such sweet compulsion took the mood
Of Pedro (tired of doing what he would).
Whether the words which that[m] strange meaning bore
Were but the poet's feigning or aught more,
Was bounden question, since their aim must be
At some imagined or true royalty.
He called Minuccio and bade him tell

What poet of the day had writ so well;[a]
For though they came behind all former rhymes,[b]
The verses were not bad for these poor times.
"Monsignor, they are only three days old,"
Minuccio said;[c] "but it must not be told
How this song grew, save to your royal ear."
Eager, the king withdrew where none was near,[d]
And gave close audience to Minuccio,[e]
Who meetly told that love-tale meet to know.[f]
The king had features pliant to confess
The presence of a manly tenderness –
Son, father, brother, lover, blent in one,[g]
In fine harmonic exaltation –[h]
The spirit of religious chivalry.
He listened, and Minuccio could see
The tender,[i] generous admiration spread
O'er all his face,[j] and glorify his head
With royalty that would have kept its rank
Though his brocaded robes to tatters shrank.
He answered without pause, "So sweet a maid,
In nature's own insignia arrayed,
Though she were come of unmixed trading blood
That sold and bartered ever since the Flood,[k]
Would have the self-contained and single[l] worth
Of radiant jewels born in darksome earth.
Raona were a shame to Sicily,[m]
Letting such love and tears unhonoured be:
Hasten, Minuccio, tell her that the king[n]
To-day will surely visit her when vespers ring."[o]

Joyful, Minuccio bore the joyous word,
And told at full, while none but Lisa heard,
How each thing had befallen, sang the song,
And like a patient nurse who would prolong

All means of soothing, dwelt upon each tone,[a]
Each look,[b] with which the mighty Aragon
Marked the high worth his royal heart assigned
To that dear place he held in Lisa's mind.
She listened till the draughts of pure content
Through all her limbs like some new being went –
Life, not recovered, but untried before,
From out the growing world's unmeasured store
Of fuller, better, more divinely mixed.
'Twas glad reverse:[c] she had so firmly fixed
To die, already seemed to fall a veil
Shrouding the inner glow from light of senses pale.

Her parents wondering see her half arise –[d]
Wondering, rejoicing, see her long dark eyes
Brimful with clearness, not of 'scaping[e] tears,
But of some light ethereal that enspheres
Their orbs with calm,[f] some vision newly learnt
Where strangest fires[g] erewhile had blindly burnt.
She asked to have[h] her soft white robe and band
And coral ornaments, and with her hand
She gave her locks' dark length a backward fall,[i]
Then looked intently in a mirror small,[j]
And feared her face might perhaps[k] displease the king;[l]
"In truth," she said, "I am a tiny thing;[m]
I was too bold to tell what could such visit bring."[n]
Meanwhile the king,[o] revolving in his thought
That virgin[p] passion, was more deeply wrought
To chivalrous pity; and at vesper bell,
With careless mien which hid his purpose well,[q]
Went forth on horseback,[r] and as if by chance
Passing Bernardo's house, he paused to glance
At the fine garden of this wealthy man,

This Tuscan trader turned Palermitan:
But, presently dismounting,[a] chose to walk
Amid the trellises,[b] in gracious talk
With this same trader, deigning even to ask
If he had yet fulfilled the father's task
Of marrying that daughter whose young charms
Himself, betwixt the passages of arms,[c]
Noted admiringly. "Monsignor, no,
She is not married; that were little woe,[d]
Since she has counted barely fifteen years;
But all such hopes of late have turned to fears;
She droops and fades;[e] though for a space quite brief –
Scarce three hours past – she finds some strange relief."[f]
The king avised: "'Twere dole to all of us,[g]
The world should lose a maid so beauteous;[h]
Let me now see her; since I am her liege lord,[i]
Her spirits must wage war with death[j] at my strong word."[k]
In such half-serious playfulness, he wends,[l]
With Lisa's father and two chosen friends,[m]
Up to the[n] chamber where she pillowed sits
Watching the open door, that now admits[o]
A presence as much better than her dreams,[p]
As happiness than any[q] longing seems.
The king advanced, and,[r] with a reverent kiss
Upon her hand, said, "Lady, what is this?
You, whose sweet youth should others' solace be,
Pierce all our hearts, languishing piteously.
We pray you, for the love of us, be cheered,
Nor be too reckless of that life, endeared
To us who know your passing worthiness,
And count your blooming life as part of our life's bliss."[s]
Those words, that touch upon her hand from him

Whom her soul worshipped, as far seraphim
Worship the distant glory, brought some shame
Quivering upon[a] her cheek, yet thrilled her frame
With such deep joy she seemed in paradise,[b]
In wondering gladness, and in dumb surprise[c]
That bliss could be so blissful: then she spoke –[d]
"Signor,[e] I was too weak to bear the yoke,
The golden yoke of thoughts too great for me;[f]
That was the ground[g] of my infirmity.
But now, I pray your grace to have belief
That I shall soon be well,[h] nor any more cause grief."[i]

The king alone perceived the covert sense
Of all her words,[j] which made one evidence
With her pure voice and candid loveliness,[k]
That he had lost much honour, honouring less
That message of her passionate distress.[l]
He stayed beside her for a little while
With gentle looks and speech, until a smile
As placid as a ray of early morn
On opening flower-cups[m] o'er her lips was borne.
When he had left her, and the tidings spread
Through all the town how he had visited
The Tuscan trader's daughter, who was sick,[n]
Men said, it was a royal deed and catholic.[o]

And Lisa? she no longer wished for death;[p]
But as a poet,[q] who sweet verses saith
Within his soul, and joys in music there,[r]
Nor seeks another heaven,[s] nor can bear
Disturbing pleasures, so was she content,[t]
Breathing the life of grateful sentiment.
She thought no maid betrothed could be more blest;
For treasure must be valued by the test
Of highest excellence and rarity,

And her dear joy was best as best could be;
There seemed no other crown to her delight
Now the high loved one saw her love aright.
Thus her soul thriving on that exquisite mood,[a]
Spread like the May-time all its beauteous good[b]
O'er the soft bloom of neck, and arms,[c] and cheek,
And strengthened the sweet body,[d] once so weak,
Until she rose and walked, and,[e] like a bird
With sweetly rippling throat, she made her spring joys[f] heard.

The king, when he the happy change had seen,[g]
Trusted the ear of Constance, his fair queen,[h]
With Lisa's innocent secret, and conferred
How they should jointly, by their deed and word,[i]
Honour this maiden's love, which,[j] like the prayer
Of loyal hermits, never thought to share
In what it gave. The queen had that chief grace
Of womanhood, a heart that can embrace
All goodness in another woman's form;[k]
And that same day,[l] ere the sun lay too warm
Informed Bernardo that the royal pair
Would straightway visit him and celebrate
Their gladness at his daughter's happier state,
Which they were fain to see. Soon came the king[m]
On horseback,[n] with his barons, heralding
The advent of the queen in courtly state;
And all, descending at the garden gate,[o]
Streamed with their feathers, velvet,[p] and brocade,
Through the pleached alleys,[11] till they, pausing,[q] made
A lake of splendour 'mid the aloes grey –[r]
When, meekly facing all their proud array,[s]
The white-robed Lisa with her parents stood,[t]

As some white dove before the gorgeous brood
Of dapple-breasted birds born by the Colchian
    flood.[12a]

The king and queen, by gracious looks and speech,[b]
Encourage her, and thus their courtiers teach
How this fair morning they may courtliest be
By making Lisa pass it happily.
And soon the ladies and the barons all
Draw her by turns,[c] as at a festival
Made for her sake, to easy,[d] gay discourse,
And compliment with looks and smiles enforce;[e]
A joyous hum is heard the gardens round;
Soon[f] there is Spanish dancing and the sound
Of minstrel's song, and autumn fruits are pluckt;
Till mindfully the king[g] and queen conduct
Lisa apart to where a trellised shade
Made pleasant resting. Then King Pedro said –[h]
"Excellent maiden, that rich gift of love
Your heart hath made us, hath a worth above[i]
All royal treasures, nor is fitly met
Save when the grateful memory of deep debt[j]
Lies still behind the outward honours done:
And as a sign that no oblivion
Shall overflood[k] that faithful memory,
We while we live your cavalier will be,
Nor will we ever arm ourselves for fight,[l]
Whether for struggle dire or brief delight
Of warlike feigning, but we first will take
The colours you ordain,[m] and for your sake
Charge the more bravely where your emblem[n] is;
Nor will we ever claim[o] an added bliss
To our sweet thoughts of you save one sole kiss.[p]
But there still rests the outward honour meet
To mark your worthiness, and we entreat

That you will turn your ear to proffered vows
Of one who loves you,[a] and would be your spouse.
We must not wrong yourself and Sicily
By letting all your blooming years pass by
Unmated: you will give the world its due
From beauteous maiden and become a matron true."

Then Lisa, wrapt in virgin wonderment
At her ambitious love's complete content,
Which left no further good for her to seek
Than love's obedience, said with accent meek –[b]
"Monsignor,[c] I know well that were it known
To all the world how high my love had flown,[d]
There would be few who would not deem me mad,
Or say my mind the falsest image[e] had
Of my condition and your lofty place.[f]
But heaven has seen that for[g] no moment's space
Have I forgotten you to be the king,[h]
Or me myself to be a lowly thing –[i]
A little lark, enamoured of the sky,[j]
That soared to sing, to break its breast,[k] and die.
But,[l] as you better know than I, the heart
In choosing chooseth not its own desert,[m]
But that great merit which attracteth it;
'Tis law, I struggled, but I must submit,
And having seen a worth all worth above,
I loved you, love you, and shall always love.
But that doth mean, my will is ever yours,[n]
Not only when your will my good insures,[o]
But if it wrought me what the world calls harm –
Fire, wounds, would wear from your dear will a charm.
That you will be my knight is full content,
And for that kiss – I pray, first for the queen's
consent."

Her answer, given with such firm gentleness,
Pleased the queen well, and made her hold no less
Of Lisa's merit than the king had held.
And so, all cloudy threats of grief dispelled,[a]
There was betrothal made that very morn
'Twixt Perdicone, youthful, brave, well-born,[b]
And Lisa,[c] whom he loved; she loving well
The lot that from obedience befell.
The queen a rare betrothal ring on each
Bestowed, and[d] other gems, with gracious speech.
And that no joy might lack, the king,[e] who knew
The youth was poor, gave him rich Ceffalù
And Cataletta, large and fruitful lands –[f]
Adding much promise when he joined their hands.
At last he said to Lisa,[g] with an air
Gallant yet noble: "Now we claim our share
From your sweet love, a share which is not small:[h]
For in the sacrament one crumb is all."
Then taking her small[i] face his hands between,
He kissed her on the brow with kiss serene,
Fit seal to that pure vision her young soul had seen.[j]

Sicilians[k] witnessed that King Pedro kept
His royal promise: Perdicone stept
To many honours honourably won,
Living with Lisa in true union.[l]
Throughout[m] his life the king still took delight
To call himself fair Lisa's faithful knight;
And never wore in field or tournament[n]
A scarf or emblem save by Lisa sent.[o]

Such deeds made subjects loyal in that land:
They joyed that one so worthy to command,
So chivalrous and gentle, had become
The king[p] of Sicily, and filled the room

Of Frenchmen, who abused the Church's trust,[a]
Till, in a righteous vengeance on their lust,
Messina rose, with God, and with the dagger's thrust.[b]

L'ENVOI.[c]

Reader, this story pleased me long ago
In the bright pages of Boccaccio,
And where the author of a good we know,[d]
Let us not fail to pay the grateful thanks we owe.[e]

A MINOR PROPHET

The extant MS version of 'A Minor Prophet' is the Jubal M.S. (Add. 34,038), which is a copy of an original manuscript now lost (see Notes to the Jubal M.S., below). The poem was published in the 1874 *Jubal* and the 1878 *Jubal*, the latter serving as the copy-text.

In her Diary 1861–77, Eliot lists the poem under 'Order of Writings': 'A Minor Prophet January 1865', and made the following entry on Sunday, 8 January 1865: 'Since last Monday I have been writing a poem, the matter of which was written in prose 3 or 4 years ago – My Vegetarian Friend' (*Journals*, pp. 96, 122). That prose work has not survived. The following Sunday, 15 January, Eliot and Lewes set off for Paris, returning home on 25 January; and on 28 January 1865 she wrote in her diary, 'Finished my poem on Utopias' (*Journals*, p. 123).

This period coincides with Eliot's struggles to write *The Spanish Gypsy*, which proved so difficult that she wrote in her diary on 21 February 1865, 'Ill with bilious headache, and very miserable about my soul as well as body. *George has taken my drama away from me*' (*Journals*, p. 123). She did not resume the latter until March 1867. Haight notes that Eliot had also written *The Spanish Gypsy* in prose before turning it into verse (*Biography*, p. 402), thereby suggesting that this was Eliot's habitual method when it came to writing verse. However, as

Secor says, there is no evidence that any of the later poems – other than 'A Minor Prophet' – were worked out in the same manner (Secor, p. 124).

As the Notes to the Jubal M.S., below, indicate, Eliot made substantial revisions while copying the poem, and more changes were made, presumably in the proofs, which have not survived.

Notes to the Jubal M.S. (Add. 34,038)

- MS numbering is ff. 118–33 (with last 3 lines of poem on reverse side of f. 133); Eliot's page numbering of poem as follows: title page and then ff. 1–16 (16 on the reverse side of 15)
- f. 118: title page 'A Minor Prophet'
- MS written in violet ink on lined paper, watermarked 'T & JH Kent', also used for 'Stradivarius' and 'The Choir Invisible' (Eliot adopted violet ink in 1872; therefore MS is copy of 1865 version)
- Date, '1865', recorded on last page of MS
- f. 122 of MS cropped, possibly removing up to 4 lines. Very top of one line partly visible
- Lines 295 and 313 have square brackets, '[Full' and '[After', respectively, in black ink. Additionally, line 313 has '225,P', which I have not been able to account for. Lines 295–7 were used as epigraph to Chapter LXXII of *Middlemarch*, which probably accounts for square bracket: however, lines 313ff. do not appear to have been used. Lines 292–4 used (with minor changes) as epigraph to Epilogue of *Felix Holt*, but they are not marked in any way. See the headnote to 'Two Lovers', which has similar notation
- f. 122: ll. 68–87 (bottom 4 lines [?] cropped)

- f. 123: ll. 88–100 (only 13 of 23 lines filled: Secor thinks Eliot deleted part of original page and rewrote remaining lines on new sheet)
- f. 133 (reverse side): ll. 323–5

A Minor Prophet

I have a friend, a vegetarian seer,
By name Elias Baptist Butterworth,[a]
A harmless, bland, disinterested man,
Whose ancestors in Cromwell's day believed
The Second Advent[b] certain in five years,
But when King Charles the Second came instead,
Revised their date and sought another world:
I mean – not heaven but – America.
A fervid[c] stock, whose generous hope embraced
The fortunes of mankind, not stopping short
At rise of leather, or the fall of gold,
Nor listening to the voices of the time
As housewives listen to a cackling hen,
With wonder whether she has laid her egg
On their own nest-egg. Still they did insist
Somewhat too wearisomely on the joys
Of their Millennium, when coats and hats
Would all be of one pattern, books and songs
All fit for Sundays, and the casual talks
As good as sermons preached extempore.

And in Elias the ancestral zeal
Breathes strong as ever, only modified
By Transatlantic air and modern thought.
You could not pass him in the street and fail
To note his shoulders' long declivity,
Beard to the waist, swan-neck, and large pale eyes;

Or, when he lifts his hat, to mark his hair
Brushed back to show his great capacity –
A full grain's length at the angle of the brow
Proving him witty, while the shallower men
Only seem witty in their repartees.
Not that he's[a] vain, but that his doctrine needs
The testimony of his frontal lobe.
On all points he adopts the latest views;
Takes for the key of universal Mind[b]
The "levitation"[c] of stout gentlemen;
Believes the Rappings[1] are not spirits' work,
But the Thought-atmosphere's, a steam of brains
In correlated force of raps, as proved
By motion, heat, and science generally;[d]
The spectrum, for example, which has shown
The self-same metals in the sun as here;
So the Thought-atmosphere[e] is everywhere:[f]
High truths that glimmered under other names
To ancient sages,[g] whence good scholarship
Applied to Eleusinian mysteries –
The Vedas – Tripitaka[h] – Vendidad –[2]
Might furnish weaker proof[i] for weaker minds
That Thought was rapping in the hoary past,
And might have edified the Greeks by raps
At the greater Dionysia, if their ears
Had not been filled with Sophoclean verse.
And when all[j] Earth[k] is vegetarian –
When, lacking butchers, quadrupeds die out,
And less Thought-atmosphere is reabsorbed
By nerves of insects parasitical,
Those higher truths, seized now by higher minds
But not expressed (the insects hindering)
Will either flash out into eloquence,

Or better still, be comprehensible
By rappings simply, without need of roots.

'Tis on this theme – the vegetarian world –
That good Elias willingly expands:
He loves to tell in mildly nasal tones
And vowels stretched to suit the widest views,
The future fortunes of our infant Earth –
When it will be too full of human kind
To have the room for wilder animals.
Saith he, Sahara will be populous
With families of gentlemen retired
From commerce in more Central Africa,
Who order coolness as we order coal,[a]
And have a lobe anterior strong enough
To think away the sand-storms.[b] Science thus
Will leave no spot on this terraqueous[3] globe
Unfit to be inhabited by man,
The chief of animals: all meaner brutes
Will have been smoked and elbowed out of life.
No lions then shall lap Caffrarian[4] pools,
Or shake the Atlas with their midnight roar:
Even the slow, slime-loving crocodile,
The last of animals to take a hint,
Will then retire for ever from a scene
Where public feeling strongly sets against him.
Fishes may lead carnivorous lives obscure,
But must not dream of culinary rank
Or being dished in good society.
Imagination in that distant age,
Aiming at fiction called historical,
Will vainly try to reconstruct the times
When it was men's preposterous delight
To sit astride live horses, which consumed

Materials for incalculable cakes;
When there were milkmaids who drew milk from cows
With udders kept abnormal for that end
Since the rude mythopœic period
Of Aryan dairymen, who did not blush
To call their milkmaid and their daughter one –
Helplessly gazing at the Milky Way,
Nor dreaming of the astral cocoa-nuts
Quite at the service of posterity.[a]
'Tis to be feared, though, that the duller boys,[b]
Much given to anachronisms and nuts,
(Elias has confessed boys will be boys)
May write a jockey for a centaur, think
Europa's suitor was an Irish bull,
Æsop a journalist who wrote up Fox,
And Bruin a chief swindler upon 'Change.[5c]
Boys will be boys, but dogs will all be moral,
With longer alimentary canals
Suited to diet vegetarian.
The uglier breeds will fade from memory,[d]
Or, being[e] palæontological,
Live but as portraits in large learned books,
Distasteful to the feelings of an age[f]
Nourished on purest beauty. Earth will hold
No stupid brutes, no cheerful queernesses,
No naïve cunning, grave absurdity.
Wart-pigs with tender and parental grunts,
Wombats much flattened as to their contour,
Perhaps from too much crushing in the ark,[g]
But taking meekly that fatality;
The serious cranes, unstung by ridicule;[h]
Long-headed, short-legged, solemn-looking curs,
(Wise, silent critics of a flippant age);[i]
The silly straddling foals, the weak-brained geese

Hissing fallaciously at sound of wheels –
All these rude[a] products will have disappeared
Along with every faulty human type.
By dint of diet vegetarian
All will be harmony of hue and line,
Bodies and minds all perfect, limbs well-turned,
And talk quite free from aught erroneous.

Thus far Elias in his seer's mantle:
But at this climax in his prophecy
My sinking spirits, fearing to be swamped,
Urge me to speak. "High prospects these, my friend,
Setting the weak carnivorous brain astretch;
We will resume the thread another day."
"To-morrow," cries Elias, "at this hour?"
"No, not to-morrow – I shall have a cold –
At least I feel some soreness – this endemic –
Good-bye."
                    No tears are sadder than the smile
With which I quit Elias. Bitterly
I feel that every change upon this earth
Is[b] bought with sacrifice. My yearnings fail
To reach that high apocalyptic mount
Which shows in bird's-eye view a perfect world,
Or enter warmly into other joys
Than those of faulty, struggling human kind.
That strain upon my soul's too feeble wing
Ends in ignoble floundering: I fall
Into short-sighted pity for the men
Who living in those perfect future times
Will not know half the dear imperfect things
That move my smiles and tears – will never know
The fine old incongruities that raise
My friendly laugh; the innocent conceits

That like a needless eyeglass or black patch
Give those who wear them harmless happiness;
The twists and cracks in our poor earthenware,
That touch[a] me to[b] more conscious fellowship
(I am not myself the finest Parian)[6]
With my coevals. So poor Colin Clout,
To whom raw onion gives prospective zest,
Consoling hours of dampest wintry work,
Could hardly fancy any regal joys
Quite unimpregnate with the onion's scent:
Perhaps his highest hopes are not all clear[c]
Of waftings from that energetic bulb:[d]
'Tis well that onion is not heresy.
Speaking in parable, I am Colin Clout.
A clinging flavour penetrates my life –
My onion is imperfectness: I cleave
To nature's blunders, evanescent types
Which sages banish from Utopia.
"Not worship beauty?" say you. Patience, friend!
I worship in the temple with the rest;
But by my hearth I keep a sacred nook[e]
For gnomes and dwarfs, duck-footed waddling elves
Who stitched and hammered for the weary man
In days of old. And in that piety
I clothe ungainly forms inherited
From toiling generations, daily bent
At desk,[f] or plough,[g] or loom, or in the mine,
In pioneering labours for the world.
Nay, I am apt when floundering confused
From too rash flight, to grasp at paradox,
And pity future men who will not know
A keen experience with pity blent,[h]
The pathos exquisite of lovely minds
Hid in harsh forms – not penetrating them

Like fire divine within a common bush
Which glows transfigured by the heavenly guest,[a]
So that men put their shoes off; but encaged
Like a sweet[b] child within some thick-walled cell,
Who leaps and fails to hold the window-bars,[c]
But having shown a little dimpled hand
Is visited thenceforth by tender hearts
Whose eyes keep watch[d] about the prison walls.
A foolish, nay, a wicked paradox!
For purest pity is the eye of love
Melting at sight of sorrow; and to grieve
Because it sees no sorrow, shows a love
Warped from its truer nature, turned to love[e]
Of merest habit, like the miser's greed.
But I am Colin still: my prejudice
Is for the flavour of my daily food.[f]
Not that I doubt the world is growing still
As once it grew from Chaos and from Night;
Or have a soul too shrunken for the hope
Which dawned in human breasts, a double morn,
With earliest watchings of the rising light
Chasing the darkness; and through many an age
Has raised the vision of a future time
That stands an Angel[g] with a face all mild
Spearing the demon.[h] I too rest in faith
That man's perfection is the crowning flower,[i]
Toward which the urgent sap in life's great tree
Is pressing, – seen in puny blossoms now,[j]
But in the world's great morrows to expand
With broadest petal and with deepest glow.

Yet,[k] see the patched and plodding citizen
Waiting upon the pavement with the throng
While some victorious world-hero makes

Triumphal entry, and the peal of shouts
And flash of faces 'neath uplifted hats
Run like a storm of joy along the streets!
He says, "God bless him!" almost with a sob,
As the great hero passes; he is glad
The world holds mighty men and mighty deeds;
The music stirs his pulses like strong wine,
The moving splendour touches him with awe –
'Tis glory shed around the common weal,
And he will pay his tribute willingly,
Though with the pennies earned by sordid toil.
Perhaps the hero's deeds have helped to bring
A time when every honest citizen
Shall wear a coat unpatched. And yet he feels
More easy fellowship with neighbours there
Who look on too; and he will soon relapse
From noticing the banners and the steeds
To think with pleasure there is just one bun
Left in his pocket, that may serve to tempt
The wide-eyed lad, whose weight is all too much
For that young mother's arms:[a] and then he falls
To dreamy picturing of sunny days
When he himself was a small big-cheeked lad
In some far village where no heroes came,
And stood a listener 'twixt his father's legs
In the warm fire-light, while the old folk talked
And shook their heads and looked upon the floor;
And he was puzzled, thinking life was fine –
The bread and cheese so nice all through the year
And Christmas sure to come. Oh[b] that good time!
He, could he choose, would have those days again
And see the dear old-fashioned things once more.
But soon the wheels and drums have all passed by
And tramping feet are heard like sudden rain:

The quiet startles our good citizen;
He feels the child upon his arms, and knows
He is with the people making holiday
Because of hopes for better days to come.
But Hope to him was like the brilliant west
Telling of sunrise in a world unknown,
And from that dazzling curtain of bright hues
He turned to the familiar face of fields
Lying all clear in the calm morning land.[a]
Maybe 'tis wiser not to fix a lens
Too scrutinising on the glorious times
When Barbarossa[7] shall arise and shake
His mountain, good King Arthur come again,
And all the heroes of such giant soul
That,[b] living once to cheer mankind with hope,
They had to sleep until the time was ripe
For greater deeds to match their greater thought.[c]
Yet[d] no! the earth yields nothing more Divine[e]
Than high prophetic vision – than the Seer[f]
Who fasting from man's meaner joy beholds
The paths of beauteous order, and constructs
A fairer type, to shame our low content.
But prophecy is like potential[g] sound
Which turned to music seems a voice sublime
From out the soul of light; but turns to noise
In scrannel pipes, and makes all ears averse.

The faith that life on earth is being shaped
To glorious ends, that order, justice, love
Mean man's completeness, mean[h] effect as sure
As roundness in the dew-drop – that great[i] faith
Is but the rushing and expanding stream
Of thought, of feeling, fed by all the past.
Our finest hope is finest memory,

As they who love in age think youth is blest
Because it has a life to fill with love.[8]
Full souls are double mirrors, making still
An endless vista of fair things before
Repeating things behind: so faith is strong
Only when we are strong, shrinks when we shrink.
It comes when music stirs us,[a] and the chords
Moving on some grand climax shake our souls
With influx new that makes new energies.
It comes in swellings of the heart and tears
That rise at noble and at gentle deeds –
At labours of the master-artist's hand
Which, trembling, touches to a finer end,
Trembling before an image seen within.
It comes in moments of heroic love,
Unjealous joy in joy not made for us –[b]
In conscious triumph of the good within
Making us worship goodness that rebukes.
Even our failures are a prophecy,
Even our yearnings and our bitter tears
After that fair and true we cannot grasp;
As patriots who seem to die in vain
Make liberty more sacred by their pangs.

Presentiment of better things on earth
Sweeps in with every force that stirs our souls
To admiration, self-renouncing love,
Or thoughts, like light, that bind the world in one:
Sweeps like the sense of vastness, when at night
We hear the roll and dash of waves that break
Nearer and nearer with the rushing tide,
Which rises to the level of the cliff
Because the wide Atlantic rolls behind
Throbbing respondent[c] to the far-off orbs.[d]

EDITORIAL NOTES

EARLY EXPERIMENT IN VERSE

As tu vu la lune se lever

1. *As tu vu … nos larmes.*:

Have you seen the moon rise
In a cloudless azure sky?
A thousand dewdrops reflect
Its light like so many stars.

Gather a spring violet
And hide it in your bosom,
You and your garments will be heavy
With its delicious fragrance.

So when a noble spirit appears,
It invests everything with its grace: –
Let us remember it that way
Even though, alas, it moves us to tears.
Translation by K. M. van den Broek.

THE LEGEND OF JUBAL (1878) POEMS

The Legend of Jubal

1. *far strand*: cf. Genesis 4:15: 'And Cain went out from the presence of the LORD, and dwelt in the land of Nod, on the east of Eden'.
2. *Tartary … Ind;*: Tartary was the vast area of Eastern Europe and northern Asia controlled by the Mongols in the thirteenth and fourteenth centuries; Ind is India.
3. *Cain's young city*: Enoch, named after Cain's son (Genesis 4:17).
4. *red brand … hand,*: 'And the LORD set a mark upon Cain' (Genesis 4:15).
5. *Lamech struck … boy,*: 'And Lamech said unto his wives, Adah and Zillah, Hear my voice; ye wives of Lamech, hearken unto my speech: for I have slain a man to my wounding, and a young man to my hurt' (Genesis 4:23).
6. *And the last parting … tenderness.*: These lines were used by Eliot in her dedication to Lewes (cf. Jubal M.S., f. 1).
7. *Jabal … Tubal-cain*: 'And Adah [one of Lamech's wives] bare Jabal: he was the father of such as dwell in tents, and *of such as have* cattle' (Genesis 4:20); 'And Zillah [Lamech's other wife], she also bare Tubal-cain, an instructor of every artificer in brass and iron' (Genesis 4:22).
8. *Jubal*: 'And his [Jabal's] brother's name *was* Jubal: he was the father of all such as handle the harp and organ' (Genesis 4:21).
9. *sister;*: Jabal's half-sister was Namaah (Genesis 4:22).

10. *till his eyes … only listened to*: cf. Introduction, pp. xliii–xlviii and ll. 726–7, above.
11. *From out … energies.”*: iambic hexameter.
12. *With glad … good.*: iambic hexameter. Cf. Dryden’s ‘Song for Saint Cecilia’s Day’:

    When Jubal struck the chorded shell
    His listening brethren stood around,
    And, wondering, on their faces fell
    To worship that celestial sound.
    Less than a god they thought there could not dwell
    Within the hollow of that shell
    That spoke so sweetly and so well. (ll. 17–23)

13. *And thus … utterance.*: cf. two deleted couplets at line 458, above; see Textual Variants, pp. 197–8.
14. *Seth;*: the third son of Adam and Eve, given to them to replace Abel, who was murdered by Cain. Since Cain led his family from Eden to the land of Nod, Seth’s ‘region’ is, therefore, Eden.
15. *heavenly chime … pathway,*: The ancients believed that the stars and planets rotated around the Earth on spheres moved by angels, and that the movement of the spheres caused, or was accompanied by, heavenly music.
16. *guided by the steadfast spheres,*: see note 15, above.
17. *rune-writ … man.*: a man resembling a character in an ancient and mysterious tale.
18. *psalteries,*: ancient stringed instruments, resembling lyres or zithers.
19. *Still ’mid … flesh.*: In a letter to John Cross, dated 29 April 1878, Eliot thanked him for a basket of flowers, adding, ‘Yet I like to be loved in this faulty, frail (yet venerable) flesh’ (cf. *Letters*, Vol. IX, p. 226; noted by Bonnie J. Lisle in ‘Art and Egoism in George Eliot’s Poetry’, *Victorian Poetry*, 22:3 (Autumn 1984), p. 273).

20. *to hear … ecstasy:*: cf. Introduction, pp. xliii–xlviii and ll. 248–51, above.
21. *"Jubal … last.*: This voice is not unlike the LIFE in Eliot's 'Self and Life', and offers a similar consolation (see Vol. 2, pp. 57–60).

Agatha

1. *faces as Griselda mild,*: A medieval icon of misfortune, Griselda is the long-suffering heroine of romances by, among others, Boccaccio, Petrarch, Chaucer and Thomas Dekker. Her husband tested her fidelity and devotion by setting her numerous trials.
2. *Saint Ursula … Saint Elizabeth,*: Wiesenfarth notes that Eliot recorded lengthy extracts from Mrs [Anna] Jameson's *Sacred and Legendary Art*, 2 vols (London, Longman, Brown, Green and Longmans, 1848), in her Notebook 1854–79, including the following: 'St. Ursula, with her eleven thousand Virgins, is the patroness of girls & teachers' (*A Writer's Notebook*, pp. 63–4, 186). Saint Elizabeth was the mother of John the Baptist and kinswoman to the Virgin Mary.
3. *lets her girdle down … burial.*: During her assumption into Heaven, the Virgin Mary is sometimes depicted as being received by God while lowering her belt or girdle down to St Thomas, who asks for proof of her assumption.
4. *Francis … wounds;*: St Francis of Assisi (1182–1226), founder of Franciscan order, embraced poverty and, reportedly, in 1224 had the stigmata stamped on his skin by a seraph.
5. *Einsiedeln*: A town in the canton of Schwyz, Switzerland, Einsiedeln is an important place of pilgrimage

to the site, now in the town's Benedictine Abbey, where the reclusive St Meinrad was martyred in AD 861.

6. *troubles with her husband too.*: According to the second century apocryphal document, the Protoevangelium of James, Saint Ann, mother of the Virgin Mary, did not conceive until late in life, after she and her husband, Saint Joachim, began to despair at the prospect of remaining childless.
7. lily-laden,: The Archangel Gabriel is often depicted as carrying lilies, symbolizing the purity of the Virgin Mary.

Armgart

1. *The* Orpheus: The best known of Christoph Willibald Gluck's (1714–87) more than 100 operas, *Orfeo ed Euridice* was first performed in Vienna on 5 October 1762. The libretto was by Ranieri de Calzabigi (1714–95). In 1774 Gluck expanded and rewrote sections for the Paris production of *Orphée*. In the nineteenth century, the part of Orpheus was sung by a female alto or tenor.
2. *Mænad*: the word means 'raving ones'. The Maenads were the highly dangerous, because riotous and orgiastic, women who worshipped and followed Dionysus, the ancient Greek god of wine and revelry.
3. Enter LEO … bouquets.: Creel draws attention to the fact that in *Daniel Deronda* (chapter XXXIX), another Leo taught Mirah and once wrote music for Leopardi's *Ode*: 'Both are Viennese; both lived at the same time. Leo may have been suggested by the life of Leonardo Leo, 1694–1744' (Creel, p. 125 n.). See also Sandra M. Gilbert and Susan Gubar, *The Madwoman in the Attic: The Woman Writer and the*

Nineteenth-Century Imagination (New Haven and London, Yale University Press, 1979), p. 454.

4. *burying them ... Midas' secret,*: alluding to one of the stories of Midas, a pleasure-loving king in Greek mythology. He once attended a musical contest between Apollo and Marsyas and pronounced his preference for the latter's music, for which Apollo punished him with the ears of an ass. Midas kept his dishonour a secret by hiding his ears under his cap, but his barber, unable to contain himself, dug a hole in a riverbank and whispered into it what only he and Midas knew. After filling up the hole, reeds sprouted on the bank, betraying Midas's shame to all who passed by.
5. *Schroeder-Devrient*: Wilhelmine Schröder-Devrient (1804–60), popular opera singer.
6. *chiton."*: a knee-length, woolen tunic worn by men and women in ancient Greece.
7. *Sintram.*: Leo refers to music he composed as a young man, with the Greek hero of the German romance, *Sintram and his Companions,* by Baron Friedrich de la Motte Fouqué (1777–1843), as focus – cf. ll. 841–52. In fact, the American composer George Templeton Strong (1856–1948) did compose a symphony called *Sintram* in 1887–8.
8. *thalers.*: also talers; silver coins, serving as units of currency in some Germanic countries between the fifteenth and nineteenth centuries.
9. *Fidelio*: Ludwig van Beethoven's (1770–1827) opera in two acts, first performed in Vienna on 29 March 1806. The German libretto is by Joseph Sonnleithner (1776–1835) from the French of Jean-Nicolas Bouilly (1763–1842). The opera concerns Leonore, disguised as a prison guard called 'Fidelio',

rescuing Florestan, her husband, threatened with death in a political prison. Louise Hudd observes that the reference to *Fidelio* may have special significance: 'It could be argued that her [Armgart's] failure to to sing the role is precisely due to the fact that she has rejected the wifely devotion represented by Leonora, when she spurned the Graf' ('The Politics of a Feminist Poetics: "Armgart" and George Eliot's Critical Response to *Aurora Leigh*' in Kate Flint (ed.), *Poetry and Politics* (Cambridge, D. S. Brewer, 1996), p 77). See also the entry, 'Poetry of George Eliot', by Margaret Reynolds, in John Rignall (ed.), *Oxford Reader's Companion to George Eliot* (Oxford, Oxford University Press, 2000), pp. 304–8.

10. *feuilletonist*: a writer of feuilletons, fiction designed to entertain with a familiar or reminiscent content, catering to popular taste.
11. *droshkies*: a Russian or Polish open horse-drawn carriage.
12. *Breisgau?*: a district in the grand duchy of Baden, Germany.

How Lisa Loved the King

1. *Calpe's rock*: ancient Gibraltar and one of the Pillars of Hercules.
2. *Bosporus*: the strait connecting the Mediterranean and the Black Sea, separating the European and Asian parts of Turkey.
3. *Pedro, King of Aragon,*: Pedro III, 'The Great', King of Aragon and Sicily (1239–85).
4. *Hyads*: a cluster of five stars in the constellation Taurus, thought at one time to indicate the coming of rainy weather when they rose with the sun.

5. *Roland ... Amadis,*: chivalric heroes: Roland was the eighth-century French hero immortalized in *Chanson de Roland* (eleventh or twelfth century); the 'warriors of Troy' alludes to the heroes in Homer's *Iliad* and *Odyssey*; Cid (El Cid Campeador, *c.* 1045–99) was the important Castilian knight Rodrigo (or Ruy) Díaz de Vivar, hero of the epic *Poema de Mio Cid*; and Amadis is the hero in the entirely fictional Spanish or Portuguese prose romance, *Amadis de Gaule* (thirteenth or fourteenth century), which also deals with honour and knightly perfection.
6. *fair boy ... Moors.*: Alexander the Great (356–323 BC) died young, of a sudden fever, in Babylon, having conquered all before him.
7. *Raona's royalty,*: In the *Decameron*, King Pedro is referred to as 'Pietro di Raona' (cf. *Decima Giornata*, *Novella Setima*, l. 5).
8. *Costanza,*: Costanza Moranon (b. *c.* 1035) married Sancho IV Garces (*c.* 1030–73), King of Navarre.
9. *Asklepios*: the ancient Greek god of medicine.
10. *canzòn*: a song, which can have a variety of verse forms, usually dealing with serious topics such as war, love and virtue.
11. *pleached alleys,*: alleys shaded by interlaced branches or vines.
12. *dapple-breasted birds ... Colchian flood.*: Cochis, site of an ancient country where Jason sought the Golden Fleece, is on the Black Sea south of the Caucasus, not far from Mount Ararat, the traditional site where the arks of Xisuthros, hero of the Sumerian Flood legend, and Noah and his family, survivors of the biblical Flood, came to rest. In both Noah's story and Deucalion's, survivor of yet another mighty del-

uge, doves bring reassurance to the survivors that the waters are receding.

A Minor Prophet

1. *Rappings*: technical term describing the sounds (thumping, knocking, bumping or tapping) purportedly made by spirits in response to questions at a séance.
2. *Vedas – Tripitaka – Vendidad –*: The four Vedas are primary texts of Hinduism; Tripitaka is the formal term for the Buddhist canon of scriptures; Vendidad is a holy text in Zoroastrianism, containing phrases and formulas to protect against demons and other inhabitants of darkness.
3. *terraqueous*: consisting of land and water.
4. *Caffrarian*: or Kaffrarian; Kaffraria is a region in South Africa.
5. *Europa's suitor … Æsop … Fox … Bruin … 'Change.*: Europa was a Phoenician princess abducted to Crete, where Zeus, who had assumed the form of a white bull, raped her. Over thirty fables involving one or more foxes are attributed to Aesop, the legendary sixth century BC Greek fabulist. Bruin (Dutch for brown) is the conventional name for a bear (cf. the fourteenth-century beast epic Reynard the Fox). 'Bear' is also an early eighteenth-century term for someone who speculated on Exchange Alley, London's Stock Market, selling 'stock for delivery at a future date, in the expectation that meanwhile prices will fall, and he will be able to buy in at a lower rate what he has contracted to deliver at a higher' (*OED*). In this poem, Eliot's impatience at ignorance is playfully expressed. In a letter to Harriet Beecher Stowe, dated 29 October 1876, she was far

more forthright about her culture's stupidity. With reference to Jews, she said,

> Can anything be more disgusting than to hear people called 'educated' making small jokes about eating ham, and showing themselves empty of any real knowledge as to the relation of their own social and religious life to the history of the people they think themselves witty in insulting? They hardly know that Christ was a Jew. And I find men educated at Rugby supposing that Christ spoke Greek. To my feeling, this deadness to the history which has prepared half our world for us, this inability to find interest in any form of life that is not clad in the same coat-tails and flounces as our own lies very close to the worst kind of irreligion. The best that can be said of it is, that it is a sign of the intellectual narrowness – in plain English, the stupidity, which is still the average mark of our culture. (*Letters*, Vol. VI, p. 302)

6. *Parian)*: ceramic ware resembling unglazed porcelain.
7. *Barbarossa*: Frederick Barbarossa, King of Germany and Italy and Holy Roman Emperor (1152–90).
8. *Our finest hope ... fill with love.*: cf. the Epilogue to *Felix Holt*: 'Our finest hope is finest memory; / And those who love in age think youth is happy, / Because it has a life to fill with love' (see Vol. 2, p. 139).

TEXTUAL VARIANTS

EARLY EXPERIMENT IN VERSE

Knowing that shortly I must put off this tabernacle

The copy-text has been compared with the *Christian Observer* edition, referred to as *CO* in the notes below.

11a *CO* does not identify biblical reference
11b Farewell!"] *Farewell!*" *CO*
11c I'd] I *CO*
11d Farewell!] *Farewell! CO*
11e below, –] below, *CO*
11f bow,] bow – *CO*
11g Farewell!] *Farewell! CO*
11h blossoms,] blossoms *CO*
11i breeze,] breeze – *CO*
11j Farewell!] *Farewell! CO*
11k creation's] Creation's *CO*
11l lord] lord, *CO*
11m food] food, *CO*
11n afford,] afford – *CO*
11o Farewell!] *Farewell! CO*
12a Fairy like] Ye gaudy *CO*
12b shine, and frolic there,] shine and frolic there – *CO*
12c Farewell!] *Farewell! CO*
12d Books] Books, *CO*

12e them] you *CO*
12f sold,] sold – *CO*
12g Farewell!] *Farewell! CO*
12h Blest ... page,] Blest tome, to thee, whose truth-writ page *CO*
12i To thee ... alone,] I say not of God's earthly gifts alone, *CO*
12j Farewell!] *Farewell! CO*
12k given,] giv'n, *CO*
12l Must ... us,] Must the strong tie that binds us *CO*
12m I ... heaven,] I – only till we meet in heaven – *CO*
12n Farewell!] *Farewell! CO*
12o There] Then *CO*
12p sounds, new sights] sights, new sounds *CO*
12q Farewell!] *Farewell!* / M.A.E. [right justified, and editor's comment below (see headnote, p. 8)] *CO*

Question and Answer

The copy-text has been compared with the version published in Cross's *Life*, referred to as *Cross* in the notes below.

19a "Where] "'Where *Cross*
19b rose?"] rose?' *Cross*
19c "That] 'That *Cross*
19d beguiled."] beguiled.' *Cross*
19e "Would] 'Would *Cross*
19f lie!] lie, *Cross*
19g thorn;] thorn: *Cross*
19h defy,] defy; *Cross*
19i forlorn."] forlorn.' *Cross*
19j "Not] 'Not *Cross*
19k child,] child – *Cross*
19l entwine –] entwine; *Cross*

19m sister pain,] sister, pain – *Cross*
19n thine!"] thine.'" *Cross*

Mid the rich store of nature's gifts to man

The copy-text has been compared with the version published in Cross's *Life*, referred to as *Cross* in the notes below.

25a man] man, *Cross*
25b resemblance] resemblance, *Cross*

THE LEGEND OF JUBAL (1878) POEMS

The Legend of Jubal

The copy-text has been compared with the MS, the editions printed in the *Atlantic Monthly* and *Macmillan's Magazine*, and the 1874 *Jubal* edition. See headnote above (pp. 33–9) for details of the editions, which are referred to respectively in the notes below as *MS*, *AM*, *MM* and *1874 Jubal*.

41a offerings] offering. *AM*
41b field-fruit,] field=fruit *MS*
41c things,] things *AM*
41d within,] within *MS*
41e some to Ind;] some, to Ind, *MS*
41f ran,] ran *AM*
41g Arts] arts *MS*
41h Man's … world:] Man's […] world: *MS*; Life ~~xxxxx~~ in the early world [left margin] *MS*
41i star-paces] star=paces *MS*
41j And grew] ~~Growing~~ {And grew↑} *MS*

41k Death] death *MS*
41l here, … law,] here […] law *MS*
42a time-fraught] time fraught *MS*
42b gold;] gold *MS*
42c gently,] gently *MS*
42d palm] hand *MS*
42e Then] Or *MS*
43a Till, … joy,] Till […] joy *MS*
43b smile] smile, *MS*
43c press,] press *MS*
43d His … 'tis] his […] tis *MS*; his […] 'tis *AM*
43e He] he *MS*, *AM*
43f He] he *MS*, *AM*
43g Him] him *MS*, *AM*
43h Death His … He … again!"] death his […] he […] again! *MS*
43i care,] care *MS*
43j Life,] life *MS*; life, *AM*, *MM*
44a close.] Now glad [bottom, indicating line 92 follows on] *MS*
44b Content … Haste] content […] haste *MS*
44c Work … eager, … Device] work […] eager […] device *MS*
44d before,] before *MS*
44e 'Twill] Twill *MS*
44f the] that {the↑} *MS*
44g understand,] understand *MS*
44h kiss,] kiss *MS*
44i Thus … seed] Thus […] seed *MS*; ~~To Cain's race death was their tear-watered seed~~ [left margin] *MS*
44j Of … need.] ~~Of life more various and act=shaping need~~. *MS*; Of […] need. [left margin] *MS*
44k ambition,] ambition *MS*
44l In] In {From↑} *MS*

44m said,] said *MS*
44n eager … closed] prisoned {eager↑} […] barred {closed↑} *MS*
45a graves,] graves *MS*
45b be,] be *MS*
45c still."] *MS*, *AM*, *MM* no stanza break
45d Tubal-Cain] Tubalcain *MS*
45e Strong … o'erthrew,] *MS* has line in left margin, circled with arrow to text
45f His … grew,] His urgent ~~xxxxx~~ {limbs↑} like ~~xxxxx~~ granite {boulders↑} grew, *MS*; His […] granite boulders grew, *AM*, *MM*, *1874 Jubal*
45g Such … wears] ~~xxxxx xxxxx xxxxx~~ {Such boulders as the plunging torrent wears↑} *MS*; Such boulders […] wears *AM*, *MM*, *1874 Jubal*
45h years.] ~~xxxxx xxxxx xxxxx~~ tears[?] / ~~xxxxx xxxxx xxxxx~~ [below; another couplet in left margin also cancelled] *MS*
45i Tubal-Cain.] Tubalcain. *MS*
45j senses,] senses *MS*
46a would,] would *MS*
46b Which, eastward] That, eastward *MS*, *AM*, *MM*
46c Near … are,] And with him dwelt his sister Naamah *MS*
46d Plied her quick] Who plied her *MS*
46e young, … bent,] young […] bent *MS*
46f He caught … young] He caught […] tent / ~~Tamed her by kindness to companionship~~ {~~xxxxx xxxxx~~ [left margin]} / And {~~xxxxx~~↑} cherished […] young *MS*
46g be,] be *MS*
47a helpfulness.] *MM* no stanza break
47b Tubal-Cain] Tubalcain *MS*
47c soft, … hard,] soft […] hard *MS*

47d would,] would *MS*
47e hold, dark, obstinate,] hold dark obstinate *MS*
47f within,] within *MS*
47g revealed,] revealed *MS*
47h spring] spring {spring↑} [for sake of clarity] *MS*
47i Then … cry,] Then […] cry, *MS*; ~~Then spring with wondering triumphant shout~~ / ~~And seeing xxxxx about~~ [left margin] *MS*
47j labour] labor *AM*
47k can] doth {can↑} *MS*
47l Of various … earth,] *MS* numbers line '216' [bottom, centre]
47m pain;] pain, *MS*, *MM*
47n And near … spade,] And near […] spade, *MS*; ~~And close beside them lay the share and spade~~ / ~~The mighty bar, the saw, the sickle's blade~~ / ~~Holding the laughter of the harvest-home~~ [left margin] *MS*
48a deep-curved] sickle's {deep-curved↑} *MS*
48b As,] As *MS*
48c discs;] disc's; [apostrophe partially erased] *MS*; disks *AM*
48d appetite,] appetite *MS*
48e withering,] withering *MS*
48f Tubal-Cain] Tubalcain *MS*
48g Nor … nor] Or […] or *MS*
48h nought,] nought *MS*
48i young:] young *MS*; *MS* numbers line '242' [bottom, centre]
48j tools,] tools *MS*
48k Till, … rules,] Till […] rules *MS*
48l breath,] breath *MS*
48m Jubal, too, … hammer, … eyes,] Jubal too […] hammer […] eyes *MS*

48n rise,] rise *MS*
48o see,] see *MS*
48p to – some melody,] to, some melody *MS*; to, – some melody, *AM*
48q found,] found *MS*
49a grew,] grew *MS*
49b skyey] skiey *MS*, *MM*
49c enlargèd] enlarged *AM*, *MM*
49d being,] being *MS*
49e rise,] rise *MS*; *MS* numbers line '266' [bottom, centre]
49f growth within unborn] ~~birth~~ {growth↑} within unborn, *MS*
49g wandering, listening,] wandering listening *MS*
49h seemed] seems *MS*
49i tears, smiles,] tears smiles *MS*
49j night,] night *MS*
49k Pondering,] Pondering *MS*
49l word:] word; *MS*
49m tumbling] ~~bounding~~ {tumbling↑) *MS*
50a ring.] *MS*, *AM*, *MM* insert stanza break
50b him:] him – *MS*; *MS* numbers line '290' [bottom, centre]
50c odour] odor *AM*
50d Subtler … found] Subtler […] found *MS*; The labyrinthine soul and ~~xxxxx~~ bound" / "All ~~xxxxx~~ … adding energy [left margin] *MS*
50e memory,] memory *MS*
50f Jubal, standing, … upraised,] Jubal standing […] upraised *MS*
50g there.] there: *MS*, *AM*, *MM*
50h saw:] saw; *AM* and *MM*
50i struggling] mighty *MS*, *1874 Jubal*
50j "Were] Were *MS*

50k wrestle] wrestling *MS*
50l To human … fed] *MS* numbers line '315' [bottom, centre]
51a difference –] difference, – *AM*
51b vision,] vision *MS*
51c Nay,] nay, *MS*
51d lovers'] lover's *MS*
51e energies."] energies. *MS*
51f soul-fed] soulfed *MS*
51g through] ~~for~~ {through↑} *MS*
51h yesterday;] yesterday, *MS*
51i mine;] mine, *MS*
51j fervour] fervor *AM*
51k throngèd] thronged *MM*
51l labours] labors *AM*
51m to] towards *MS*, *AM*, *MM*, *1874 Jubal*
51n Sailing … win.] *MS* numbers line '340' [bottom, centre]
51o And, … plenteous] And […] complete *MS*
51p lyre.] *MS*, *AM* insert stanza break
51q obedience.] *MS*, *AM* no stanza break [unclear in *MM* – line occurs at bottom of page]
52a song –] song, – *AM*
52b Or] ~~And~~ {Or↑} *MS*
52c "This] This *MS*
52d Song … be."] song […] be. *MS*
52e consent –] consent, – *AM*
52f blent.] space > [left margin, indicating need for stanza break] *MS*
53a too –] too, – *AM*
53b merriment,] merriment *MS*
53c went,] went *MS*
53d climbed on by] circled with *MS*, *AM*, *MM*

53e Yet … blent,] ~~But with the feast some hunger still was blent~~ {Yet […] blent.↑}; ~~Yet with joy's nectar some strange thirst was blent~~ [left margin] *MS*

53f toward] towards *MS*

53g 'mid the throng,] mid the throng *MS*; mid the throng, *MM*

53h Where the blank … song,] *MS* numbers line '415' [bottom, centre]

54a full] ~~xxxxx~~ {full↑} *MS*

54b sob,] sob *MS*

54c new] new {new↑} [for sake of clarity] *MS*

54d air,] air *MS*

54e entrancèd] entranced *MM*

54f thrilled … ends,] filled [emended to '~~thrilled~~'] {thrilled↑} […] ends *MS*

54g creature] creatures *MS*, *AM*, *MM*

54h more] ~~her~~ {more↑} *MS*

54i paused,] paused *MS*

54j Felt] Knew *MS*, *1874 Jubal*

54k Known … Unknown] known […] unknown *MS*

54l influence,] influence *MS*

54m sense,] sense *MS*

54n Enlarging … led] *MS* numbers line '441' [bottom, centre]

54o possessed,] possessed *MS*

54p swerve] ~~curve~~ {swerve↑} *MS*

55a countenance,] countenance *MS*

55b gazing elders rose] circling tribe arose *MS*, *AM*, *MM*, *1874 Jubal*

55c which he lent] which {he↑} lent *MS*

55d this –] this, – *AM*

55e bliss,] bliss *MS*

55f there,] there, / ~~And thus did Jubal to his race reveal~~ / ~~Music, their larger soul, where woe or weal~~ / ~~Fill-~~

~~ing the resonant chords, the song, the dance~~ / ~~Moved with a wider-wingéd utterance~~; Transfer to next page [left margin – cf. ll. 468–71, below] *MS*

55g this … air:] that […] air; *MS*; *MS* numbers line '465' [bottom, centre]

55h It seemed … delight] It seemed […] delight *MS*; ~~No other night was ever like this night~~ / ~~It seemed the stars were shining with delight~~ [left margin] *MS*

55i trod –] trod, – *AM*

55j All eyes … God.] All eyes […] God. *MS*; ~~xxxxx eyes can see when light flows out from God~~ [left margin] *MS*

55k wider-wingèd] ~~wider~~-wingéd {stronger↑ [and] wider-wingéd↓} *MS*; wider-wingéd *AM*

55l Now] Now {And↑} *MS*

55m Raised] Made {Raised↑} *MS*

55n "Hearing myself" … "hems] Hearing myself […] hems *MS*

55o stand] stand, *AM*, *MM*

56a symphony –] symphony, – *AM*

56b Where bees and birds] Where {bees and↑} birds *MS*

56c there,] there *MS*, *AM*

56d both] both {both↑} [for sake of clarity] *MS*

56e rise and spread … year."] spread and rise […] year. *MS*; *MS* numbers line '490' [bottom, centre]

56f raft,] raft *MS*

56g awe,] awe *MS*

56h along,] ~~among~~, {along↑} *MS*

56i sublime.] *AM* inserts stanza break

56j Seth;] Seth, *MS*

56k "Here] Here *MS*

56l rest,] rest *MS*

56m honey-bee."] honey-bee. *MS*
56n wandering … age,] in that land {wandering↑} […] age *MS*
56o And, … music,] And […] music *MS*
56p Flood –] flood – *MS*; Flood, – *AM*
57a For generations … good.] ~~For the poor human late begotten brood~~ / ~~Who taste life's weary brevity and perilous good~~ *MS*; For generations […] good [left margin] *MS*
57b And ever … ears.] ~~But xxxxx oft again xxxxx he xxxxx till the heights~~. / ~~Had shown him ocean with its liquid light~~. / ~~And till he heard its multitudenous roar~~ / ~~Its plunge and hiss upon the pebbled shore~~ *MS*; And ever […] ears [left margin] *MS*; Beating … ears] *MS* numbers line '515' [bottom, centre]
57c And … mountain] ~~And the hill's revelation~~ {And […] mountain↑} *MS*
57d earth;] earth, *MS*
57e roar,] roar *MS*
57f "The … weak,] The […] weak *MS*
57g To … plain.] For me to stand on, but this panting sea / Which sobs as if it stored all life to be. *MS*, *AM*, *MM* and no stanza break; To […] main / Like myriad […] plain *1874 Jubal*
57h "New] New *MS*, *AM*, *MM*
57i home:] home, *MS*
57j weaker,] weaker *MS*
57k its chords were all] these chords would be *MS*, *AM*, *MM*
57l Too … call.] Too poor to bear {~~speak~~↑} the gathering mystery *MS*; Too poor to bear the gathering mystery *AM*, *MM*

57m Can … lore] ~~Can soul & hand & voice with xxxxx lore~~ *MS*; Can […] lore [left margin] *MS*
57n me:] me; *MS*
57o "No] No *MS*
57p see,] see *MS*
57q Where I … youth] *MS* numbers line '539' [bottom, centre]
58a Helpless … welcoming."] Helpless to move. My tribe will welcome me / Jubal, the sire of all their melody. *MS*, *AM*, *MM*
58b weary. Many … grew.] weary; many […] grew *MS*
58c blue,] blue *MS*
58d Jubal, … spheres,] Jubal […] spheres *MS*
58e years,] years *MS*
58f floods,] floods *MS*
58g far] far [recopied for sake of clarity] *MS*
58h range,] range *MS*
58i The ancient] His precious {The ancient↑} *MS*
58j lightning] fire-orbs *MS*, *AM*, *MM*
58k Pressed … now,] *MS* numbers line '564' [bottom, centre]
59a days;] days, *MS*, *AM*, *MM*
59b flowers –] mead {flowers↑} *MS*; flowers, *AM*, *MM*
59c him, … "Thou art he!] him […] Thou art he, *MS*
59d thine,] thine *MS*
59e feeding,] feeding *MS*
59f sky-wedded … divine."] ~~heaven-~~ {sky↑} wedded […] divine. *MS*
59g plain,] plain *MS*
59h Cain,] Cain *MS*
59i Change,] change *MS*
59j old,] old *MS*; *MS* numbers line '587' [bottom, centre]

59k Like … arise] Like […] arise *MS*; ~~Like some strange heir xxxxx~~ {~~xxxxx xxxxx~~↑} [left margin] *MS*

59l "This … mine."] This […] mine. *MS*

59m made,] made *MS*

59n low] low, *MS*

59o Or monster … sleep.] Or monster […] sleep. / *MS*; ~~Or huge Leviathan in heavy breathing sleep~~ [left margin] *MS*

59p wayside on] ~~way upon~~ {wayside on↑} *MS*

59q new-raised] newraised *MS*

59r cedar wood.] cedar-wood. *AM*, *MM*

59s dry-withered] drywithered *MS*

60a That] The *MS*

60b And gladness … stream] *MS* numbers line '611' [bottom, centre]

60c dream,] dream *MS*

60d air,] air *MS*

60e strains of life] life of strains *MS*

60f listened:] listening, *MS*

60g red,] red *MS*

60h Then bursting … flower,] Then bursting […] flower *MS*; ~~Then shield bursting like xxxxx lily red~~ / ~~Burst xxxxx the trumpet's note out spread~~ / ~~xxxxx xxxxx xxxxxquire~~ [?] / ~~xxxxx xxxxx xxxxx~~ / ~~xxxxx xxxxx xxxxx~~ [left margin] *MS*

60i audible;] audible: *MS*

60j maids,] maids *MS*

60k joy,] joy *MS*

60l "Jubal!" ... "Jubal"] Jubal! Jubal *MS*

60m That grateful … again.] *MS* numbers line '636' [bottom, centre]

61a breath, … near,] breath […] near *MS*

61b dear;] dear, *MS*

61c due.] *MS*, *AM*, *MM* insert stanza break; due, – *AM*
61d him, … apart,] him […] apart *MS*
61e space,] space *MS*
61f quire? –] quire – *MS*
61g centuries,] centuries *MS*
61h Through thrice … strowed] *MS* numbers line '660' [bottom, centre]
61i Ached with its smallness] Ached smallness *MS*, *AM*, *MM*
61j him,] him *MS*
62a And, … desire,] And […] desire *MS*
62b I! . . .] I! – *MS*
62c lake;] lake: *MS*
62d he] he – *MS*
62e the] the {~~xxxxx~~↑} *MS*
62f And] All {And↑} *MS*
62g Jubal was but a] Jubal was ~~for~~ {but↑} a *MS*
62h too, … spot,] too […] spot *MS*
62i blot,] blot *MS*
62j two,] two *MS*
62k honour] honor *AM*
62l out,] out *MS*
62m need;] need: *MS*
63a speed,] speed *MS*
63b That] That {~~xxxxx xxxxx~~↑} *MS*
63c Which] ~~That~~ *MS*; Which [left margin] *MS*
63d thorny] ~~xxxxx~~ {thorny↑} *MS*
63e Of thorny … unseen.] *MS* numbers line '707' [bottom, centre]
63f die.] *MS*, *AM* insert stanza break [unclear in *MM* – line occurs at bottom of page]
63g "This] This *MS*
63h pain;] pain: *MS*

63i again.] space > [left margin, indicating stanza break] *MS*

63j “Is] Is *MS*

63k Enclose me] ~~From some~~ {Enclose me↑} *MS*

63l love,] love *MS*

63m Song?”] Song? *MS*

63n gentlest tones were … blent:] there were tones that […] blent; *MS*, *1874 Jubal*; there were tones that […] blent: *AM*, *MM*

63o calm] ~~sweet~~ {calm↑} *MS*

63p one,] one *MS*; *MS* numbers line ‘731’ [bottom, centre]

64a limbs,] limbs *MS*

64b “Jubal,” … Past,] Jubal […] past, *MS*; *AM* does not indent line

64c beside?] beside – *MS*

64d god –] god, *MS*, *AM*, *MM*

64e skies –] skies, *MS*

64f aught else for] as other *MS*, *AM*, *MM*

64g *her*] her *MS*, *AM*, *MM*

64h Buried within] And buried in *MS*

64i may sleep] that lie *MS*

64j give,] give *MS*

65a means] is {means↑} *MS*

65b Melody] melody *MS*, *AM*, *MM*

65c man’s soul,] men’s souls, *MS*

65d poverty.” –] poverty. – *MS*; poverty. *AM*

65e grave.] grave. / George Eliot {December 1869↓} [both right] *MS*; grave. / 1869 [left] *1874 Jubal*, *1878 Jubal*

Agatha

The copy-text has been compared with the MS, Trübner's 1869 edition, the *Atlantic Monthly* edition, the edition Eliot gave to Mrs Cross in January 1874 and the 1874 *Jubal* edition. See headnote above (pp. 67–71) for details of the editions, which are referred to respectively in the notes below as *MS*, *1869*, *AM*, *Cross* and *1874 Jubal*.

73a Old World] old-world *MS*, *1869*
73b hollow:] hollow; *MS*
73c steeps,] steeps *MS*
73d Pine woods] Pine-woods *MS*, *1869*
73e southwestward] south-westward *MS*, *1869*
73f France by the Rhine,] The Rhine-edged France {France by the Rhine↑} *MS*
73g monks] monks {~~Benedictines~~↑} *MS*
73h their] their {~~this~~↑} *MS*
73i Sancta Maria,] ~~The Holy Mary~~ {Santa Maria↑} *MS*
73j Sanct Märgen, –] Sanct Märgen – *MS*
74a eyes] eyes, *MS*
74b her] her, *1869*, *AM*
74c own,] own *MS*
74d fruit] fruit, *1869*
74e hill,] hill *MS*
74f hearth, –] hearth – *MS*
74g girls, –] girls – *MS*
74h Boy,] boy *MS*
74i storm,] storm *MS*
74j plagues] plagues, *MS*
74k cottage] cottage, *MS*
74l which,] which *MS*, *1869*
74m cows,] cows *1869*

75a Open] *MS* shows ‘Of h’ corrected to ‘Open’ – obvious mistake

75b Fever,] Fever *MS*, *1869*

75c love,] love *MS*

75d omnipotent,] omnipotent *MS*, *1869*

75e That cottage on the slope,] ~~This low-thatched~~ {That cottage on the slope,↑} *MS*

75f rose-tree] rose tree *MS*

75g ajar;] ajar. *MS*

75h within, –] within – *MS*, *1869*

75i Love and Duty’s] love and duty’s *MS*

75j *MS* has no line indent after ‘relic’

75k the rose-hung gate,] the {rose-hung↑} gate ~~with skirts~~ *MS*

75l With skirts … the pearl,] {With skirts [left margin]} ~~All~~ {pale↑} blue ~~and white~~, a brow to quench the ~~fresh found~~ pearl *MS*

75m soft and blonde as infants’,] ~~blond as infants’~~ [or ~~infant’s~~: apostrophe directly above ‘s’]{soft and blond as infants’↑ [or infant’s: apostrophe directly above ‘s’]} *MS*

76a To give good day.] ~~And made~~ {To give good day↑} *MS*

76b there.] there, *MS*

76c that fits a court,] ~~all lore that shapes~~ {that fits a court↓} *MS*

76d All lore that shapes] All lore that shapes {~~To delicate uses~~↑} *MS*

76e Yet quiet … dove] ~~But with a presence like~~ {~~pure & gentle as~~↑} *MS*; Yet quiet, lowly as a meek dove~~s~~, [left margin] *MS*

76f Linda;] Ida; *MS* [see note to 79h, below]

76g Mamma] Mámma *1869*, *AM*

76h Linda:] Ida: *MS*

76i few,] few – *MS*

76j budding] blossom {budding↑} *MS*; budding-time *AM*
76k homes] homes, *AM*
76l lonely;] lonely: *AM*
76m noiseless yet responsive] noiseless, yet responsive, *AM*
76n at breast that] ~~that sleeps &~~ {at breast that↑} *MS*
76o or] & {or↑} *MS*
76p and] And {Or↑} *MS*
76q bees,] bees; *MS*, *1869*
76r goods, which,] ~~objects~~ {goods, being↑} *MS*
76s Shone … beams] ~~The very ceiling, easy to be reached~~ {Shone as with glad content, the↑ ~~ceiling low~~ wooden beams↓} *MS*
76t Dark … reached,] {Dark & yet friendly easy to be reached↑ [in left margin, next to l. 118]} *MS*
76u Bore … sign;] *MS* below 'yet friendly' (l. 117), reads 'low-hanging'
76v Ursula,] Ursula *MS*
76w books,] books *MS*
77a farthest] farther *MS*
77b trust] ~~live~~ {trust↑} *MS*
77c which] ~~that~~ {which↑} *MS*
77d Rank … Duty,] rank […] duty, *MS*
77e various,] various *MS*, *1869*
77f service;] ~~xxxxx~~ {service↑} *MS*
77g souls] souls, *MS*
77h Linda] Ida *MS*
77i Close … talked] ~~And Agatha still knitting talked with her~~ {Close […] talked↑} *MS* and this line is indented
77j With … old.] ~~interchange of voices young & old~~ {With sweet antiphony of young and old↑; ~~Each~~

~~lovely with a different loveliness~~↑} *MS* and this line is indented

77k AGATHA.] ~~Countess Ida~~ [Eliot tried to correct 'Countess' to 'Aga'] Agatha *MS*

77l You] "You *1869* has quotation marks, here and elsewhere, for each subsequent speaker's lines

77m lady?] Lady? *1869*, *AM*

77n waters all] ~~very springs~~ {waters all↑} *MS*

77o Have virtues] Have {~~priceless~~↑; ~~strengthening~~↑} virtues *MS*

77p the garden] ~~& the little~~ {~~xxxxx~~ the garden↑} *MS*

78a off,] off *MS*

78b bread:] bread? *MS*

78c lady.] Lady. *1869*

78d nought,] nought; *MS*

78e house,] house *1869*

78f pair,] pair *MS*

78g slowly;] slowly *MS*

78h died,] died *MS*

78i Full … roof] ~~Left me this roof, & all the household stuff~~ – {Full […] roof↑} *MS*

78j And … stuff.] You see here now. {And […] stuff↑} *MS*

78k wealth;] wealth – *MS*

78l so] ~~then~~ {so↑} *MS*

78m COUNTESS LINDA.] C. Ida *MS*

78n how, then,] how then *MS*

78o O,] O *MS*

78p all] & [changed to 'all'] *MS*

78q children,] children *MS*

78r work;] work, *MS*

78s good, –] good, *MS*

78t scale,] scale *MS*

78u drink;] drink, *MS*

78v farm-house] farmhouse *1869*
78w When cloth] When ~~woven~~ cloth *MS*
78x piece, – this very gown, –] piece, {– this very gown – [right and ↑]} *MS*; piece – this very gown – *1869*
78y "Here, Agatha,] ~~Here Agatha~~ *MS*; 'Here, Agatha, *1869*
78z "Here, Agatha … time] ~~You old maid, pray for me – you have the time~~, – {Here, Agatha […] time} *MS*
79a The saints … do,] He needs the ~~help of~~ ~~Holy Virgin~~ & the saints {The saints […] do –↑} *MS*
79b 'Twere … besought] ~~And they have much to do~~. {'Twere […] besought↑} *MS*
79c him."] him.' *1869*
79d She] *MS* shows word superimposed over 'You'
79e spoke] speaks {spoke↑} *MS*
79f jesting,] jesting – *MS*
79g I, –] I – *MS, 1869*
79h COUNTESS LINDA.] Countess ~~Ida~~ Linda *MS*
79i Agatha;] Agatha – *MS*
79j And] Which {And↑} *MS*
79k Feel … kindly.] ~~Feel the more kindly~~ {~~The kinder & for your prayers~~↑; . . . .↓[indicating need to retain 'Feel the more kindly?]} *MS*
79l sing:] sing *MS*
79m not, –] not, *MS*
79n the Virgin's heart] ~~&~~ the ~~dear~~ Virgin's heart *MS*
79o kinder] better {kinder↑} *MS*
79p nought] *MS* shows deleted comma after word
79q towards … men,] ~~till out it comes~~ {towards helping men↑} *MS*
79r Till … hold,] {Till out it comes [left and ↑]} Like tears that will not hold *MS*
79s me, –] me – *MS*

79t COUNTESS LINDA.] Countess Ida *MS*

79u lady:] Lady: *1869*

79v Einsiedeln] Eisleben *MS*; Eislében *1869*; Einsiedeln *Cross*

80a Nay … know;] ~~O Lady you are young~~ {~~Lady, old grandames have~~↑} / Ah, but they may be greater than I know – *MS*

80b 'Tis but dim light] ~~For I have little~~ [?] {'Tis but dim light↑} *MS*

80c and pure.] & pure. {& pure↑ [for clarity]} *MS*

80d There's … somewhere:] ~~And there is perfect goodness~~ – {There's […] somewhere↑} *MS*

80e COUNTESS LINDA.] Countess Ida *MS*

80f beautiful;] beautiful, *AM*

80g You were … way.] ~~But pilgrims surely get their food for nought~~ / ~~From charity~~ [changed to '~~charitable~~'] ~~upon the way~~ {You sound [changed to 'were'] the better for that pilgrimage / You made before? The shrine is beautiful / And then you saw fresh country all the way. [in left margin]} *MS*

80h Yes,] Yes *MS*

80i greater,] greater ~~to me~~, *MS*

80j the Holy Church] the {Holy↑} Church *MS*

80k More … all,] ~~And all~~ {~~And all~~↑} ~~t~~The {heavenly↑; ~~sacred~~↑} images ~~in carven stone~~, {with books & wings↑} *MS*

80l Are … through] ~~Visit me night & day~~ {Are […] through↑} *MS*

80m time!] time, *MS*

80n back,] back – *1869*

80o After … I] After ~~I went on~~ {that↑} pilgrimage, *MS*

80p back, and yet I knew] back, {&↑} yet {I↑} knew *MS*

80q behind,] behind *MS*

80r The highest] The ~~distant~~ highest *MS*
80s O,] Oh, *1869*
80t COUNTESS LINDA.] Countess Ida *MS*
80u band.] band? *MS*
81a people … here,] ~~but out of Freiburg town~~ {~~the~~ people are busy here↑} *MS*
81b The … missed] ~~There will be pilgrims. Our good people here~~ {The beasts want tendance. ~~But one~~ One who is not missed↑} *MS*
81c to all] ~~all the~~ {to all↑} *MS*
81d old;] old: *MS*
81e thinking, –] thinking: – *MS*
81f Given] ~~Whose spirits~~ {~~Though~~ ~~g~~Given↑} *MS*
81g merry] ~~xxxxx~~ {merry↑} *MS*
81h Quiet … the] ~~Smooth down like~~ [or, '~~Smooth down~~ – ~~like~~'] {Quiet it ~~all~~, as the↑} *MS*
81i why,] why *MS*
81j citherns,] zitterns, *MS*
81k lutes,] lutes *MS*
81l have young] have the young *MS*
81m baby] Baby *1869*
81n him.] him! *MS*
81o COUNTESS LINDA.] Countess Ida *MS*
81p To care] You ~~xxxxx~~ cannot long *MS*
81q you well.] you. {well↑} *MS*
81r away:] away – *MS*
81s 'Tis] ~~And~~ {~~It~~↑} ~~is like~~ {'Tis↑} *MS*
81t home] home, *MS*
81u beyond the grave,] ~~the other world~~ {beyond the grave –↑} *MS*
81v lights, –] lights, *MS*
81w rags:] rags, *MS*
81x pictures.] {~~holy~~↑} pictures. *MS*
81y is] ~~was~~ {is↑} *MS*

81z had] *MS* shows word superimposed on 'saw'
81aa younger] younger, *MS*
81ab and willingness] ~~'tis sweet to obey~~ – {and willingness↑} *MS*
81ac burden] burthen *MS*
82a in] on *MS*
82b pilgrimage,] pilgrimage *MS*
82c Come] I ~~xxxxx~~ ['Come' superimposed] *MS*
82d friends] friends, *MS*
82e lady.] Lady. *1869*
82f COUNTESS LINDA.] Countess Ida *MS*
82g best:] best – *MS*
82h velvet] ~~broidered~~ {velvet↑; ~~a cap gold broidered~~↑} *MS*
82i none, –] none – *MS*
82j Never] *MS* 'Never' superimposed on 'I never'
82k Good clothes] ~~'Tis true, they~~ {Good clothes↑} *MS*
82l I … things] ~~But maybe I was wrong~~ {I […] things↑} *MS*
82m More] ~~xxxxx~~ {More↑} *MS*
82n some] ~~xxxxx~~ {some↑} *MS*
82o wearing … they,] ~~putting on fine clothes~~ {wearing […] they,↑} *MS*
82p hands;] hand. *MS*
82q good-bye.] Goodby. *MS*
83a hills;] hills. *MS*
83b saints,] saint *MS*
83c with] ~~xxxxx~~ {with↑} *MS*
83d behave] ~~be good~~ {behave↑} *MS*
83e folk] folks *MS*
83f God] good {God↑} *MS*
83g one] one, *1869*
83h her,] her ~~a~~ *MS*
83i vale,] valley, {vale↑} *MS*

83j good country] ~~good~~ {good country↑} *MS*
83k wine,] wine *MS*
83l Being] ~~Was~~ {Being↑} *MS*
83m made … along] ~~they would~~ [gap] ~~song~~ ~~{& made simple~~↑; made […] along [below both crossed-out fragments]} *MS*
83n In … piety,] {In↑} Mingling [changed to 'Mingled'] ~~rough~~ {quaint of↑} mirth & piety *MS*
83o maids;] maids, [superimposed on 'maidens,'] ~~but with voice subdued~~ ~~yet good-will by far~~ {~~so strong~~↑} but when ~~they came~~ {the moment came↓} *MS*
83p sport] ~~joke~~ ~~jest~~ {sport↓} *MS*
83q nature] nature ~~has such~~ *MS*
83r Hans, the tailor,] Hans the tailor *MS*
83s grew] grow *MS*
83t crocuses] daisies grow *MS*
83u From … song] Grow in the {meadows'↑} moistness{.} ~~of the~~ 'Twas his song *MS*
83v The … feast, –] They often [changed to 'oft'] sang ~~a wedding~~ {wending homeward and ~~a coming~~ from the [overwritten to 'a'] feast –↑} *MS*
83w It … see,] You will see {It brings in, you see↑} *MS*
83x Their … maids.] ~~Their jest with Agatha & Kate & Nell~~. {~~Nell~~↑ [heavy ink]} {Their […] maids.↓} [These are the only lines on the page] *MS*
83y Midnight] *MS* shows song on left side of the page, with alternative lines in right margin, from here until the end of the poem
84a night] Night *MS*
84b Home … time] Hurry home & make the time {Home they hurry, making time [right margin]} *MS*

84c *star*,] star! {~~Good~~ {Strong↑} Saint Michael with the spear / Make us brave when danger's near! [right margin]} *MS*

84d *Brother*,] Brother *MS*

84e murk] murk, *MS*

84f Nell;] Nell – *MS*

84g *joy*,] joy! {Heart of Mary by thy pain / Keep us all from mortal {wicked↓} stain! [right margin]} *MS*

85a *Meek*] *MS* has word superimposed on 'Good'

85b sweet dreams!] ~~xxxxx~~ {sweet↑} dreams! *MS*

85c Little … beams.] ~~Little maidens, old, sleep well!~~ / ~~Mothers, too, who love us all~~ *MS*

85d *lily-laden*,] lily-laden *MS*

85e *Holy Gabriel … mother-maiden!*] Holy Gabriel … mother-maiden! *MS*; Little […] *mother-maiden!*[right margin] *MS*

85f hillside] hill-side *MS*

85g Swift … ride.] Swift~~ly~~, ~~like~~ ~~xxxxx~~ ~~xxxxx~~ ~~xxxxx~~ {as soldiers when they ride↑} *MS*

85h *sorrow*,] sorrow *MS*

85i *through*] thro *MS*

85j *Heart of Mary … the morrow!*] Heart of Mary […] the morrow! {Jesus, hope of all the nations / Keep us from amid temptations! [right margin]} *MS*

85k suddenly] suddenly, *1869*, *AM*

85l knee,] knee: *MS*

85m Now … night!] ~~Here we part~~ – ~~good night~~ – ~~good night!~~ Here the ['the' superimposed on 'our'] roads branch off – good night! *MS*

85n *Mary*,] Mary *MS*

85o *Give … place!*] ~~Keep us all a heavenly place!~~ Give … place! [right margin] *MS*; *Give* […] *place!* / 1868 [left] *1874 Jubal*, *1878 Jubal*

Armgart

The copy-text has been compared with the MS, the editions printed in the *Atlantic Monthly*, *Macmillan's Magazine* and the 1874 *Jubal* edition. See headnote above (pp. 87–92) for details of the editions, which are referred to respectively in the notes below as *MS*, *AM*, *MM* and *1874 Jubal*.

93a SCENE I.] Scene I. *MS*
93b morning,] evening, *MS*, *AM*, *MM*
93c WALPURGA.] WALP. *AM*, *MM* [here and elsewhere]
93d What … returned?] ~~xxxxx~~ ~~xxxxx~~ {What, so soon ~~xxxxx~~ returned?↑} *MS*
93e WALPURGA.] Walp. *MS* [here and elsewhere]
93f to-night?] tonight? *MS*
94a half-past] half past *MS*
94b *Orpheus*] Orpheus *MS*
94c As] As, *AM*
94d breast,] breast *MS*
95a be,] be *MS*
95b exquisite,] exquisite *MS*
95c limbs –] limbs, *AM*
95d singing,] singing *MS*
96a comes.] comes. / SCENE II. *AM*
96b ARMGART,] Armgart *MS*
96c *mantle,*] mantle *MS*
96d *hair*).] hair) *MS*
96e ARMGART.] Armg. *MS* [here and elsewhere]; ARMG. *MM* [here and elsewhere]
96f linkèd] linked *MS*, *MM*
97a Give me … *bust of* GLUCK.)] Give me the wreath. (She crowns the bust of Gluck.) *MS*
97b wrong:] wrong – *MS*, *AM*

97c *Orpheus*] Orpheus, *MS*
97d full-fed] full=fed *MS*
97e *taking*] Taking *MS*
97f deep-dug] deep=dug *MS*
98a *turning*] Turning *MS*
98b *room with* … dear Armgart.] room with the flowers). Yes, tell us all, dear Armgart~~?~~. [obvious error] *MS*
98c Did you feel] ~~xxxxx~~ ~~xxxxx~~ {Did you feel↑} *MS*
98d man] ~~one~~ {man↑} *MS*
98e ARMGART … that!] Armg. (scornfully). I knew that! *MS*
99a Judgment-day:] judgment day – *MS*; judgment day, – *AM*; Judgment Day *MM*
99b paraphrase,] commentary – *MS*; saraphrase, [obvious misprint] *MM*
99c demi-semi-quavers.] demi=semi quavers *MS*; demisemiquavers. *AM*
99d *uplifting*] ~~&~~ uplifting *MS*
99e *mouth* … Mum!] mouth ^) {And {^↓} turning away. [left margin]} Mum! *MS*
99f Leo … heard;] Leo, – what you saw and heard: *AM*
99g Armgart –] Armgart, – *AM*
99h forth.] forth, *AM*, *MM*
99i mute,] mute *MS*
99j new-created] new=created *MS*
99k taught:] taught – *MS*
100a changed:] changed! *AM*
100b demi-god] demigod *AM*
100c *advancing*,] Advancing, *MS*
100d *turning*] wheeling *MS*
100e ARMGART … bride,] Armg. […] I was a bride – *MS*

100f lady,] lady – *MS*
100g draught!] draught . . . *MS*
100h (*Snaps his fingers.*)] (snaps his fingers.) [right margin] *MS*
100i it –] it, – *AM*
100j Sintram.Well!] Lear. – *MS*; Sintram. Well, *AM*
100k Oh,] O, *AM*, *1874 Jubal*
100l ARMGART … souls,] Armg. […] Oh, pleasure has cramped dwelling in our ~~souls~~ {souls↑} *MS*
100m Being] being *MS*, *AM*
101a afire,] afire *MS*
101b ARMGART … truth:] Armg. […] truth! *MS*
101c end –] end, – *AM*
101d LEO … raving.] Leo (shaking his finger). I was raving. *MS*
101e glad,] glad *MS*, *AM*, *MM*
101f applause –] applause, – *AM*
101g many-coloured] many-colored *AM*
101h around –] around, – *AM*
102a Paradise,] paradise, *MS*
102b power –] power, – *AM*
102c LEO … *prima donna* came] Leo […] prima donna came *MS*
102d summer's sun,] summer sun's, *MS*
102e ripens] ripes *MS*
102f myrrh –] myrrh, – *AM*
103a (*taking … it*).] (Taking […] it) *MS*
103b Milky Way,] milky way, *MS*
103c splendours] splendors *AM*
103d splendour!] splendor! *AM*
103e lie?] lie? – *MS*
103f obscurity –] obscurity, – *AM*
103g One] one *MS*
103h Many?] many? *MS*

103i joy;] joy, *MM*

103j Muse . . .] Muse . . . . *AM*

104a LEO … supper.] Leo (going to the table). Who needs supper? *MS*; LEO […] supper? *AM*

104b come?] sit? *AM*

104c SCENE II.] Scene III. *MS*; SCENE III. *AM*

104d ARMGART] Armg. *MS*

104e GRAF] Graf *MS*

104f versatile,] various, *MS*

105a but others] ~~another~~ {but others↑} *MS*

105b The truth … he] ~~xxxxx xxxxx~~ {The truth, I hope ~~that~~ ; he↑} *MS*

105c "Could … would?"] 'Could […] would?' *MS*, *AM*

105d It … all,] It breathes in wholeness like an unborn child *MS*, *AM*, *MM*

105e stand,] stand *MS*

105f mart] fair *MS*

105g Absent … Possible,] absent […] possible, *MS*

105h all,] all – *MS*

105i Panting] Panting [smudged, recopied in left margin] *MS*

105j flavours] flavors *AM*

105k through;] through: *MS*

105l its] ~~the~~ {its↑} *MS*

105m upon.] upon. ['u' recopied above for sake of clarity] *MS*

106a failed –] failed, – *AM*

106b pitiable.] pitiable [obvious misprint] *1878 Jubal*

106c Have … throw.] Have won not lost in ~~xxxxx~~ {your↑} decisive throw. *MS*

106d gaze –] gaze, – *AM*

106e "The pearl … then."] 'The pearl […] then.' *MS*

106f (*rising*).] (Rising.) [left margin, with arrow to text] *MS*

106g Oh,] O, *MS*, *MM*

106h The talk … eyes] The talk of cynics, ~~men with~~ {who↑} ~~with~~ {~~show~~↑} insect-eyes *MS*

106i Explore] ~~Who see~~ {Explore↑} *MS*

106j rubbish-heap?] rubbish heap *MS*, *AM*

106k Confess] Confess, *MS*

107a I … merely] I ~~xxxxx xxxxx~~ quoted, ~~xxxxx~~ {merely↑} *MS*

107b achieved –] achieved, – *AM*

107c Though … deaf.] ~~xxxxx~~ {Though [left margin]} Armgart striving in the race was deaf ~~xxxxx~~. *MS*

107d the] ~~by~~ the *MS*

107e I ought to bear] And I will bear *MS*

107f The task … womanhood:] This worthily done. A woman's highest-rank / Is to be fully perfectly a woman: *MS*

108a kind –] kind, – *MS*

108b "Woman, thy desire … willed it so!"] 'Woman, thy desire […] willed it so!' *MS*

108c night,] night. *MS*

108d add,] add *MS*, *AM*

108e GRAF. / No!] Graf. No! [bottom right of f. 101 and top of f. 102] *MS*

108f me;] me. *MS*, *AM*; me: *MM*

109a a-twin … thought,] atwin […] thought *MS*

109b sovereignty –] sovereignty, – *AM*

109c What!] What, *AM*

109d ill-sung] ill=sung *MS*

109e honourable] honorable *AM*

109f strength –] strength, – *AM*

109g birth –] birth, – *AM*

109h comes,] comes *AM*

109i Perish –] Perish, – *AM*

109j Oh,] O *MS*, *AM*

110a me.] me *MS*
110b suit] suit, – *MS*
110c disdained –] disdained, – *AM*
110d save] than *AM*
110e Any] Other *MS*, *MM*
110f other] ~~every~~ {other↑} *MS*
110g "Wait" –] "Wait," – *AM*
111a Graf –] Graf, *MS*; Graf, – *AM*
111b me –] me, – *AM*
111c just] but *MS*
111d reasoners:] reasoners – *MS*
111e conclusion –] conclusion, – *AM*
111f me –] me, – *AM*
111g freedom" –] freedom," – *AM*
112a Again –] Again, – *AM*
112b Oh,] O, *MS*, *AM*
112c No;] No, *MS*, *AM*
112d music,] music *MS*
112e good –] good, – *AM*
112f love –] love, – *AM*
113a chafe the union.] ~~xxxxx guard the tenderness~~. {chafe the union↑} *MS*
113b steadfastness] stedfastness *MS*
113c will] ~~xxxxx~~ {will↑} *MS*
113d wed] love {wed↑} *MS*
113e Art –] art, – *AM*; art – *MM*
114a And] ~~Yes~~ {And↑} *MS*
114b Oh,] O *MS*, *MM*
115a SCENE III.] Scene IV. *MS*; SCENE IV. *AM*
115b A YEAR … DOCTOR GRAHN.] A Year Later / Scene IV. The same salon. Walpurga is standing looking / towards the window with an air of uneasiness. Doctor / Grahn enters. *MS*

115c swept] swept [blotted; recopied for sake of clarity] *MS*
115d bill –] bill, – *AM*
115e down-stairs.] *MS* has two half lines heavily crossed out following on; down stairs *AM*
116a I will come again,] I will again [obvious misprint] *AM*
116b again.] again, [obvious misprint] *1878 Jubal*
116c SCENE IV. … LATER.] Scene V. Two hours later *MS*; SCENE V. – *Two Hours later*. *AM*; SCENE IV. – TWO HOURS LATER. *MM*
116d *door,*] door – *MS*
116e WALPURGA *starts* … *mantle.*] *MS* has stage directions with 'Italics ' in left margin
116f Oh,] O *MS*
117a ARMGART *looks* … GRAHN *enters.*)] (Armgart looks […] Walpurga rising and standing near her in mute sorrow for a moment, is moving towards Leo, when the door opens & the Doctor enters.) *MS*
117b thick.] thick – *MS*
117c *starting*] standing *MS*
117d voice –] voice, – *AM*
117e me,] me *MS*
117f films –] films, – *AM*
117g dead'ning] deadening *MS*
117h blight –] blight, – *MS*
117i me,] me *MS*
117j Oh,] O *MS*
117k devil's] devils' *MS*, *AM*
117l torture –] torture, – *AM*
117m loss –] loss, – *AM*
117n *chair.*)] *chair*)*!* *AM*
117o wake –] wake, – *AM*

117p words] words, *MM*

118a sense,] sense *MS*

118b Oh,] O, *MS*, *AM*, *1874 Jubal*

118c cures –] cures, – *AM*

118d pain –] pain, – *AM*

118e Oh,] O *MS*

118f once,] once *MS*

118g air.] air! *AM*

118h thistle-seed,] thistle seed, *MS*, *AM*, *MM*

119a Oh,] O *MS*, *MM*, *1874 Jubal*; O, *AM*

119b for;] for: *MS*

119c SCENE V. … WALPURGA.] Scene VII. – Armgart, Walpurga *MS*; SCENE VI. – ARMGART, WALPURGA *AM*

120a resolve –] resolve, – *AM*

120b Oh,] O *MS*, *1874 Jubal*

120c No;] No, *MS*

120d bearable.] tolerable *MS*

120e throw into] ~~xxxxx xxxxx~~ {throw into↑} *MS*

120f nay] nay, *MM*

121a All] all *MS*

121b Oh,] O, *MS*, *AM*, *MM*

121c as mothers] ~~xxxxx xxxxx~~ {as mothers↑} *MS*

121d Armgart –] Armgart, – *AM*

121e girl –] girl, – *AM*

121f plain] plain, *AM*

121g words,] words *MS*

121h thing –] thing, – *AM*

121i Will] will *MS*; Will, *AM*

121j That,] That *MS*, *AM*

121k off,] off *MS*

121l hurl –] hurl, – *AM*

121m forms,] forms *MS*

121n renounce!] renounce! ~~xxxxx~~ *MS*

122a generous –] generous, – *MS*
122b ARMGART … until –] Armgart […] until – {~~xxxxx xxxxx xxxxx~~↓} *MS*; ARMG. He […] until – *MM*
123a lover.] tenor. *MS*
124a thence] ~~from~~ thence *MS*
124b hope –] hope, – *AM*
124c Time –] Time, – *AM*
124d pain –] pain, – *AM*
124e If] if *AM*
124f them] them! *MS*
124g dear.] ~~Walpurga~~ {dear.↑} *MS*
124h out – for a walk.] out – ~~xxxxx~~ for a walk. *MS*
125a Everyday:"] everyday": *AM*
125b chick-weed] chickweed *MS*
125c pot-herb] potherb *AM*
125d slate.] slate: *MS*
125e droschkies] droschkys *MS*
125f "Pretty?" … charity."] *MS* omits quotation marks in these lines
126a As] ~~xxxxx~~ As *MS*
126b doll-clothes] doll=clothes *MS*
126c do –] do, – *AM*
126d royal –] royal, – *AM*
127a who] who~~m~~ *MS*
127b you,] you *MS*
127c gladness –] gladness, – *AM*
127d love,] love~~?~~ – *MS*
127e Love … self] {Love [left margin]}~~N~~nurtured ~~xxxxx~~ even with ~~the~~ {that [superimposed on 'the']}strength of self *MS*
127f Oh,] O *MS*, *AM*, *1874 Jubal*
128a accept –] accept, – *AM*
128b Oh,] O, *MS*, *AM*
128c sum] sum – *MS*; sum, – *AM*

128d Of claims … myriads;] The sum of claims unpaid for myriad lives *MS*, *MM*; The sum of claims unpaid for myriad lives; *AM*

128e gone –] gone, – *AM*

129a pang –] pang, – *AM*

129b did] ~~xxxxx~~ {did↑} *MS*

129c Leap] Leap~~ed~~ *MS*

129d flight,] flight *MS*

129e to-day,] today, *MS*

130a consolation:"] consolation": *AM*

130b truth –] truth, – *AM*

130c said:] said; *MS*

130d cross-grained] cross-grained, *MS*

130e you –] you, – *AM*

130f destinies –] destinies, – *AM*

130g heart –] heart, – *AM*

130h fellowship?] fellowship? – *MS*

130i lame –] lame, – *AM*

130j birth –] birth, – *AM*

130k Self] self *MS*

130l Armgart –] Armgart, – *AM*

130m tremble –] tremble, – *AM*

130n Some one … come in!] Someone knocks. Come in! *MS*, *MM*

131a mean] meant *MS*

131b *immediately.*] meditatively. *MS*

131c *pause, speaking*] pause, {speaking↑ [right]} *MS*

131d Schubert … came] Well – Schubert wrote for silence while he lived: / His tunes hung frozen till the summer came *MS*

132a old] ~~good~~ {old↑} *MS*

132b act –] act, – *AM*

133a Oh,] O, *MS*, *AM*, *MM*, *1874 Jubal*

133b "This] "this *MS*

133c well –] well, – *AM*
133d singing –] singing, *MS*
133e singing … here,] singing, what I can, – not here *AM*
133f place –] place. *MS*; place, *AM*, *MM*
134a *surprise*).] surprise). *MS*
134b Oh,] O, *MS*, *MM*, *1874 Jubal*
134c me." / She sings . . .] me." She sings . . . *MS*, *AM*, *MM*
135a far.] far. / George Eliot / August 1870 *MS*; far. / George Eliot [right] *AM*; far. / August 1870 [left] *MM*; far. / 1870 [left] *1874 Jubal*, *1878 Jubal*

How Lisa Loved the King

The copy-text has been compared with the MS, the *Blackwood's Edinburgh Magazine* edition, the 1874 *Jubal* edition and the edition Eliot gave to Mrs Cross in January 1874. The corrections Eliot made to the *Blackwood's* proofs while she was in Rome have also been noted. See headnote above (pp. 137–41) for details of the editions, which are referred to respectively in the notes below as *MS*, *BEM*, *1874 Jubal*, *Cross* and *Rome*.

143a rhyme –] rhyme, *MS*
143b hand-painted … air-sown,] hand=painted […] air=sown, *MS*
143c full-blown,] full=blown, *MS*
143d earth,] earth *MS*
143e Aragon,] Aragon *MS*
143f Was welcomed … chivalry.] *BEM* has '}' next to these lines [right margin; to indicate triplet]
143g race;] race, *MS*
143h mutual spirit,] By one high spirit, *MS*

143i Afresh … expectancy.] That moves in ever fresh fulfilled expectancy. *MS*

143j Afresh … festival,] Afresh […] festival *MS* and reads 'space of a line>' [left margin]

144a tournament,] tournament *MS*

144b blent,] blent *MS*

144c song,] song *MS*

144d cavaliers:] cavaliers; *MS*; cavaliers: *Rome*

144e shows] tells {shows↑} *MS*

144f Hyads are.] Hyads are; *Rome*, *BEM*

144g jennet,] jennet *MS*

144h weapons, … rest,] weapons […] rest *MS*

144i watching,] watching *MS*

144j long-watched] slow sweet *MS*

144k Such rich … flies.] Such rich […] Of light from twilight when the last star dies / of vernal […] flies. *MS*; ~~as the opened shrine / That his within its gaze divine / A gaze~~ / ~~that melts in love before the prayerful eyne.~~ [left margin] *MS*; *BEM* has '}' next to these lines [right margin; to indicate triplet]

144l broad] *MS* has correction to 'b' of 'broad'

144m With innocent … glow,] The {~~From~~↑ ['With' superimposed]} innocent […] felt ~~that~~ {the↑}deep mysterious sting, *MS*; With […] arow, […] glow, *BEM* and has '}' next to these lines [right margin; to indicate triplet]

144n The … with supernal fire] ~~Thy~~ {The↑} […] ~~xxxxx~~ xxxxx ['by', 'with'?] fire *MS*

144o love – … desire,] love, […] desire *MS*

144p Best] best *MS*

144q Florentine,] Florentine *MS*

144r merchant-city] merchant city *MS*

144s try] try {~~mix~~↑} *MS*

144t And had … riches well,] And had […] well, *MS*; ~~As having virtue / Drugs that he knew had none. He loved gold well~~ – [left margin] *MS*

145a Lisa's] ~~daughter's~~ {Lisa's↑) *MS*

145b For still … higher strain] For traders {~~xxxxx xxxxx~~↑} like to mix with blood more rare / Whose ~~xxxxx xxxxx~~ moved to {~~xxxxx xxxxx xxxxx~~↓} *MS*

145c gain.] gain, *MS*

145d come:] come – *MS*

145e Lords'] Lords's *BEM*

145f head,] head *MS*

145g bred;] bred, *MS*

145h Nor,] Nor *MS*

145i A trader's … rude instead.] *MS*, *BEM* have '}' next to these lines [right margin; to indicate triplet]

145j Bernardo; so one] Bernardo: so ~~each~~ {one↑} *MS*

145k Lisa;] Lisa: *MS*

145l little birds] {little↑} birds *MS*

145m The hearts … would rouse] The hearts […] rouse *MS*; ~~It seemed to speak of some deep-seated~~ {~~tender~~↑} ~~joy~~ / ~~To which mere gaity were base alloy~~ [below] *MS*

145n Parting her] And parted {Parting her↑} *MS*

145o slight,] slight *MS*

145p sky,] sky *MS*

145q choir] crowd {choir↑} *MS*

145r But in … the dark] ~~Save that~~ {But in↑} the olive of her cheek, the dark *MS*

145s a] ~~the~~ {a↑} *MS*

146a Of kinship … mother earth,] Of kinship {close↑} to the {dear↑}dark warm ~~mother~~ earth *MS*; That ~~she was~~ {Which showed her↑} kin to the dear dark warm earth [left margin] *MS*

146b The fervid … birth.] The fervid soil that {~~ar-id~~↑}gives the {the pluméd↓}palm ~~{& old fervid~~↑} trees birth *MS*
146c Perdicone;] Perdicone, *MS*
146d Who] Who~~se~~ *MS*
146e Cid,] Cid *MS*
146f sun,] sun *MS*
146g somehow,] somewhere, [corrected to read 'somehow'] *MS*
146h wrong –] wrong *MS*
146i That Evil One who … strong;] ~~Who made the tyrant Charles of Anjou strong~~. { ~~The same~~ [?] ~~who made Anjou, the tyrant, strong~~↑} {That evil one […] strong; [left margin]} *MS*
146j be he] he be *BEM*
146k those tyrants from dear Sicily,] ~~the violent French~~ {those tyrants↑} from dear {~~xxxxx~~↑}Sicily, *MS*
146l might walk to vespers] to vespers might walk *MS*
146m And now … tranquilly.] *BEM* has '}' next to these lines [right margin; to indicate triplet]
146n this hero] that hero *MS*
146o And as … bring] And as {~~xxxxx~~ ~~the~~ wood [word circled]↑}lilies that sweet odours bring *MS*
146p Was lily-odoured … miniature] Was lily-odoured {and as rites divine / On {Round↑} turf-laid altars, or 'neath roofs of stone / Draw […] worships, [left margin with lines indicating where they belong in text]} so the miniature *MS*
146q Filled … form,] Filled with {~~xxxxx xxxxx that King Pedro xxxxx xxxxx~~↑ {~~the~~↑}} heroic virtues that bright form, *MS*
146r horsemanship – … chivalry:] horsemanship, – […] chivalry; [dash superimposed on comma] *MS*

146s For … be,] For […] be ['F' heavily written for sake of clarity] *MS*
146t Save as God's messengers … fleet? –] ~~Of xxxxx xxxxx~~ {Save as God's messengers↑}[…] fleet *MS*
146u These, scouring earth,] ~~That scoured the Earth,~~ {scouring earth↑} *MS*
147a sway,] sway *MS*
147b more;] more. *MS*
147c The soul … reverence.] *MS*, *BEM* have '}' next to these lines [right margin; to indicate triplet]
147d guest,] guest *MS*
147e arms, and plumèd helm,] arms and plumed helm *MS*
147f Their commoner … king] Their […] King *MS*; *BEM* has '}' next to these lines [right margin; to indicate triplet]
147g soul,] soul *MS*
147h love-mixed] love=mixed *MS*
147i citron-leaves,] citron leaves *MS*
147j Oh,] O *MS*, *BEM*; O, *1874 Jubal*
147k wingèd … wingèd] winged […] winged *MS*
147l hope;] hope: *MS*
147m love,] love *MS*
147n Wailed … throng] Wailed for loved beings ~~as the~~ who have joined the throng *MS*
147o ones. . . . Nay … weak –] ones – Nay […] weak; *MS*
148a ballads –] ballads, *MS*
148b have,] have *MS*
148c "Alas!] "Alas, *MS*, *BEM*
148d music-touch] music=touch *MS*
148e hearing.] hearing: *MS*
148f was –] was, *MS*

148g And he will … disclose.] *MS*, *BEM* have '}' next to these lines [right margin; to indicate triplet]
148h "For … deep-breasted] For […] deep=breasted *MS*
148i A-horseback, with blonde hair,] A-horseback with blonde hair *MS*
148j Who … grace] ~~Who nobly love the noblest, yet have grace~~ {Who nobly love the noblest, yet the grace [at end of line]} *Cross*
148k The] That *MS*
148l evermore,] evermore *MS*
148m tender] gentle *MS*
148n lone,] lone *MS*
148o With tender … stone."] *BEM* has '}' next to these lines [right margin; to indicate triplet]
149a pain;] pain, *MS*
149b morn;] morn, *MS*
149c come,] come; *MS*
149d Else] Else, *MS*
149e for,] for *MS*
149f at] at, *BEM*
149g snow,] snow *MS*
149h blow –] blow *MS*; blow, *BEM*
149i day,] day *MS*
149j And … her] Told of such dreamy joy {~~And little flutterings of her~~↑} *MS*
149k skyey] skiey *MS*
150a as in utterance dumb] in sweet prelude dumb *MS*
150b Of] To *MS*
150c "What] What *MS*
150d Minuccio, … me."] Minuccio […] me" *MS*
150e thought,] thought *MS*
150f reach, … touch,] reach […] touch *MS*
150g soul,] soul; *MS*

150h Dying … kind.] Dying, might ~~leave~~ {have↑}[…] mind, / ~~Some sweetness from her being leave behind~~ / ~~As violets do – some tender thoughts some memories kind~~. *MS*; A little […] kind. [right margin, with arrow to replace] *MS*; *MS*, *BEM* insert stanza break after ‘kind.’; *BEM* has ‘}’ next to these lines [right margin; to indicate triplet]

150i A … brokenly,] ~~Some~~ {A↑} strain that falling on her brokenly *MS*

150j blossoms lightly blown … tree,] petals gently blown […] tree [‘b’ of ‘blown’ superimposed on ‘f’] *MS*

150k was] seemed {was↑} *MS*

150l tournament;] tournament. *MS*

150m me –] me, *MS*

150n messenger;] messenger: – *MS*

150o medicinal;] medicinal, *MS*

150p instrument;] instrument, *MS*

150q In brief, good] In short, {~~xxxxx short~~↑}~~that~~ {good↑} *MS*; In short, good *BEM*

150r with … enough!] & {with↑} […] Enough! *MS*

150s came.] came: *MS*

150t (He … fame –] He […] fame, {~~(A singer of most honourable name~~↑} [no closing bracket] *MS*

151a great –] great, – *MS*

151b alone,] alone *MS*

151c vibrant] palpable *MS*; ~~palpable~~ {vibrant↑} *Cross*

151d listener,] listener *MS*

151e voice, … rush,] voice […] rush *MS*

151f passion, … felt,] passion […] felt *MS*

151g but cool] as cooler *MS*

151h melt.] *MS*, *BEM* insert stanza break

151i palm,] palm *MS*

151j hope,] hope *MS*

151k Which] That *MS*
151l rest,] rest *MS*
151m lone,] lone *MS*
151n my best of life,] ~~that poor small bird~~, {~~like tame~~↑} {my best of life↑} *MS*
151o See … unfledged] But it is all unfledged, it has no {See […] unfledged↑} *MS*
152a But … secretly,] ~~Lest~~ ['But,' superimposed] […] secretly *MS*
152b king,] King, *MS*
152c safe,] safe *MS*
152d know."] know. *MS*
152e loyally;] loyally, *MS*
152f your] ~~thy~~ {your↑} *MS*
152g fulfil,] fulfil *MS*
152h still."] *MS* numbers line '~~297~~' [?; bottom, right]
152i Mico,] Mico *MS*
152j sadness] sadness, *MS*
152k But cannot … lord."] *BEM* has '}' next to these lines [right margin; to indicate triplet]
153a When … lay,] *MS* has line in right margin with arrow to text
153b moments] moments {pauses↑} *MS*
153c dinner to the king.] ~~dinner~~ {~~meal~~↑} ~~to the King~~ slct ['select'? lightly crossed out with series of dots below, to indicate restoration of fragment?] *MS*
153d This … bring] ~~This was the occasion when~~ ~~xxxxx~~ ~~xxxxx~~ ['he had'?] ~~to sing~~ {This […] bring↓}[more ~~xxxxx xxxxx~~ above crossed-out line] *MS*; *MS* has alternative lines crossed out, right margin
153e To ringing … incline.] *BEM* has '}' next to these lines [right margin; to indicate triplet]
153f *Love, … me, … breath,*] Love […] me […] breath *MS*

153g *child,*] child; *MS*

153h *Death.*] death. *MS*

153i *Love, … own,*] Love […] own *MS*

153j *away,*] away *MS*

153k *thee,*] thee *MS*

153l *Death!*] death! *MS*

153m *king*] King *MS*

154a *lord,*] Lord, *MS*

154b *Death.*] death. *MS*

154c *springtime,*] spring-time *MS*

154d *love,*] love *MS*

154e *blissful*] blissful ~~thing~~ *MS*

154f *Love, thou didst … Death.*] *MS* centred on page; vertical line in right margin and 'Ital' [instruction to printer]

154g cry,] cry *MS*

154h tear-filled] tear-~~washed~~ {filled↑} *MS*

154i first, … rose,] first […] rose *MS*

154j grows,] grows *MS*

154k hall,] hall *MS*

154l That … there,] That not one living breathing {conscious↑} soul was there, *MS*

154m that] some {that↑} *MS*

155a well;] well, *MS*

155b rhymes,] rhymes *MS*

155c said;] said, *MS*

155d near,] near *MS*

155e Minuccio,] Minuccio *MS*

155f Who meetly … know.] *MS* numbers line '400' [bottom, right]

155g one,] one *MS*

155h exaltation –] exaltatiön – *BEM*

155i tender,] tender *MS*

155j face,] face *MS*

155k Flood,] flood, *MS*, *BEM*
155l self-contained and single] sole & self=containéd *MS*
155m Sicily,] Sicily *MS*
155n king] King *MS*
155o To-day … ring."] Today […] ring. *MS*
156a tone,] tone *MS*
156b look,] look *MS*
156c glad reverse:] sweet reverse: *MS*
156d arise –] arise, *MS*
156e 'scaping] scaping *MS*
156f calm,] calm – *MS*
156g fires] fire *MS*
156h have] ~~give~~ {have↑} *MS*
156i She gave … fall,] She gave her long dark locks a backward fall, *MS*, *BEM*
156j small,] small *MS*
156k perhaps] ~~perhaps~~ {half↑} *Cross*
156l king;] King *MS*
156m thing;] thing, *MS*
156n And feared … bring."] *BEM* has '}' next to these lines [right margin; to indicate triplet] and inserts stanza break
156o king,] King *MS*
156p virgin] innocent *MS*, *BEM*
156q well,] well *MS*
156r horseback,] horseback *MS*
157a But, … dismounting,] But […] dismounting *MS*
157b trellises,] trellises *MS*
157c arms,] arms *MS*
157d woe,] woe *MS*
157e She droops and fades] ~~xxxxx~~ she is songsick: 'tis true her ~~xxxxx~~ {~~xxxxx xxxxx xxxxx~~↑} *MS*; ~~For she~~

~~has drooped~~ {She droops & fades↑} [right margin] *MS*

157f Scarce … relief –"] ~~xxxxx xxxxx xxxxx~~ *MS*; Scarce […] relief –" [right margin] *MS*

157g The king … of us,] ~~The King who said 'twere~~ {~~xxxxx xxxxx xxxxx~~↑} *MS*; The King […] of us, [right margin] *MS*

157h The world … beauteous;] ~~The world should lose a maid so beauteous~~. *MS*; The world […] beauteous, [right margin] *MS*

157i Let me … liege, lord,] ~~Let me now see her; since she is my liege~~ {~~xxxxx xxxxx xxxxx~~↑} *MS*; Let me […] ~~liege~~ {liege↑}, lord, [right margin] *MS*

157j Her spirits … death] She must ~~xxxxx xxxxx~~ {Her spirits↑} must {wage↑} war with death – *MS*

157k word."] *MS* inserts stanza break

157l In … wends,] ~~With~~ {In↑} […] wends {~~So, with a playful seriousness, he wends~~↑} *MS*

157m With Lisa's … friends,] With ~~Lisa's~~ the maid's […] friends [line smudged, repeated in right margin as 'With Lisa's […] friends'] *MS*

157n Up to the] ~~To Lisa's~~ {Up to the↑} *MS*

157o Watching … admits] Watching the door that ~~opens &~~ {opening↑} admits *MS*

157p dreams,] dreams *MS*

157q any] ~~hopeless~~ {any↑} *MS*

157r advanced, and,] advanced and *MS*

157s bliss."] *MS*, *BEM* insert stanza break

158a Quivering upon] ~~A~~ = ~~quivering to~~ {Quivering upon↑} *MS*

158b joy … paradise,] joy […] paradise *MS* ; joy, […] paradise, *Cross*

158c surprise] surprize. *MS*; surprise. *BEM*

158d bliss … spoke –] aught {bliss↑} […] spoke. *MS*

158e “Signor,] Signor *MS*

158f yoke … great for me;] ~~weight~~ {yoke↑} […] ~~high~~ {great↑} for me: *MS*; But her {when such↑}such courage came, that she could speak / ‘Signor, she said, ‘I only was too weak {it was that I was weak↑} / To bear {and took↑} the golden weight of thought too high [in right margin] *MS*

158g ground] ~~source~~ {ground↑} *MS*

158h well,] well *MS*

158i But now … grief.”] ~~But now, I thank your grace, I xxxxx believe~~ / ~~I shall xxxxx xxxxx~~ [right margin] *MS*

158j words,] words *MS*

158k loveliness,] loveliness *MS*

158l With her pure … distress.] *BEM* has ‘}’ next to these lines [right margin; to indicate triplet]

158m flower-cups] petals *MS*

158n The Tuscan trader’s … sick,] The {Tuscan↑} trader’s […] sick *MS*

158o said, … catholic.] said […] catholic *MS*

158p she … death;] She […] death: *MS*

158q poet,] poet *MS*

158r soul, … there,] soul […] there *MS*

158s heaven,] heaven *MS*

158t content,] content *MS*

159a mood,] mood *MS*

159b Thus her … good] *MS* has lines against crossed out against left margin, rewritten against right margin [mistake in placement]

159c neck, … arms,] neck […] arms *MS*

159d body,] body *MS*

159e walked, and,] walked and *MS*

159f throat, … spring joys] throat […] spring-joys *MS*

159g seen,] seen *MS*

159h Constance, … queen,] Constance […] queen *MS*
159i word,] word *MS*
159j which,] which *MS*
159k form;] form, *MS*
159l day,] day *MS*
159m king] King *MS*
159n horseback,] horseback *MS*
159o all, … gate,] all […] gate *MS*
159p velvet,] velvet *MS*
159q alleys, till they, pausing,] alleys till they pausing *MS*
159r grey –] grey: *MS*
159s array,] array *MS*
159t white-robed … stood,] white=robed Lisa, with her parents, stood *MS*
160a The white-robed … flood.] *BEM* has '}' next to these lines [right margin; to indicate triplet]
160b king … speech,] King […] speech *MS*
160c turns,] turns *MS*
160d easy,] easy *MS*
160e enforce;] enforce: *MS*
160f Soon] ~~xxxxx~~ {Soon↑} *MS*
160g king] King *MS*
160h said –] said, *MS*
160i hath a worth above] ~~is too far above~~ {hath a worth above↑} *MS*
160j Save … debt.] *Rome* Eliot alerted Blackwood about 'the omission of a word on page 14, where line 16 should read 'Save when the grateful memory of deep debt' (*Letters*, Vol. V, p. 23)
160k overflood] over=flood *MS*
160l fight,] fight *MS*
160m ordain,] ordain *MS*
160n emblem] emblem {honour↑} *MS*

160o will we ever claim] we claim from you *MS*
160p Charge the … kiss.] *MS*, *BEM* have '}' next to these lines [right margin; to indicate triplet]
161a you,] you *MS*
161b meek –] meek *MS*
161c "Monsignor,] Monsignor, *MS*
161d flown,] flown *MS*
161e image] image {pictures↑} *MS*
161f lofty place.] loftiness, *MS*; loftiness. *BEM*
161g for] in {for↑} *MS*
161h king,] King *MS*
161i thing –] thing, *MS*
161j lark, … sky,] lark […] sky *MS*
161k sing, … breast,] sing […] breast *MS*
161l But,] But *MS*
161m desert,] desert *MS*
161n yours,] yours *MS*
161o insures,] ensures, *MS*, *BEM*
162a dispelled,] dispelled *MS*
162b well-born,] well=born, *MS*
162c Lisa,] Lisa *MS*
162d and] ~~with~~ {and↑} *MS*
162e king,] King *MS*
162f lands –] lands, *MS*
162g last … Lisa,] last, […] Lisa *MS*
162h small:] small, *MS*; small; *BEM*
162i small] ~~pure~~ [?] {sweet↑} *MS*
162j Then taking … seen.] *MS*, *BEM* have '}' next to these lines [right margin; to indicate triplet]
162k Sicilians] And many *MS*, *BEM*
162l union.] union *MS*
162m Throughout] ~~And~~ Through{out↑} *MS*; Through~~out~~ {all↑} *Cross*

162n And never ... tournament] ~~Nor ever~~ {~~And never~~↑} ~~wore in field~~ {~~field any xxxxx~~↑} ~~or tournament~~ {And never [...] tournament↓} *MS*
162o sent.] *MS* no stanza break
162p king] King *MS*
163a Frenchmen, ... Church's trust,] Frenchmen [...] church's trust *MS*
163b Of Frenchmen ... thrust.] *BEM* has '}' next to these lines [right margin; to indicate triplet]
163c L'ENVOI.] L'Envoi. *MS*
163d *know,*] know *MS*
163e *owe.*] *owe.* / George Eliot / 25 January 1869–14 February 1869 *MS*; *owe.* / GEORGE ELIOT. [right justified] *BEM*; *owe.* / 1869. [left] *1874 Jubal*, *1878 Jubal*

A Minor Prophet

The copy-text has been compared with the MS and the 1874 *Jubal* edition, which are referred to respectively in the notes below as *MS* and *1874 Jubal*.

169a Butterworth,] *MS* has the 'worth' of 'Butterworth' written over again, possibly to correct mistake
169b Second Advent] second advent *MS*
169c fervid] virtues *MS*
170a he's] he is *MS*
170b Mind] mind *MS*
170c "levitation"] 'levitation' *MS*
170d generally;] generally: – *MS*
170e Thought-atmosphere] Thought=atmosphere *MS*
170f everywhere:] everywhere – *MS*
170g sages,] seers, *MS*
170h Tripitaka] ~~Rounddhiem, and the~~ {Tripitaka↑} *MS*
170i proof] proofs *MS*

170j all] ~~the whole~~ {all↑} *MS*
170k Earth] earth *MS*
171a order coal,] order ~~xxxxx~~ coal, *MS*
171b sand-storms.] sandstorms. *MS*
172a posterity.] *MS* shows 'Quite at the service', bottom right corner, indicating next sheet to follow
172b boys,] boys *MS*
172c Æsop … 'Change.] Heenan a giant poisoned with a shirt, / And Hercules a big Far-Western Celt. *MS*
172d memory,] memory *MS*
172e being] be quite *MS*
172f Distasteful … age] Living as portraits in large dusty books *MS*
172g ark,] Ark, *MS*
172h ridicule;] ridicule, *MS*
172i age);] age) *MS*
173a rude] crude *MS*
173b Is] ~~Has to be~~ {Is↑} *MS*
174a touch] bind {touch↑} *MS*
174b to] in {to↑} *MS*
174c all clear] quite clear *MS*
174d bulb:] bulb: – *MS*
174e nook] nook, *MS*
174f desk,] desk *MS*
174g plough,] plough *MS*
174h with pity blent,] that is blent with pity *MS*
175a guest,] guest *MS*
175b sweet] ~~xxxxx~~ {sweet↑} *MS*
175c window-bars,] window bars *MS*
175d keep watch] are keen *MS*
175e Warped … love] ~~Since~~ {Quite↑} warped from its true nature, turned to love *MS*
175f food.] *MS* inserts stanza break
175g Angel] angel *MS*

175h demon.] Demon. *MS*
175i flower,] flower *MS*
175j now,] now *MS*
175k Yet,] Yet – *MS*
176a arms:] arms; *MS*
176b Oh] O *1874 Jubal*
177a land.] *MS* inserts stanza break
177b That,] That *MS*
177c thought.] *MS* inserts stanza break
177d Yet] But {Yet↑} *MS*
177e Divine] divine *MS*
177f Seer] seer *MS*
177g potential] ~~eternal~~ {potential↑} *MS*
177h mean] means *MS*
177i great] ~~xxxxx~~ {great↑} *MS*
178a us,] us *MS*
178b Which, trembling … us –] Which […] us, *MS*; See Back [bottom right corner of page, to indicate that these lines are on reverse of page] *MS*
178c respondent] resistless *MS*
178d orbs.] orbs. / 1865 [right] *MS*; orbs. / 1865. [left] *1874 Jubal*, *1878 Jubal*